FDR and the Modern Presidency

FDR
and the
MODERN
PRESIDENCY

Leadership and Legacy

Edited by
Mark J. Rozell and William D. Pederson

Westport, Connecticut
London

Library of Congress Cataloging-in-Publication Data

FDR and the modern presidency : leadership and legacy / edited by Mark
    J. Rozell and William D. Pederson.
        p. cm.
    Includes bibliographical references and index.
    ISBN 0–275–95873–6 (alk. paper)
    1. Presidents—United States—History—20th century.
    2. Roosevelt, Franklin D. (Franklin Delano), 1882–1945.
    3. Political leadership—United States—History—20th century.
    4. United States—Politics and government—1945–1989. 5. New Deal,
    1933–1939. I. Rozell, Mark J. II. Pederson, William D., 1946–.
    JK516.F39   1997
    324.6′3′097309043—dc21   96–53620

British Library Cataloguing in Publication Data is available.

Library of Congress Catalog Card Number: 96–53620
ISBN: 0–275–95873–6

First published in 1997

Praeger Publishers, 88 Post Road West, Westport, CT 06881
An imprint of Greenwood Publishing Group, Inc.

Printed in the United States of America

The paper used in this book complies with the
Permanent Paper Standard issued by the National
Information Standards Organization (Z39.48–1984).

10 9 8 7 6 5 4 3 2 1

Contents

Part II: Leadership and Presidential Powers

FDR and the Modern Presidency

1

FDR's Leadership and Legacy

Mark J. Rozell and
William D. Pederson

Franklin D. Roosevelt's unparalleled impact on the modern presidency is the theme of this volume. Of all the modern presidents, FDR looms largest. Indeed, scholarly accounts date the origins of the modern presidency to FDR and many find that no one since has achieved his level of greatness in office. Candidates for public office, Democrat and Republican alike, invoke his name and accomplishments in campaign appeals, as Ronald Reagan frequently did in his successful run for the presidency in 1980.

Although FDR himself requested that no major monument be erected to commemorate him, on May 2, 1997 President Bill Clinton dedicated the elaborate Roosevelt memorial near the Tidal Basin of the Potomac in Washington, D.C. Impassioned debates continue over how the memorial should have portrayed FDR—for example, whether he should have been seated in a wheelchair, or shown holding a cigarette. At the dedication ceremony activists for the disabled community protested to show their displeasure that the memorial did not portray FDR—who had been stricken with polio—in a wheelchair. Those honoring Roosevelt wanted to be sure that the memorial achieved just the right measure of dignity and respect and some pointed out that FDR himself went to great lengths to hide his disability from the public. There was no controversy over whether this man deserved to be honored—just how he should be remembered.

Among scholars, FDR's influence is so strong that Sidney Milkis and Michael Nelson, the authors of a leading textbook, felt compelled to correct the common assumption that 1933 was A.D. 1 of the American presidency.[1] It is lamentable but true that many academic texts on the presidency give very short shrift, and in some cases no coverage at all, to FDR's predecessors. David Nichols has written a rebuke of the tendency among many scholars to treat FDR's administration as a fundamental break from the constitutional framers' conception of the office of the presidency.[2]

Although it is correct that FDR did not singularly create the powers of the modern presidency, it is considerable testimony to his impact that many accounts give him credit for having inaugurated what we call the modern presidency and look to his leadership as a model of achievement. His efforts to plant the seeds of an activist federal government fundamentally changed the national dialogue about the proper role of government in solving economic and social problems. For years there was a widespread consensus that the national government should take an active role. The major difference between liberals and conservatives was no longer over whether government should have an active role in solving domestic problems, but over the purpose for which big government should be used.

Nonetheless, Nichols and other scholars have correctly argued that the foundations for the powers exercised by modern presidents preceded Roosevelt's actions. Yet it is unarguable that FDR appropriated extraordinary authority to meet the challenges of his era. That he did so and successfully led the country through domestic economic calamity and threats from abroad have secured for him a place among America's greatest presidents. He is therefore among the relatively few presidents in American history who loom large and have established the standards by which others who served in the Oval Office have been judged (and those in the future will be judged).

To some degree, to use Leuchtenburg's phrase, it is unfair that the modern presidents must serve "in the shadow of FDR."[3] The circumstances under which FDR served were extraordinary and called for exceptional leadership. Few disagree that he largely met the challenges of his era and deserves high praise for his achievements. Nonetheless, the infatuation with Roosevelt's model of leadership is so pervasive in our modern culture that every new president is judged at the 100-day point of his term by how well his achievements stand up to those of FDR's extraordinary first 100 days in office.

Modern presidents are acutely aware that journalists and scholars will judge a chief executive's leadership against the backdrop of FDR's achievements. In 1989, when reporters asked President George Bush about his first 100 days' agenda, the president responded that he didn't think in terms of promoting a Roosevelt-style aggressive agenda. In trying to lower what he considered unreasonable expectations of performance, Bush said—in reference to the most recent vice president to succeed to the presidency by election—that he would be happy to promote a first 100 days' agenda similar to that of Martin Van Buren. During Van Buren's first 100 days as president, the nation's banking system collapsed, the country fell into a deep depression, and riots broke out—facts of which Bush was unaware when he made his comment. Bush nonetheless had been aware of the need to lower expectations for Roosevelt-style activism because he had a cautious, status-quo agenda.

As a candidate for the presidency in 1992, Bill Clinton understood the appeal of the Roosevelt-style activist model of leadership—especially for a Democrat during a period of Democratic control of Congress—and promised that with partisan control of the political branches, he could effect an aggressive domestic policy agenda similar to FDR's. During the transition period, aware of the inevitable disappointment, President Clinton went to considerable lengths to downplay expectations for an aggressive first 100 days' agenda and made it clear that he did not plan to achieve a series of major reforms in such a short time frame.

Some recent scholarship questions the wisdom of this reliance on an activist model of leadership as the basis for judging each president's performance.[4] Fred Greenstein's study of the Eisenhower presidency broke important scholarly ground in convincingly showing that a president can be acutely political and a successful leader without the use of bold leadership gestures and without bulldozing a massive domestic agenda through the Congress in a short period of time.[5] Different times call for different leadership approaches, and there are various methodologies that presidents may employ to achieve their ends.

For better or worse, the FDR model of leadership still pervades our political culture. In 1995, fifty years after the death of FDR, over 150 scholars from a variety of disciplines gathered at Louisiana State University–Shreveport to present research papers commemorating Roosevelt's presidency. This volume is a collection of eleven original papers from that conference and one additional paper commissioned by the editors. The essays that make up the chapters—from scholars of history, political science, political theory, and sociology—provide impressive testimony to the continuing widespread interest in Roosevelt scholarship. In them a balanced portrait of the Roosevelt legacy emerges, although it becomes clear why we remain in awe of FDR.

The chapters in this volume are organized into two broad sections: the first includes analyses of FDR's impact on the creation and development of the administrative presidency as well as the New Deal legacy. The second emphasizes FDR's legacy to presidential leadership and the exercise of presidential powers.

Part I begins with political scientist Matthew J. Dickinson's analysis of the roots of the "presidential branch"—largely portrayed as an outgrowth of the FDR era. Dickinson maintains that FDR deserves much of the credit for the institutionalization of presidential staff support. FDR appointed the Brownlow Committee, and he used its recommendations to establish (with congressional approval) the Executive Office of the President (EOP), including the White House Office (WHO).

Dickinson shows that, contrary to the conventional wisdom, FDR did not lay the foundation for the presidential branch. FDR in fact went to great lengths to prevent excessive White House growth and differentiation. Dickinson explains why FDR did so, and describes the alternative staff system that the president used. Chapter 2 shows how the underlying principles of FDR's staff system can be used to remedy the defects typically associated with the modern White House-centered advisory system.

Political scientist Margaret C. Rung explores the construction of authority in the executive branch during the Roosevelt administration. By focusing on a series of ideological debates concerning the professionalization of the civil service, she illustrates the ways in which the modern civil service developed. Administrators fought among themselves and with other civil servants over the best means of organizing and developing a nonpartisan, professionally based civil service that would be consistent with democratic, rather than authoritarian, values.

Rung emphasizes that administrators' struggles for professional authority and for a more democratic civil service mirrored FDR's attempts to balance his aristocratic background with his desire to appear as a democratic leader deeply respectful of ordinary Americans. His struggle to balance these opposing ideologies was a part of a larger battle waged within the executive branch over the meaning and exercise of power in a democratic state. Over time, these battles intensified as Americans searched for a means of preserving individualism in an organizational society. FDR's successors searched for a means of preserving their power and authority as the institution of the presidency and the administrative state expanded and matured.

Historian Martin Halpern analyzes the significance of an unlikely meeting between FDR and Henry Ford in 1938. The meeting seemed unlikely because it brought together the architect of the New Deal and a prominent antiunion advocate of self-reliance. FDR had come from an aristocratic background, but he recognized government's responsibility to the less fortunate. Ford had been reared in a middle-class family, had earned enormous wealth, and believed that his approach to success was the answer for others.

In the context of explaining how this meeting took place, Halpern examines the antipathy of the conservative business community toward FDR and the New Deal as well as the president's motivations for holding a lengthy discussion with a leading antagonist. Although FDR had hoped to build business support for his leadership, Halpern concludes that the meeting produced "no meeting of the minds." The differences between FDR and Ford in background and philosophical orientation were too strong to overcome. Over time their differences grew more substantial, as Ford's foreign policy orientation became isolationist and anti-British, the opposite of the president's policies.

Differences between FDR and the business community continued throughout his terms in office, despite efforts to reach out to business leaders. The New Deal approach to labor relations nonetheless had a profound impact on the industrial economy, although the death of FDR and the onset of the long Cold War led to a renewed and largely successful effort by the business community to restrict prolabor legislation for years.

Sociologist Michael Lewis examines FDR's creation of the Civil Works Administration (CWA), a federally funded and administered work relief program against the backdrop of contemporary debates over state autonomy. Created in 1933, the CWA drew opposition from both the business community and social workers. Lewis examines the forces that led to the elimination of the program after a brief period and the creation of an alternative work relief program in 1935, the Works Progress Administration (WPA). He shows how the lack of business and social worker input doomed the CWA and how these groups shaped the development of the more successful WPA.

The case of the CWA, he concludes, was one of state autonomy in which state managers had agendas separate from those of societal elites. The state managers who devised the program were primarily career civil servants who did little consultation with societal elites. The CWA failed because it both put government in competition with the private sector and failed to include social workers in the implementation process.

Although hero worship of FDR's leadership still prevails, some scholars take a more cautious view of the New Deal. Political theorist James F. Pontuso explores FDR's statements on the causes and cures of the Great Depression and finds that the president was too willing to accept that the capitalist system made economic collapse inevitable. Not only was FDR critical of the tendency toward monopoly, with its attendant harm to the working class; Pontuso shows that "Roosevelt [also] came to doubt the efficacy of an economy made up of small entrepreneurs and businesses." FDR believed that capitalism created overproduction, flat wages for the working class, and ultimately high unemployment and huge income disparities.

For FDR, the cure for the depression was to alter the foundations of the free-market system. Indeed, he was the first president explicitly to link economic security for the working class with basic constitutional rights. Market forces could not ensure a decent standard of living, but government could. Government, in FDR's view, had to adopt the role of manager to prevent economic collapse and the end of free and democratic government.

Pontuso argues that FDR was wrong about the origins of the Great Depression because "the free market had not reached the outer limits of its useful productive capacity." Ironically, perhaps, it was Herbert Hoover who argued presciently that the country had not experienced the vast developments in scientific inventions and technology that would fuel the future growth of the capitalist economy and ensure the stability of liberal democracy. Yet, as Pontuso concludes, the welfare state survived and FDR has had the greater impact on our history and thinking.

Part II opens with political scientist Sean J. Savage's essay on FDR's party leadership. Savage challenges the leading interpretation of James MacGregor Burns that FDR was not a successful party leader because the president had failed to define the Democratic Party in terms of key voting blocs and in terms of a philosophical commitment to a liberal policy agenda. Savage examines FDR's public addresses and leading sources on the New Deal era in order to paint a portrait of a president who indeed had a vision of a united national Democratic Party founded on the liberal principles of governmental intervention in the economy and broader distribution of societal wealth. Indeed, FDR was not blindly loyal to the Democratic Party; he was willing to break with his own party when it appeared to stray from the liberal principles he espoused.

Chapter 8 examines FDR's controversial exercise of prerogative powers. Although many scholars argue that FDR acted improperly and even unconstitutionally on many occasions, an examination of the constitutional framers' understanding of executive power makes it clear that presidents may take extraordinary actions in extraordinary circumstances. The political theorists from whom the framers took many of their cues—especially Locke and Montesquieu—allowed for the exercise of prerogative powers. The writings of the framers lend credibility to the view that presidents may exercise substantial discretion for the public good during emergencies, but that the usual checks and balances must be maintained during normal times.

Political theorist Ethan Fishman maintains that FDR's leadership was compatible with the classical definition of prudence: a situation in which the leader tries to achieve the best possible outcome given the circumstances with which he or she is confronted. FDR himself said, "I have no expectation of making a hit every time I come to bat. . . . What I seek is the highest possible batting average not only for myself but for the team." Consequently, he was not hampered in his leadership by dogmatism or rigid ideology. His successes were not due to superior ideas or even luck. He adopted his approach according to the needs of the times and was not afraid to experiment with different policies.

The profound implication of Fishman's argument is that FDR perceived a need for government action in 1933, but today he might choose a very different course of action. Fishman concludes that FDR saw the need for certain government actions during the Great Depression to relieve hardship. If he were president today, he would be disturbed about welfare dependency and possibly would advocate a different role for government.

Political scientist Samuel B. Hoff examines FDR's extensive use of one of the president's most formidable powers: the veto. As Hoff demonstrates, FDR's use of the veto contributed to presidential power in an unprecedented fashion and shaped the use of that weapon for future chief executives. Indeed, FDR set the standard for future presidents in the exercise of private and pocket vetoes. He also established precedents in the use of technology (i.e., radio) and in interaction with Congress (i.e., addressing a joint session) as they pertained to the publicizing of vetoes. Hoff concludes that although other presidents exercised this power, and in some cases impressively so, none did so as extensively or effectively as FDR.

Historian William E. Ellis challenges the common academic view that FDR used subordinates for self-serving purposes, often at their own expense. Much has been written about FDR's staffing procedure and of how he purposefully employed a competitive staff system that encouraged subordinates to challenge one another for the president's favor. Ellis focuses on the case of Robert Worth Bingham, who served FDR at the Court of St. James's from 1933 through 1937.

As Ellis demonstrates, Bingham willingly acted as the president's point man for diplomacy in Great Britain. Bingham did and said things that FDR was either unwilling or unable to do or say during the years when isolationist sentiment in the United States was still strong. He was much more than just a conduit of information for the president, and he worked hard for better U.S.–British relations by pushing FDR toward closer ties with Great Britain.

No examination of the leadership and legacy of FDR would be complete without an analysis of the important role of the first lady, Eleanor Roosevelt. Historian Allida M. Black, the author of a well-received two-volume biography of Mrs. Roosevelt, writes that "More than any other politician in the wartime Roosevelt White House, Eleanor Roosevelt understood the fragile underpinnings of the American home front." Mrs. Roosevelt best understood the need to prepare the nation for war by taking care of domestic social and economic needs. She lamented the contradiction of a society that simultaneously detested Hitler and embraced Jim Crow laws.

Although most interpretations of Mrs. Roosevelt's role in the White House label her an idealist or a spokesperson for the less fortunate, Black shows that the first lady was a savvy politician who was pragmatic and influential. She interprets Mrs. Roosevelt's role through an examination of the first lady's actions on two racial issues: segregation and internment of Japanese Americans. She was not only the voice of conscience on both issues but also an advocate who pressured her husband to change his policies. She was somewhat successful in promoting reforms in the former, and disappointed in the outcome of the latter.

Black shows that Mrs. Roosevelt was such a formidable player that those in the White House who opposed her actions made efforts to shut her out of policy circles. That was testimony to her political acumen, and ultimately her influence was curtailed on these civil rights matters. Nonetheless, she established the first lady as a substantive player in the policy process, a role that other first ladies—perhaps most prominently Hillary Rodham Clinton—have tried to emulate.

At this writing, President Bill Clinton has become the first Democratic president since FDR to be reelected to the office (Truman and LBJ had earned their second—and first complete—terms in their elections to the presidency in 1948 and 1964, respectively). Once again, political observers have invoked the legacy of FDR as the standard by which Clinton should be measured, without regard to historic or political context. Over half a century after his presidency ended, FDR's legacy to the office looms large.

NOTES

1. Sidney Milkis and Michael Nelson, *The American Presidency* (Washington, D.C.: Congressional Quarterly Press, 1990), xi.

2. David Nichols, *The Myth of the Modern Presidency* (University Park: Pennsylvania State University Press, 1994).

3. William Leuchtenburg, *In the Shadow of FDR: From Harry Truman to Ronald Reagan* (Ithaca, N.Y.: Cornell University Press, 1983).

4. See Charles O. Jones, *The Presidency in a Separated System* (Washington, D.C.: Brookings Institution, 1994); David Mervin, *George Bush and the Guardianship Presidency* (New York: St. Martin's Press, 1996); Mark J. Rozell, *The Press and the Carter Presidency* (Boulder, Colo.: Westview Press, 1989), *The Press and the Ford Presidency* (Ann Arbor: University of Michigan Press, 1992), *The Press and the Bush Presidency* (Westport, Conn.: Praeger, 1996).

5. Fred I. Greenstein, *The Hidden-Hand Presidency: Eisenhower as Leader* (New York: Basic Books, 1982).

PART I

The Administrative Presidency and the New Deal

2

Uprooting the Presidential Branch? The Lessons of FDR

Matthew J. Dickinson

Since at least the 1974 Watergate scandal, with its revelations regarding ethical and legal improprieties by Richard Nixon's closest aides, political scientists and other presidency watchers have warned about the dangers of excessive White House staff size, politicization, and functional specialization.[1] The growth of this "presidential branch," critics argue, has warped the constitutionally mandated system of separate institutions sharing power.[2] Rather than the "energetic" executive envisioned by the framers of the Constitution, we have instead an "imperial" presidency, supported by a White House-centered staff system frequently lacking ethical guidelines, analytic capacity, or democratic accountability.[3]

Presidents are not oblivious to these warnings. Even before Watergate, Nixon, alarmed at the rapid growth of his White House staff, had begun scaling it back. However, he also proposed investing more authority in a few senior White House aides, thus elevating them in power above most of his cabinet secretaries.[4] The sentiments underlying Nixon's administrative strategy have been shared by most of his successors; while almost all agreed to trim the size of the presidential branch, none seriously considered plans to uproot it.[5] Bill Clinton's effort to reduce the size of the White House office by some 25 percent is a case in point. Critics carped that by obfuscating what was actually meant by the "White House staff," Clinton did not actually cut staff as deeply as he claimed.[6]

In defense of presidents, however, their cautious attitude toward real White House staff reform is easily understood. As a number of scholars have pointed out, many White House staff services have proved indispensable, and it is not immediately obvious who or what else could provide them.[7] Lacking administrative alternatives, then, presidents are hesitant to respond to charges of presidential branch weaknesses with anything more than symbolic gestures. Clinton is no exception. Confronted with scandals, misjudgments, and other staff-related miscues, he has opted to shuffle senior aides while eschewing more significant staff structural changes.[8]

As this chapter argues, however, there *is* an alternative to the White House staff-centered presidential branch—one that promises to provide the political and administrative services that presidents seek, but without the associated costs. That presidents have so far failed to embrace it reflects in part historical ignorance—ignorance aided and abetted by political science. The alternative to which I refer is the staff system devised by FDR in consultation with the Brownlow Committee, and implemented via Executive Order 8248 and Reorganization Plan I of 1939.[9]

Some undoubtedly will find irony in this assertion. After all, conventional wisdom holds FDR culpable—through Brownlow—for planting the seed from which the presidential branch grew.[10] Roosevelt, however, is wrongly blamed in this regard; as I argue below, he nurtured a staff system, here labeled "competitive adhocracy,"[11] that was antithetical to the White House-centered presidential branch in almost all respects.

The primary goal of this chapter, then, is to document FDR's system of competitive adhocracy by isolating the ten principles that underlay it and to illustrate each briefly with historical examples. I wish also, however, to suggest why those principles proved so effective, and consider whether they might be implemented today. One cannot, of course, fully explore the topic in a chapter of this length. But given FDR's historical ranking as one of our greatest presidents, it behooves us to begin trying to understand how much of his leadership effectiveness was predicated on his skill in organizing and utilizing a presidential staff. What lessons, if any, can be extracted for use by his successors? Much more is at stake in this enterprise than simply correcting the historical misperception regarding FDR's role in founding the modern presidential staff. If critics are correct that the growth of the presidential branch is linked to the rise of an imperial presidency, then it is in presidents' interest—and ours—to see whether that growth can be countered without stripping presidents of the staff resources they need to govern effectively. Roosevelt suggests it can be done.

COMPETITIVE ADHOCRACY—TEN PRINCIPLES

Although FDR's administrative strategy evolved throughout his presidency, its maturation can be dated to the 1937 Brownlow Report, whose findings were largely incorporated into the creation of the Executive Office of the President and White House Office. This provided the blueprint by which FDR administered the executive branch through his remaining time in office. Although details of that blueprint were adapted to the changing political context induced by World War II, it was nevertheless predicated on a relatively fixed set of administrative tenets or, more properly, instincts that, while never articulated by FDR, can be deduced from his staff choices. Ten such principles are discussed here.

1. Resist Delegating Presidential Authority to Subordinates

The president, by virtue of the Constitution and subsequent statute and tradition, is held solely accountable for any inherently presidential act. Accordingly, Roosevelt would not allow aides to act in his name unless administrative safeguards were built in to protect him from possible repercussions. As he explained to Jim Rowe, an administrative assistant: "I do not have to do it your way and I will tell you the reason why. The reason is that, although they may have made a mistake, the people of the United States elected me President, not you."[12]

The historical record demonstrates Roosevelt's stubborn commitment to this principle. In the fall of 1939, for instance, with the United States on the brink of World War II, he rejected carefully laid plans to delegate oversight of defense production to the business community under the direction of a "mobilization czar."[13] Instead, FDR created government agencies—the National Defense Advisory Commission (NDAC), the Office of Production Management (OPM), the Supplies, Priorities, and Allocations Board (SPAB)—with multiple chairmen and weak or overlapping statutory authority.[14] The effect was to force any controversial mobilization decisions to him for resolution. Even when Donald Nelson was ostensibly granted full mobilization authority as director of the War Production Board (WPB) in 1942, FDR allowed—even encouraged—Nelson's authority to be challenged by administrators ostensibly under Nelson's charge.[15]

Only at the war's peak in late 1943, when the economy was fully mobilized and FDR was increasingly preoccupied with foreign affairs and postwar planning, did he finally delegate partial administrative control on the home front to James Byrnes and the Office of War Mobilization (OWM). Even here, however, FDR was careful to do so on his own terms. Byrnes's authority, though broad, was tempered by his understanding of what FDR expected Byrnes to do—an understanding made possible by Byrnes's long acquaintance with the president and his own vast reservoir of political experience, and by the fact that Byrnes's power was conferred by executive order rather than congressional statute.[16]

The wartime story is the same in the international arena. It was Roosevelt who personally integrated the military and diplomatic decision streams to produce national security policy. Almost all his major foreign policies during World War II were worked out personally with other heads of state at summit meetings, rather than by negotiations entrusted to military and diplomatic professionals. Indeed, Secretary of State Cordell Hull attended almost none of the major wartime conferences. Roosevelt's generals did participate, but to provide military—not diplomatic—expertise. Although FDR informally established the Joint Chiefs of Staff (JCS), consisting of the heads of the three major military branches, there was no "national security" staff per se.[17]

2. Employ Multiple Communication Channels to Extend the Range of Information Received

Roosevelt devised administrative means to glean information beyond what his official channels provided.[18] One method was to parallel official communication channels with informal sources. For instance, Sumner Welles, Chip Bohlen, and others reported directly to FDR from the State Department, bypassing Hull.[19] Similarly, Lend-Lease officials, including Harry Hopkins and Averell Harriman, were used to double-check State Department communiqués from overseas embassies and military estimates regarding the defense capabilities of Britain and the Soviet Union.[20]

Moreover, FDR jealously guarded his information sources. The Map Room, his military command post at the White House during World War II, was organized so that incoming messages came through one military channel and outgoing communications were handled by another. In this way the only complete set of military-related messages remained in FDR's hands.[21]

And, as indicated by his private correspondence and the testimony of others, FDR nurtured a wide assortment of individuals situated across all levels of government, and within the private sector, as intelligence sources. His wife, Eleanor, is perhaps the most famous example, but the names of many others—Felix Frankfurter,[22] Bernard Baruch,[23] Basil O'Connor[24]—

come up repeatedly in Roosevelt's papers. Indeed, a careful study of the Roosevelt archives reveals the amazing number of intelligence sources on which he relied.

3. Overlap Staff Functions to Two or More Agencies or Individuals

Roosevelt invariably assigned government tasks to two or more individuals or agencies. He did so to exert effective influence on governmental outcomes through more than one pressure point. Overlapping assignments also induced competition among staff vying to win FDR's confidence. As he noted, "There is something to be said . . . for having a little conflict between agencies. A little rivalry is stimulating. . . . It keeps everyone going to prove that he is a better fellow than the next man. It keeps them honest too."[25]

In this regard, FDR was reluctant to assign war procurement responsibility to either the military or the civilian production agencies alone. By splitting procurement powers among several agencies, he was alerted to production controversies in time to formulate solutions and protect his political interests. For the same reason FDR's work-relief policies during his first presidential term were entrusted to both Harold Ickes at the Public Works Administration and Hopkins, head of the Civil Works Administration (later the Works Progress Administration). And Hugh Johnson and Ickes split management of the National Industrial Recovery Act.[26]

Of course, administrative competition had drawbacks. It sometimes demoralized staff, and festering disputes often erupted publicly, as was the case with Hull and his assistant, Sumner Welles, and Nelson and the Army and Navy Munitions Bureau.[27] Nor was it always the most efficient way to expend scarce resources. But, on balance, FDR judged the benefits to outweigh the costs.

4. "Experts" Do Not Protect Presidential Interests

Roosevelt made extensive use of professionals with specialized political, policy, or administrative expertise. But he did not let their expertise distort his judgments. For example, he refused to accept predictions by his military professionals, concerned in 1940–1941 with conserving U.S. resources, that both Great Britain and the Soviet Union were likely to wilt before the German military blitzkrieg.[28] Similarly, FDR in 1942 proposed production targets that most businessmen thought quite unfeasible but that nonetheless were largely obtained.[29]

Roosevelt felt confident discounting experts' advice because he subjected it to the scrutiny of his personal assistants, whose perspective more nearly matched his. Hopkins analyzed military and diplomatic issues. Lauchlin Currie double-checked economic forecasts. James Rowe and later Samuel Rosenman reviewed domestic legislative proposals. Byrnes adjudicated production disputes.

Evidently FDR reasoned that because experts were trained in one particular area—diplomacy, economics, military strategy, and so on—they were less likely to render advice that addressed Roosevelt's broader needs. Defense preparation in the two years prior to Pearl Harbor is a case in point. Roosevelt continually prodded his service chiefs to expand aviation production for overseas shipment, despite the insistence of General George Marshall and others that planes were not a defense priority at that time, and would do the United States little good if shipped elsewhere. In a purely military sense, of course, his generals' judgments were justified. But their objections did not address FDR's concern, which was to stiffen British and French resistance to the German onslaught as soon as possible. He therefore used Treasury Secretary Henry Morgenthau, and later Currie and Hopkins, to spur plane production rather than entrust the task to the War Department.[30]

5. Do Not Institutionalize White House Staff Positions

Roosevelt retained administrative flexibility by refusing to institutionalize White House staff positions through statutory grants of power.[31] As Richard Neustadt notes, Roosevelt's White House aides were organized around recurring decision-making processes rather than by functional or programmatic specialty.[32] Beginning in 1943, Hopkins used munitions shipments as his vehicle for intervening across the spectrum of war production and military strategic issues. When Rosenman joined the White House staff full-time in 1943, he utilized the flow of executive orders, bill signings, presidential speeches, and other recurring action processes to help FDR shape a domestic program. Harold Smith, director of the Bureau of the Budget, organized his job around budget deadlines. Byrnes responded to production disputes that flowed upward to him. And Admiral William Leahy, FDR's military liaison to the JCS, saw his duties structured by the military decisions forced on FDR by the war.

This system precluded White House staff differentiation and specialization because these administrative processes did not fall within neat substantive or functional areas. For instance, Hopkins's role as munitions allocation chair required some knowledge of budgeting, military strategy, diplomacy, and production and price control processes—all under the purview of other presidential aides.

Moreover, FDR thought a formal staff assignment difficult to revoke.[33] That explains his unwillingness to statutorily convert the JCS into a permanent advising body despite Marshall's advice to the contrary. Similarly, he resisted giving Byrnes or the OWM statutory footing.[34] Roosevelt evidently thought aides interpreted formal staff designations as hunting licenses authorizing them to exercise full control of particular administrative processes or policy spheres. To prevent this, he eliminated the attempt in a early draft of the Brownlow Report to specify White House staff functions.[35] Instead, by diluting Brownlow's description of advising roles, FDR served notice that he reserved the right to assign staff tasks according to his needs at the moment.

This aversion to staff institutionalization pertained to public descriptions of staff duties, including formal titles, as well. Except for Rosenman, whose title—special counsel—was in deference to his background as a state judge, and Hopkins, who technically was not a member of the White House staff, all of Roosevelt's White House aides were listed as either secretaries or administrative assistants.[36] Thus none could claim, by virtue of title or job description, an exclusive mandate to manage certain policies or processes.

Moreover, these titles were granted only to those who worked directly for FDR in the White House. Roosevelt would not give White House privileges to anyone who did not have regular access to him. It was too risky to designate someone a White House staff member, only to have that person operate without presidential supervision.[37]

This aversion to staff institutionalization forced Roosevelt's White House assistants to encroach on their colleagues' turf in order to do their own jobs well. Thus staff parochialism, close-mindedness, and complacency were less likely to take root. To be sure, some role specialization was helpful, but not to the point that aides began attributing unwarranted preeminence to their particular functions. From the president's perspective, staff tasks were important only to the extent that they addressed a *president's* interests.[38]

Moreover, FDR's aides were recruited primarily on the basis of a demonstrated loyalty to his interests and a track record of government service, not on the basis of particular "expertise." Indeed, except for Louis Howe, Steve Early, Marvin McIntyre, and Rosenman—each of whom had worked for FDR prior to his becoming president—promotion to the White House staff for all of FDR's political assistants came only after extended apprenticeship.[39] Most first went through a baptism of fire serving FDR in other government capacities. He wanted his presidential assistants fully capable of operating across a broad range of activities, and thus it helped to have extensive government experience.[40]

6. Keep the White House Staff Small

This principle follows directly from the previous two. For all the reasons mentioned above—distrust of specialization, wariness of institutionalization, and his desire to manage staff personally—FDR did not allow his White House staff to grow so large that he could not personally supervise each member's activities. As a result, even at the height of the war, his senior White House staff, not counting clerical aides, numbered no more than a dozen. And they had few assistants of their own; there was little of the staff layering so common today.

These senior aides served three primary functions, each related to a daily activity that FDR could not escape. The White House staff secretaries—Early, "Pa" Watson (actually a military aide), and William Hassett—oversaw FDR's daily appointments, media relations, and correspondence.[41] Roosevelt's administrative assistants—who never numbered more than a handful—served as FDR's eyes, ears, and legs, gathering intelligence, running errands, performing liaison to departments and agencies, and generally serving as in-house office boys.[42]

Finally, FDR had a quintet of senior advisers—Byrnes, Hopkins, Leahy, Rosenman, and Smith—organized around recurring decision-making streams. While their functional areas were somewhat bounded, none of them was a policy or program specialist. Nor did they—with the exception of Smith, who headed the Bureau of the Budget—build extensive staffs. Instead, as noted above, each assisted FDR in handling events and processes—budgeting, program development, war production, and allocation—that flowed to the presidency on a somewhat regular basis. Roosevelt gave these senior aides extensive leeway to handle second-level issues within their areas of responsibility, but with the provisos that he could intervene at any moment and that their licenses to operate on his behalf were subject to revocation as he saw fit.

Production and price control, handled by Byrnes, and munitions allocations, which Hopkins oversaw, were directly related to actions predicated on U.S. participation in World War II. It is therefore difficult to predict with certainty what would have become of these positions after 1945. Near the end of the war, some individuals discussed turning the Office of War Mobilization and Reconversion (the OWM's successor) into a presidential program- or policy-development staff. But there is no evidence that FDR supported such proposals. Instead, he evidently preferred that policy development remain the special province of the executive branch departments and agencies; they proposed legislation, and FDR was free to accept or reject it as his interests dictated. To be sure, he used aides like Ben Cohen and Tom Corcoran to extract, synthesize, and refine ideas that were working their way through the bureaucracies' policy mill.[43] And he expected his White House aides to work with the permanent government to hatch legislative proposals. The closest he came to sanctioning a permanent White House-centered policy staff was his effort to institutionalize the National Resources Planning Board (NRPB), responsible for long-range policy planning. However, even this effort wavered in the face of congressional opposition.[44]

Because he accepted "happy thoughts" from any source, Roosevelt showed no inclination to create White House domestic or foreign policy staffs.[45] Moreover, freed from White House domination, his Cabinet secretaries played a more integral policy formulation and implementation role than is now the case. At the same time, however, FDR stopped short of sanctioning "Cabinet government." After his unhappy first-term experience with the National Emergency Council, he never again encouraged the development of a Cabinet-level coordinating council similar to today's National Security Council or National Economic Council.

7. Keep Institutional and Personal Staff Functions Separate

Roosevelt actively nurtured two types of staff: personal and institutional. He thought both were necessary to govern effectively. Institutional staff protected the presidency as an institution. Personal staff, in contrast, were more sensitive to the interests of the sitting president.[46]

Because institutional staff were largely career-based, they were more responsive to congressional and executive branch entreaties than was FDR's White House staff. This meant that institutional staff gave FDR a more accurate picture of how his choices would be received by Congress and the bureaucracy. This explains why FDR made sure the Brownlow Committee recommendations primarily augmented his institutional staff-based resources pertinent to budgeting, personnel, policy planning, and administrative management.[47] Indeed, after a shaky start, the Bureau of the Budget grew more than tenfold during FDR's presidency, and Harold Smith, its director, became one of FDR's most important aides. In contrast, the White House staff grew much more slowly during this same period, never numbering more than about 60 full-time aides, supplemented by approximately 120 detailees.

8. Be Your Own Staff Coordinator

Roosevelt immersed himself in the actual day-to-day work of his assistants. This meant actively managing staff activities: assigning tasks, hearing reports firsthand, and personally correlating the inflow of information and expertise. At the same time, he sabotaged almost every Cabinet- or White House-level coordinating body that he ostensibly sanctioned. Donald Richberg, for instance, had a brief tenure as the "assistant president," responsible for coordinating the National Emergency Council (NEC) during FDR's first presidential term. Richberg's authority was undercut by FDR's tendency to deal directly with those nominally under Richberg's supervision.[48]

Similarly, FDR thwarted General Marshall's attempt in 1942 to make Admiral William Leahy a chief of staff to the JCS in order to coordinate military advice to Roosevelt. Instead, Leahy became FDR's personal military aide, keeping the president abreast of divisions among the military services that he then was free to exploit for his own purposes.[49]

In short, there was no room in Roosevelt's system for an "executive assistant" charged with managing the staff on his behalf. Today, of course, scholars argue that presidents cannot hope to function effectively without a chief of staff to supervise and coordinate staff activities.[50] But that claim is premised on the existence of a large White House staff bureaucracy, functionally specialized and hierarchically arranged. If, in contrast, White House staffs are kept small and composed primarily of generalists—precisely the impact of FDR's administrative principles—the rationale for an executive assistant becomes suspect.

Moreover, Roosevelt felt that active presidential oversight improves staff work; aides tend to understand presidential objectives in proportion to the amount of time they interact with the president. It also gives staff a greater sense of involvement in presidential decision-making.

In short, by directly managing both personal *and* institutional staff, FDR served their needs and his own. Aides gained personal access to the Oval Office, professional fulfillment, and a better sense of what the president wanted. And Roosevelt was generally well positioned to gauge the importance of their work for his interests. This, in turn, allowed him to shift staff arrangements as dictated by his needs.

9. When Politically Possible, Place New Government Functions Within New Institutions

By placing new governmental functions within new government organizations that reported directly to him, Roosevelt increased his implementation and management capacities. This was the purpose behind his creation of the alphabet-soup Depression-era emergency agencies, almost all of which were established outside the existing governmental framework, and which reported directly to him. Similarly, during World War II, the industrial production and price control agencies were placed within the Office of Emergency Management, an administrative "holding company" whose de facto head was FDR.[51] In this way new tasks were entrusted to new agencies that were directly under Roosevelt's control rather than to existing bureaucratic departments that might have their own agendas. Moreover, FDR was able to attract new blood into government by promising recruits freedom to work within agencies dedicated solely to tasks that interested them. Finally, by placing these functions within agencies and departments that reported directly to him, Roosevelt was better positioned to see that they operated in his interest. He also was free, at least initially, to circumvent civil service regulations by making unabashedly partisan appointments. Once the emergency agencies were brought within the fold of permanent government, this influx of Democratic personnel was locked in by the extension of civil service.

10. Set Internal Staff Deadlines But Remain Publicly Flexible

The effective use of time was FDR's final staff maxim. Repeatedly, as when developing the U.S. military strategy in World War II, Roosevelt imposed internal deadlines on presidential staff work to force consideration of issues that were important to him. In the eighteen months before Pearl Harbor, FDR's military staff actively formulated military strategic plans based on Roosevelt's assumptions regarding who would be in the war. Likewise, as early as 1936, prior to the outbreak of the European war, FDR directed Brownlow (and later Currie) to examine his war mobilization plans. In each case, Roosevelt set internal staff deadlines so as to be more fully prepared when actual decision-making deadlines appeared.

At the same time, however, Roosevelt was careful not to commit himself publicly to specific strategies or plans unless he sensed political support had crystallized behind them. By refusing formal endorsement of long-range plans, he retained administrative flexibility in the face of changing circumstances. Thus, he reviewed but did not formally approve any of the military strategic plans presented to him by his commanders in the months preceding U.S. entrance into the war. He ordered the Brownlow Committee report withheld until immediately after the November 1936 presidential election, so that he could implement a new staff system without jeopardizing his reelection chances. In 1940 he let Marshall lobby Congress for a military draft, without formally supporting him, for several months. Nor did he actively commit to the defense buildup his generals so desperately wanted in this period.

FDR's basic philosophy was to set internal deadlines to move staff work ahead while publicly refusing to tie himself to any plan of action until circumstances made such a commitment favorable to him.

COMPETITIVE ADHOCRACY: AN ASSESSMENT

Conventional wisdom views FDR's staff choices as manifestations of his unique temperament and operating style.[52] There is probably some truth to this, but gratification of psychological needs does not explain why FDR's staff system worked. To understand that, we need a conceptual framework linking presidential staff to presidential power. This final section takes on that task, albeit in an introductory fashion.

I start with Richard Neustadt's oft-cited dictum that presidential power is the power to persuade, and persuasion is tantamount to bargaining within a system of separate institutions sharing power.[53] In Neustadt's framework, as amplified by subsequent research, bargaining effectiveness is almost entirely attributable to a president's judicious use of what scholars label political capital: the resources he controls that others value (either positively or negatively). These are largely derived from a president's formal powers, but they become more or less fungible according to his public prestige and reputation for bargaining skill.

The focus on capital, however, gives short shrift to a second set of resources necessary for presidents to bargain effectively. These include (but are not limited to) time, energy, information, and expertise.[54] These additional resources help reduce bargaining uncertainty by allowing presidents to better gauge the likely impact of their bargaining choices on their desired objectives.

Where do presidents obtain these resources? One source is presidential aides.[55] Neustadt recognized this, of course, but he cautioned that advisers do not automatically provide the bargaining resources presidents seek: "On the one hand, [a president] can never assume that anyone or any system will supply the bits and pieces he needs most; on the other hand, he must assume that much of what he needs will not be volunteered by his official advisers."[56]

This is because the Constitution, statutes, and political tradition center political accountability in the president, not his advisers. As John Kennedy observed, "No matter how many advisers you have, the President must finally choose. . . . [He] bears the burden . . . the advisers may move on to new advice."[57] Because presidential assistants do not fully share responsibility for a president's choices, they do not necessarily provide the resources that presidents need to reduce bargaining uncertainty without active presidential oversight. But oversight is a costly activity; presidents do not have unlimited time and energy to expend looking over their assistants' shoulders, nor do they always have the expertise to properly evaluate what their assistants are saying.[58]

It was in limiting these staff oversight costs that FDR's competitive adhocracy proved so effective. First, by controlling White House staff size, layering, and functional specialization, FDR rendered his personal aides more likely to understand his bargaining objectives, and thus more likely to provide the resources he needed to obtain them. And by inducing intrastaff competition, FDR encouraged his aides to supervise one another on his behalf, thus lowering his management costs.[59] Finally, by nurturing a separate staff composed of career civil servants, FDR ensured ready access to sources of institutional memory and resources devoted to the interests of the presidency, not just of the president.

Competitive adhocracy had critics of course, especially among FDR's own advisers. It could be demoralizing to staff, it encouraged public airing of their disputes, and it sometimes led to the duplication and inefficient use of staff resources.[60] But on the whole, the evidence suggests that competitive adhocracy served him well. Consider three broad-gauge measures: electoral success, historical legacy, and decision-making effectiveness. On each FDR compares favorably with his successors in utilizing the White House-centered presidential branch for staff support.

Roosevelt was, of course, elected to an unprecedented four terms in office, and his historical reputation is higher than that of any other modern president. True, these accomplishments are not solely or even primarily attributable to his administrative approach, but neither can one dismiss the possibility that his success on both counts had something to do with his staff strategy.

Moreover, a closer look at specific instances of FDR's use of assistants suggests how well his staff system served him. Consider his handling of domestic economic production and the Allied military effort during World War II. By creating a series of war production agencies, each marginally more powerful than its predecessor, FDR was able to mobilize U.S. economic might without outpacing public opinion, which, until Pearl Harbor, remained highly ambivalent about U.S. involvement overseas. Thereafter, as the United States became an active military participant, Roosevelt oversaw the emergence of the United States as the "arsenal of democracy," meeting or exceeding almost every production target and paving the way for postwar prosperity.

At the same time, by devising an administrative strategy for vesting command of the Army, Navy, and Air Force in the single JCS, and integrating it with British military counterparts, FDR was able to coordinate military action on a global basis. Yet by refusing to formalize this arrangement, and by exploiting divisions between the military branches (in part by skillfully using Leahy as an information source), Roosevelt widened his political-military options beyond his generals' often parochial interests.[61]

Roosevelt's experiences, as conceptualized here, help pinpoint the flaw inherent in the White House-dominated presidential branch. By increasingly centralizing bargaining support within the White House staff, FDR's successors gradually lost the ability to distance themselves from staff actions. More aides were acting in the president's name, but with less knowledge of his bargaining needs. Accordingly, staff management costs went up, but without a corresponding increase in the bargaining resources that aides provided. Indeed, White House staff growth, specialization, and layering may have made the provision of presidentially oriented bargaining resources less likely. Comparatively speaking, Roosevelt's competitive adhocracy was more efficient; it enabled him to extract bargaining resources from aides at a lower management cost.

Do we have reason to believe that FDR's staff tenets are applicable today? Short of an actual test, of course, one cannot be sure. However, the growth of government size and responsibilities in the half-century after FDR's death did *not* significantly alter the constitutional and statutory foundation of presidential power; presidents continue to operate in a system of separate institutions sharing power, in which their effective influence on governmental outcomes remains largely dependent on their bargaining effectiveness. That effectiveness, in turn, is partly predicated on how well presidents can extract the necessary resources from their advisers.

Indeed, a strong case can be made that Roosevelt's administrative strategy unfolded at a time when bargaining was as costly as it has ever been, at least as measured by the number of government personnel, budget outlays, regulations, and the sheer importance of the bargaining outcomes for which he was responsible. It is true that the number of federal regulations (as approximated by the number of pages in the *Federal Register*) has increased dramatically since FDR's presidency, although it was not until 1967 that the peak total number of pages listing regulations during his tenure in office was eclipsed.

Roosevelt's wartime national government expenditures (adjusted for inflation) were not matched until 1980, long after the appearance of the presidential branch. As a percentage of the gross domestic product (GDP), peak government outlays under Roosevelt have never been matched.

Although the number of public sector employees has increased at a steady clip since 1945, federal employment under FDR was not matched until the early 1980s, again well after the most extensive growth in White House staff and influence.

Finally, the significance of the policy decisions that FDR confronted on a daily basis during the Great Depression and the war years—decisions in which the future of the free world hung in the balance—have arguably not been matched since. And although many of these critical decisions were made during a time of war, it is not the case that they unfolded in an atmosphere of political consensus; indeed, precisely because the stakes were so high, the policy and political bickering and disagreements that characterized wartime decision-making were in many respects more virulent than during peacetime.[62]

Of course, the proof of the conceptual pudding is in the empirical eating. Unfortunately, recent presidents have not seriously tried to implement FDR's administrative system, in part because it has often been mischaracterized by scholars. If we wish to help presidents "reinvent" the White House, then, it behooves us first to portray past administrative strategies, especially Roosevelt's, accurately, so that presidents can make realistic judgments as to their utility. From time to time during the last three decades, presidents have sought an administrative alternative to the presidential branch. It is reassuring to know that a feasible, time-tested candidate exists.

NOTES

1. The most recent alarm, which linked the growth of the White House staff to an "imperial presidency," was sounded by Michael Lind in "The Out-of-Control Presidency," *New Republic* (August 1995): 18–23. Lind's jeremiad is the latest in a series of such warnings. See, for example, George Reedy, *The Twilight of the Presidency* (New York: World, 1970); Thomas Cronin, *The State of the Presidency* (Boston: Little, Brown, 1975); Hugh Heclo, "The Changing Presidential Office," in Arnold J. Meltsner (ed.), *Politics and the Oval Office* (San Francisco: Institute for Contemporary Studies, 1981); Thomas Cronin, "The Swelling of the Presidency: Can Anyone Stop the Tide?" in Peter Woll (ed.), *American Government: Readings and Cases*, 8th ed. (Boston: Little, Brown, 1984); Stephen Hess, *Organizing the Presidency*, 2nd ed. (Washington, D.C.: Brookings Institution, 1989); and John Hart, *The Presidential Branch*, 2nd ed. (Chatham, N.J.: Chathan House, 1995).

2. Although the phrase was coined by Nelson Polsby, the use of "presidential branch" as a synonym for the White House-centered presidential staff was popularized by John Hart's indispensable book on the topic. See Polsby's "Some Landmarks in Modern Presidential-Congressional Relations," in Anthony King (ed.), *Both Ends of the Avenue* (Washington, D.C.: AEI, 1983), p. 20; and Hart's *The Presidential Branch*. The phrase "separate institutions sharing power" is taken from Richard Neustadt, *Presidential Power and the Modern Presidents: The Politics of Leadership from Roosevelt to Reagan* (New York: Free Press, 1990), p. 1.

3. On the necessity for an energetic executive, see Alexander Hamilton's *Federalist* paper #70.

4. For details, see Richard P. Nathan, *The Plot That Failed: Nixon and the Administrative Presidency* (New York: John Wiley, 1975); Peri Arnold, *Making the Managerial Presidency: Comprehensive Reorganization Planning, 1905–1980* (Princeton: Princeton University Press, 1986), ch. 9; and Harold Seidman and Robert Gilmour, *Politics, Position, and Power*, 4th ed. (New York: Oxford University Press, 1986), pp. 108–111. Eventually, Nixon's plan fell prey to congressional intransigence fed by Watergate.

5. Gerald Ford, following in Watergate's wake, also embraced staff reductions, in part to end repeated clashes between Nixon holdovers and Ford appointees. Although he trimmed almost 100 people from the White House Office, these were largely peripheral cuts affecting second-level aides. Jimmy Carter campaigned in 1976 on a promise of staff reductions, but once in office, rather than reduce staff numbers, he shifted aides from the White House to other executive staff agency payrolls.

Although talk of White House staff cuts was temporarily quelled during Reagan's first term, Iran-contra resurrected the issue. Ultimately, rather than reduce White House staff size, Reagan opted for more staff hierarchy and a reversion to regularized staffing procedures. Finally, after one term plagued by the failings of key aides, most notably chief of staff John Sununu and his replacement, Samuel Skinner, George Bush promised a major overhaul of his White House office, only to be denied reelection. For details, see Richard P. Nathan, *The Administrative Presidency* (Princeton: Princeton University Press, 1983); Robert Hartmann, *Palace Politics: An Inside Account of the Ford Years* (New York: McGraw-Hill, 1980), pp. 34–36, 272–302; Dom Bonafede, "White House Reorganization: Separating Smoke from Substance," *National Journal* 10, no. 46 (1977): 1307–1311; Arnold, *Making the Managerial Presidency*; Seidman and Gilmour, *Politics, Position, and Power*; Hart, *The Presidential Branch*.

6. See "Clinton Trimming Lower-Level Aides," *New York Times*, February 10, 1993, pp. A1, A20; Ann Devroy, "Defining the Quarter Among the Dollars; White House Says Pledge to Cut Staff Has Been Met; Critics Counter That Spending Will Rise," *Washington Post*, April 14, 1993, p. A19; Ann Devroy, "Pruning the White House Vineyard," *Washington Post*, August 26, 1993, p. A25;

and Rogelio Garcia, "President Clinton's Proposed Reduction in White House Staff," Congressional Research Service (May 6, 1993).

7. On this point, see Hart, *The Presidential Branch*; Terry Moe, "The Politicized Presidency," in John E. Chubb and Paul E. Peterson (eds.), *The New Direction in American Politics* (Washington, D.C.: Brookings Institution, 1985), pp. 235–271; Samuel Kernell and Samuel L. Popkin, *Chief of Staff: Twenty-five Years of the Managerial Presidency* (Berkeley: University of California Press, 1986); and Samuel Kernell, "The Evolution of the White House Staff," in John E. Chubb and Paul E. Peterson (eds.), *Can the Government Govern?* (Washington, D.C.: Brookings Institution, 1989).

8. Those "staff-related miscues" include (but are not limited to) attempts by presidential aides to influence FBI investigations of the White House travel office; the bungled handling of White House aide Vincent Foster's papers in the aftermath of his suicide; the contacts between White House legal counsel Bernie Nussbaum and federal officials investigating Arkansas land deals made by Clinton and his wife prior to his becoming president; the series of ill-fated nominations (Zoe Baird, Kimba Wood, Lani Guinier, and Henry Foster) based in part on White House aides' recommendations; the ill-advised use of White House helicopters by White House aides for golf excursions; and allegations that key advisers used poor judgment during the botched raid on David Koresh's Branch Davidian complex at Waco, Texas. In response, three significant staff shuffles have taken place since Clinton took office: in May 1993, in June 1994, and in September 1995.

For details regarding the first, see Ruth Marcus, "GOP Insider to Be Clinton Counselor," *Washington Post*, May 30, 1993, p. A1; John M. Broder, "Gergen Reveals He Has Sweeping Power," *Los Angeles Times*, June 8, 1993, p. A16; Michael Kranish, "Clinton to Reduce White House Staff," *Boston Globe*, February 10, 1993, p. 3; and Carl P. Leubsdorf, "It Can Be Too Much Fun," *Dallas Morning News*, December 23, 1993, p. 17A. On the second staff shuffle, see Douglas Jehl, "Clinton Shuffles His Aides, Selecting Budget Director as White House Staff Chief," *New York Times*, June 28, 1994, p. A1; Michael Kranish, "McLarty Out, Panetta in as Clinton Shakes Staff," *Boston Globe*, June 28, 1994, p. 1; Marshall Ingwerson, "Deficit Hawks Rise to the Top in White House," *Christian Science Monitor*, June 29, 1994, p. 1; and Suzanne Garment, "Starting Over: Is Lack of Focus the Problem?" *Los Angeles Times*, July 3, 1994, p. M1. An overview of the third reshuffling is contained in transcripts of the White House press briefing announcing the changes (September 23, 1994).

9. See the Report of the President's Committee on Administrative Management (Washington, D.C.: U.S. Government Printing Office, 1937), hereafter the Brownlow Report; and Executive Order 8248 (September 8, 1939), issued under Reorganization Plan I, pursuant to authority granted Roosevelt by the 1939 Reorganization Act.

10. See, for example, Terry Moe, "Presidents, Institutions and Theory," in George C. Edwards, John H. Kessel, and Bert A. Rockman (eds.), *Researching the*

Presidency: Vital Questions, New Approaches (Pittsburgh: University of Pittsburgh Press, 1993), p. 341; John Burke, *The Institutional Presidency* (Baltimore: Johns Hopkins University Press, 1992), pp. 3, 12; and Hess, *Organizing the Presidency*, p. 6.

11. The term "competitive adhocracy" is drawn from Roger Porter, *Presidential Decisionmaking* (New York: Cambridge University Press, 1980), Appendix, pp. 229–235.

12. Quoted in Arthur Schlesinger, Jr., *The Coming of the New Deal*, vol. III of his *The Age of Roosevelt* (Boston: Houghton Mifflin, 1959), p. 531.

13. This was the "M-Day" Plan, drafted in 1931 and revised in 1933, 1936, and 1939. See "Industrial Mobilization Plan Revision of 1939," Senate Document no. 134, 76th Cong., 2nd sess. (Washington, D.C.: U.S. Government Printing Office, 1939). A copy is in the Hopkins Papers, Sherwood Book Collection, Book 2: Organization of NDAC #3 File, FDR Library (FDRL).

   In the event of war, the plan proposed creating a War Resources Administration under the direction of a civilian appointed by the president. This individual would be assisted by an Advisory Council consisting of individuals selected to oversee conversion in the areas of industrial facilities, commodities, power, fuel, and transportation. Representatives from the State, War, and Navy departments, and from the Army chief of staff and chief of naval operations would report to the defense czar, as would representatives of other emergency agencies handling public relations, selective service, finance, trade, labor, and prices. Although the plan provided only general guidelines for economic mobilization, detailed annexes held by the armed services fleshed these out considerably.

14. The NDAC, a seven-person advisory committee, was established in May 1940, to advise FDR on defense mobilization. It was largely replaced by the OPM, established by Executive Order 8629 (January 7, 1941), which in turn was superseded by SPAB, via Executive Order 8875 (August 28, 1941).

15. The WPB, created January 16, 1942, by Executive Order 9024, replaced both SPAB and OPM as the primary war production agency. See Donald Nelson, *Arsenal of Democracy* (New York: Harcourt Brace, 1946), pp. 195–197.

16. The OWM, created on May 27, 1943, became responsible for overseeing all aspects of war production. Byrnes resigned from the Supreme Court to head the OWM. Previously he had served in the U.S. Senate and House of Representatives. See James Byrnes, *Speaking Frankly* (New York: Harper & Brothers, 1947), pp. 16–19.

17. For details regarding FDR's use of a national security advisory system, see Matthew J. Dickinson, *Bitter Harvest: FDR and the Growth of the Presidential Branch* (New York: Cambridge University Press, 1997), chs. 7–8.

18. One of the most important intelligence sources, of course, was his wife. Eleanor Roosevelt served effectively as FDR's eyes and ears during her national and global trips. See Doris Kearns Goodwin, *No Ordinary Time* (New York: Simon and Schuster, 1994).

19. Welles was assistant secretary of state until Hull forced his resignation in 1943. When Hull subsequently resigned due to ill health, Bohlen, FDR's interpreter at the 1943 Teheran conference with Stalin, reprised Welles's role under Secretary of State Edward Stettinius.

20. Lend-Lease, created in March 1941, was administered through the Defense Aid Division within the EOP's Office of Emergency Management. On March 27, 1941, FDR designated Hopkins "to advise and assist me in carrying out the responsibilities placed upon me by the act of March 11, 1941 [the Lend-Lease Act]. . . ." See the copy of the memo (March 27, 1942) from FDR to Hopkins, PSF Subject File, Hopkins Folder, FDRL. Averell Harriman, stationed in London to oversee the Lend-Lease mission there, reported directly to Hopkins through naval communications, thus bypassing Ambassador John Winant. Churchill, knowing of the arrangement, used Harriman to communicate with Hopkins and FDR. When a Lend-Lease mission was established in Moscow, similar communications arrangements were used. See Robert Sherwood, *Roosevelt and Hopkins* (New York: Harper & Brothers, 1947), pp. 268–270, 755–756; Rudy Abramson, *Spanning the Century: The Life of W. Averell Harriman* (New York: William Morrow, 1992).

21. Impressed by the portable maps and communications equipment Churchill brought to the Acadia conference, Roosevelt in January 1942 implemented a comparable communication center on the ground floor of the White House. This "Map Room" was used by FDR to track his troops across the globe. His naval aides, beginning with Captain John L. McCrea, handled the daily communications flowing in and out of this command post. See the Finding Aid, Map Room, FDRL; and Admiral William Leahy, *I Was There* (New York: McGraw-Hill, 1950), p. 99.

22. A Harvard Law School professor later appointed by FDR to the Supreme Court.

23. A consultant to presidents from Wilson through Eisenhower.

24. Roosevelt's former law partner.

25. Quoted in Schlesinger, *The Coming of the New Deal*, p. 535.

26. See Harold Wilensky, *Organizational Intelligence: Knowledge and Policy in Government and Industry* (New York: Basic Books, 1967), pp. 50–53.

27. The Army and Navy Munitions Board, created on July 22, 1922, by administrative action, coordinated Army and Navy mobilization efforts.

28. For details regarding FDR's relations with his generals, see Eric Larrabee, *Commander-in-Chief: Franklin Delano Roosevelt, His Lieutenants, and Their War* (New York: Harper & Row, 1987); Ed Cray, *General of the Army: George C. Marshall, Soldier and Statesman* (New York: W. W. Norton, 1990); Forrest Pogue's multivolume work on Marshall, especially *Ordeal and Hope, 1939–1942* (New York: Viking Press, 1965); Thomas Parrish, *Roosevelt and Marshall: Partners in Politics and War* (New York: William Morrow, 1989); and Robert William Love, Jr. (ed.), *The Chiefs of Naval Operations* (Annapolis, Md.: Naval Institute Press, 1980).

29. In his State of the Union address to Congress on January 6, 1942, Roosevelt laid out America's war production goals: 60,000 planes in 1942 and 125,000 the following year; 45,000 tanks, followed the next year by 75,000; 20,000 antiaircraft guns in 1942 and 35,000 the following year; and 8 million deadweight tons of shipping in 1942. For more detailed breakdown, see the memorandum from FDR to Henry Stimson (January 3, 1942), listing projections for 1942 and 1943 (Hopkins Papers, Special Assistant to the President, 1941–45, Production File, FDRL). For the skeptical reaction to FDR's figures, see "The Feasibility Dispute: The Determination of War Production Objectives for 1942 and 1943" (Washington, D.C.: Committee on Public Administration Cases, 1950).

30. Dickinson, *Bitter Harvest*, ch. 7.

31. Institutionalization of staff roles refers either to formal designations of authority, as by executive order, or to informal grants, including presidential statements, that publicly place specific responsibility for particular policy or processes with a single assistant.

32. Richard Neustadt, "Approaches to Staffing the Presidency: Notes on FDR and JFK," *American Political Science Review* 57, no. 4 (1963): 855–863.

33. This is the prime reason why presidents should be reluctant to formally place the vice president in charge of critical staff areas: once in place, they are difficult to remove. President Gerald Ford's problems with Vice President Nelson Rockefeller, who was formally appointed to head Ford's Domestic Council, is instructive in this regard. See Kernell and Popkin, *Chief of Staff*, pp. 173–176.

34. Indeed, when Byrnes was made statutory head of the OWMR, established by Congress on October 3, 1944, through the War Mobilization Act (58 Stat. 785), he offered his resignation to FDR. Roosevelt persuaded Byrnes to stay only because he wanted him to attend the Yalta conference. (Conversation with Richard Neustadt, based on his discussion with those who worked with Roosevelt.)

35. See Brownlow's thoughts in his "Memo, Nov. 5, 1939. Brownlow. Dictated in New York," Document A-II-33, pp. 1–3, PCAM (President's Committee on Administrative Management), FDRL; and accompanying organizational chart titled "Possible Organization of President's Staff" (November 5, 1936). See also Brownlow, *A Passion for Anonymity* (Chicago: University of Chicago Press, 1955), p. 376; and "Organization of President's Staff," with chart and memorandum from Herbert Emmerich to Joseph Harris (Oct. 29, 1936), Document G-XX, PCAM, FDRL.

36. See the White House staff listings in *U.S. Government Manual* (Washington, D.C.: U.S. Government Printing Office) for the years 1940–1945.

37. As Ted Sorensen warns, "More important than who gets a White House parking permit or who eats in the White House mess is who is able to invoke the president's name, who is using the president's telephone, and who is using the president's stationery. That's serious. If you have hundreds of people doing that, there is no way you can keep them out of mischief" (Kernell and Popkin, *Chief of Staff*, p. 106).

38. This aversion to staff specialization explains Hopkins's value to FDR during World War II. Hopkins's lack of military and diplomatic expertise, combined with his broad mandate, encouraged him to question the assumptions of experts in both fields with impunity. It also helps explain why FDR frequently shifted staff to new, unfamiliar assignments, as when Lauchlin Currie was moved from domestic economic advice to liaison with the Chinese during World War II, and why Rosenman, primarily a domestic adviser, was sent overseas to investigate Allied relief policy in 1945. These aides' lack of familiarity with the issues may have allowed them to bring a fresh perspective.

39. FDR's son James, hired as a White house assistant during FDR's second term, was a conspicuous exception to this rule.

40. Again, Hopkins is a prime example. He started as a New Deal bureaucrat specializing in work relief, but after several years achieved preeminence as FDR's primary foreign policy consultant.

41. McIntyre, who handled appointments prior to Watson, died early in the war.

42. For a description of their duties, see Grace Tully, *FDR, My Boss* (New York: Charles Scribner and Sons, 1949), p. 169.

43. Corcoran, a Hoover appointee working in the Reconstruction Finance Corporation, and Cohen, first with the Public Works Administration and later with the National Power Policy Committee within the Interior Department, drafted significant chunks of New Deal legislation on FDR's behalf, and helped sell it on Capitol Hill. See "The Draftsmen," in Katie Louchheim (ed.), *The Making of the New Deal: The Insiders Speak* (Cambridge, Mass.: Harvard University Press, 1983), pp. 105–118; Tully, *FDR, My Boss*, pp. 141–142; the Samuel Rosenman Oral History, FDRL; Schlesinger, *The Coming of the New Deal*, pp. 440–441, 456–467; and, regarding Corcoran, Louis Koenig, *The Invisible Presidency* (New York: Rinehart & Co., 1960), pp. 249–298.

44. The five-member NRPB was established through Reorganization Plan I by absorbing the duties and personnel of the National Resources Committee, except for the committee itself, and some of the functions carried out by the Federal Employment Stabilization Office, then located in the Department of Commerce. But because only those functions performed by the stabilization office had a statutory basis, FDR continued to seek congressional legislation for an NRPB. Due to various factors, however, including congressional reluctance to spend money for "planning," Roosevelt's disinclination to fight for that money during World War II, and the competition from other agencies, especially the Bureau of the Budget and the Office of War Mobilization, the NRPB expired in 1943, never to be resurrected. See Harold H. Roth, "The Executive Office of the President" (Ph.D. diss., The American University, 1953), pp. 175–176.

45. In fact, Roosevelt evidently did not see a distinction between the two areas; his most important advisers—Hopkins, Rosenman, Byrnes, Smith—were as likely to deal with domestic as with foreign policy issues.

46. On this distinction, see Colin Campbell, *Managing the Presidency: Carter, Reagan and the Search for Executive Harmony* (Pittsburgh: University of Pittsburgh Press, 1986), esp. pp. 3–24.

47. True, Roosevelt was less successful at institutionalizing either a planning or a personnel staff; neither the NRPB nor his White House liaison for personnel management fulfilled his expectations in these regards. But their failures reflect the opposition he encountered more than his own staff utilization.

48. Richberg, former counsel to the National Recovery Administration, was appointed by FDR as executive secretary to the NEC, authorized to make any rules and regulations necessary to achieve the president's objectives. Although dubbed the "assistant president," within six months Richberg had resigned, effective May 1935, a victim of sniping from Cabinet members and FDR's lukewarm administrative backing. See Donald Richberg, *My Hero: The Indiscreet Memoirs of an Eventful But Unheroic Life* (New York: Putnam, 1954), p. 178.

49. For details, see Leahy, *I Was There*.

50. See James Pfiffner, "The President's Chief of Staff: Lessons Learned," *Presidential Studies Quarterly* 23, no. 1 (Winter 1993): 77–102; and the viewpoints expressed by several former White House staff members in Kernell and Popkin, *Chief of Staff*; compare with Richard Neustadt, "Does the President Need a Chief of Staff?" 29–32, and Bruce Buchanan, "Constrained Diversity: The Organizational Demands of the Presidency," 78–104, both in James Pfiffner, ed., *The Managerial Presidency* (Pacific Grove, Calif.: Brooks-Cole, 1991).

51. A little-noted provision in E.O. 8248 empowered the president, in times of national emergency, to activate an "office of emergency management." Roosevelt used this in May 1940 to create the OEM.

52. See, for example, Alexander George, *Presidential Decisionmaking in Foreign Policy: The Effective Use of Information and Advise* (Boulder, Colo.: Westview Press, 1980); Richard Tanner Johnson, *Managing the White House* (New York: Harper & Row, 1974); Porter, *Presidential Decisionmaking*, esp. Appendix, pp. 231–235; Schlesinger, *The Coming of the New Deal*, pp. 511–573; Hess, *Organizing the Presidency*, pp. 23–39; Neustadt, *Presidential Power*, pp. 128–135, and his "Approaches to Staffing the Presidency"; and Louis Wann, *The President as Chief Administrator* (Washington, D.C.: Public Affairs Press, 1968).

53. Neustadt, *Presidential Power*, p. 1.

54. Compare with Paul Light, *The President's Agenda: Domestic Policy Choice from Kennedy to Carter* (Baltimore: Johns Hopkins University Press, 1983), pp. 14–29.

55. Presidents must utilize aides, of course, because presidential resources are finite—for any given bargain in any specified period, they have but limited time, energy, information and expertise. Hence the need for assistance.

56. Neustadt, *Presidential Power*, p. 129.

57. Quoted in Theodore Sorensen, *Decision-making in the White House* (New York: Columbia University Press, 1963), p. 82.

58. The need to manage staff is a specific example of the more general issue addressed in the principal–agent literature developed mainly by economists. For an introduction to the issues, see John W. Pratt and Richard Zeckhauser, "Principles and Agents: An Overview," in Pratt and Zeckhauser (eds.), *Principles and Agents: The Structure of Business* (Boston: Harvard Business School Press, 1985), pp. 1–36.

Political economists typically assume that agents pursue their own interest, quite consciously subverting the terms of the contract with their principal. This, I argue, is rarely the case with presidential advisers. Instead, it is more common for overzealous aides to pursue what they *believe* to be the president's interest, when in fact it is not.

59. As Schlesinger puts it, "The competitive approach to administration gave Roosevelt great advantages. It brought him an effective flow of information; it kept the reins of decision in his own hands; it made for administrative flexibility and stimulated subordinates to effective performance" (*The Coming of the New Deal*, p. 537).

60. For criticisms of FDR's administrative habits, see Dean Acheson, *Present at the Creation* (New York: W. W. Norton, 1987), pp. 46–47; Frances Perkins, *The Roosevelt I Knew* (New York: Harper & Row, 1964), p. 357; Henry Stimson with McGeorge Bundy, *On Active Service in Peace and War* (New York: Octogon Books, 1971), p. 495; and Harold Ickes, *The Secret Diary of Harold Ickes: The First Thousand Days* (New York: Simon and Schuster, 1953) vol. I, p. 308, and vol. III, p. 433.

61. For details, see Dickinson, *Bitter Harvest*, chs. 4–8.

62. For evidence on this point, see ibid., esp. chs. 6–7.

3

Administering Democracy: Personnel Management in the Federal Civil Service, 1933–1953

Margaret C. Rung

To many who suffered during the Great Depression, President Franklin D. Roosevelt's New Deal illustrated the president's desire to address the needs of the dispossessed. He seemed to champion the "forgotten" people and turn his back on the upper crust. Ironically, Roosevelt himself was a member of the elite. Early in his career, one of his supporters noted that Roosevelt's greatest political handicap was his patrician background.[1] By 1933, however, he seemed to have overcome the handicap. Indeed, Roosevelt's leadership talents rested upon his ability to convince people that he could be as forceful and dignified as a monarch while still respecting ordinary citizens and democratic rule.

"Roosevelt's all-embracing strategy was to appear as the patron of the average American, commanding attention not merely because he was the nation's leader, blessed with a benignly superior, cultivated background, but also by suggesting that he could help define the true average."[2] This tension between liberal democratic principles, on the one hand, and aristocratic rule, on the other, caused significant conflict within the federal government during the 1930s and 1940s. Yet it represented just one set of a series of oppositional ideologies that undergirded the debate over authority. Over time, totalitarianism, on the one hand, and individualism, on the other, also informed this debate. These issues were not exclusive to the presidency, but extended deep into the foundations of the federal bureaucracy.

In 1936 former Assistant Secretary of the Treasury Russell Leffingwell endorsed this approach to civil service staffing: "The Government ought to be out for the triple A men," he stated, and should recruit these "triple A men out of the graduating classes of our great universities, as they do in England and in France."[3] Two years earlier, Secretary of the Treasury Henry Morgenthau, commenting on the creation of the Social Science Research Council's Commission of Inquiry on the Public Service, noted that the expansion of government activities would make the public more interested in the sources from which the government recruited its workforce.[4] Indeed, when Roosevelt recruited his brain trust and created the Committee on Administrative Management to examine, among other issues, recruitment in the civil service, he reinforced a Progressive Era faith in expertise.[5]

This preoccupation with professionalism was bolstered by the growing strength of the field of public administration, which advocated extensive training and education for career civil servants. Using money from the Rockefeller Foundation's Spelman Fund, public administrative specialist Frederick Davenport established the National Institute of Public Affairs (NIPA), which selected college students to intern in government agencies. Once they graduated, Davenport hoped, they would apply their professional administrative skills in the career civil service.[6]

The creation of professional administrators sparked an often venomous discussion among federal civil servants.[7] During the 1930s they bitterly debated the advantages and disadvantages of hiring "triple A men" out of "great universities." One reporter warned that the government was establishing a "caste system," in which favored individuals from "favored schools" were "handpicked" to take jobs at the top that might have gone to employees who through years of effort had prepared themselves for a promotion. A union leader claimed that there was "a total absence of any system of promotion in the Federal civil service," and those few who did manage to rise from rags to riches, did so with "considerable" political aid.[8]

Longtime civil service staffers, along with the chair of the Civil Service Commission, Harry Mitchell, pointed to organizations like the NIPA as evidence of this elitist trend.[9] Helen Miller, representing the Congress of Industrial Organizations's United Federal Workers of America Local 12, concluded in 1940 that NIPA and similar programs gave "special privileges to a favored few in disregard of the interests of the thousands of government employees now in the service who are qualified for promotion." Indeed, she charged, the method of selection was "undemocratic and noncompetitive."

Only those with money, she said, could afford to work without pay. Blacks and students from free metropolitan universities were noticeably absent from NIPA intern registers. Consequently, Miller claimed, the program was susceptible to "favoritism, intrigue and politics—the very evils which the merit system was designed to eliminate." On behalf of union members, she requested that the Labor Department cease its participation in the program. Two Southern congressmen echoed these concerns, urging government recruiters to select those with proven ability and the "necessary character qualifications," even if they had been "denied a college education."[10]

Among public administration reformers committed to a merit system, it was not clear whether the Roosevelt administration should recruit a more professional workforce or whether, as some argued, the civil service was to be a democratic institution, used as a means of upward mobility for ordinary Americans. Elite reformers wanted to develop an administrative aristocracy by recruiting highly educated individuals into the career service.[11] This issue was especially problematic during the Great Depression because the crisis encouraged Americans to reexamine not only issues of class but also the meaning and workings of democracy. Reformers struggled to find a way to organize and develop a nonpartisan, professionally based civil service system that would be consistent with democratic, rather than authoritarian, values.

This dilemma was most evident among federal personnel administrators, who were themselves trying to identify the proper credentials for their occupation. Personnel managers neither obtained professional status automatically nor acquired it with ease.[12] They haggled among themselves and with the outside world in their efforts to define and legitimate their profession. Ultimately they achieved their peculiar professional status by creating a demand for their services, by establishing networks of power within and between departmental personnel divisions, and by building a distinct body of knowledge. Among public personnel administrators in the New Deal era, the most elite group of managers had a special role in this process. They took advantage of their positions within the bureaucracy to establish a particular occupational identity that put them in a position to control the establishment and administration of federal personnel policies.

In addition to these elite public administrators, two other groups of personnel managers had an impact on the development of administrative professions during the New Deal era. A coterie of Horatio Alger-like civil service staffers and a group of quasi-professionals eventually joined the elites in an aggressive search for professional authority. The group with the least formal training, the "Algers," consisted of lifelong civil servants who had started their government careers in low-level positions. They included Navy Department personnel director Charles Piozet, who began by earning 25 cents an hour as a messenger for the Navy Department when he was fifteen, and Julia Atwood Maulding, personnel director for the Interior Department, who started out as a stenographer and typist in 1917 for the Bureau of Mines. Their stories became the Horatio Alger lore of the civil service.[13] Gradually these servants rose from "rags" to modest riches as government personnel directors. From their perspective, the ideal career rewarded hard work. As their experience demonstrated, the government bureaucracy provided an opportunity for those with initiative to rise to positions of prominence.

Washington Post columnist Scott Hart illustrated this bias in a series of articles profiling personnel directors. He commended Thomas McNamara's commonsense approach to management at the Railroad Retirement Board and his deep commitment to a government service "wherein practical and competent men can demonstrate what they've got on the ball, and having demonstrated it, move up." In Hart's view, McNamara vocalized the necessity of retaining opportunities for low-level civil servants by favoring a system of career development that would be free of "red tapes of technicality and theory." This approach, Hart believed, would appeal to those upset about the federal government's trend toward hiring bureaucrats "with pockets full of college degrees."[14]

Hart emphasized the upward mobility theme. He detailed the childhood of Maritime Commission personnel director Justice Chambers, noting that the "little boy . . . had a long way to go before he could get to town. But leaving Horatio Alger out of it, he's here." Russell Herrell of the Government Printing Office "went up in the ranks under his own steam," as did Theodore Wilson of the Farm Credit Administration, who got to his position "on his own footing, step by step," because "[n]obody smoothed his way to the desk he holds now." Of John Switzer, personnel director at the Interstate Commerce Commission, who started as a messenger in the Congressional Library in 1904, Hart wrote: "He is typical of the merit system, in its best workings, as any man could be. . . . He knows all the bumps of starting at the very bottom and working wherever the way leads." Hence, Switzer could look any crowd in the eye and state, I took it the hard way." Achieving success the "hard way" gave these managers a particularly strong commitment to the creation of a fluid administrative civil service and the maintenance of an open profession.[15]

The next group—the quasi-professionals—included personnel officials who had not only achieved educational success at a younger age but also had had careers in the private sector. They therefore entered government service at higher grades than did the Algers. These administrators had held a variety of positions ranging from corporate personnel administrator to journalist. Some had academic degrees in personnel administration. This middle group of personnel specialists was not entirely cohesive; it was driven by a common interest in perfecting and utilizing the latest techniques in personnel management. They were devoted to the development of distinct tasks for personnel administrators and concentrated their efforts on extending their administrative authority over programs at the agency level. Their commitment to the personnel field provided a critical base of support for a professionalization movement.

This new breed of managers was more self-assured than the Algers and less worried about the danger of hiring administrators with "pockets full of college degrees." Instead the quasi-professionals highlighted the need to create distance between managers and employees. This appealed to the Algers, who welcomed recognition of their accomplishments and were intent on achieving and maintaining high-level administrative positions.

Because specialized administrative occupations such as personnel management existed only within large-scale organizations, their professional development followed a path different from the one normally associated with academic disciplines. Their search for authority ended, but did not begin, with the capture of the coveted prize of professionalism: a body of knowledge. Prodded by a desire for authority and status, personnel administrators started their rocky road toward professionalism, somewhat strangely, by solidifying their right to elite staff positions within their departments.[16] Their professional development was based initially on their success at manipulating the organization. By doing so, they built jurisdictional boundaries, educational supports, professional networks and associations, and, eventually, their own knowledge base. Slowly, they transferred their base of authority from the organization to professional competence.

During this early phase of profession building, personnel managers desperately sought to make themselves indispensable. They knew that they could not automatically accrue status by virtue of their white-collar jobs. In America, occupation and class had never been fully merged, and the increasing presence of white-collar occupations in the early twentieth century clouded, rather than clarified, this issue. Lower-salaried clerical and sales workers, while seemingly part of a white-collar workforce, over time became segmented into a sphere that was separate from elite "professional" white-collar workers.[17] Technical tasks, such as personnel management, then, occupied a nebulous and precarious position in the world of early twentieth-century work. Ever conscious of the possibility that they might tumble into the growing pink-collar workforce, personnel managers worked desperately to solidify their place within the organization's structure. By creating organizational authority, they hoped to cement their position within a broadly defined middle class.[18]

Their pursuit of prestigious positions within the organization helped this disparate group of public personnel managers forge a common occupational identity. At first, internal divisions created tension among government personnel administrators. Those with less training in personnel administration initially hesitated to construct professional barriers around their jobs. But they, like their more professionally oriented colleagues, wanted to be permanently elevated above clerical workers.

Personnel managers received assistance in their effort to secure high-level posts from the President's Committee on Administrative Management. Most historians have focused intently on the committee's attempt to build a stronger presidency.[19] Management of the bureaucracy was to be streamlined and structured to bolster the president's authority, as the committee's head, Louis Brownlow, advocated. But the Brownlow Committee also recommended the development of specialized personnel offices, with authority vested in a departmental personnel director. Commissioner Samuel Ordway, among others, promoted the creation of specialized and professional departmental personnel offices capable of modernizing all aspects of personnel administration within agencies. Six months before Roosevelt issued his order, Ordway concluded that the fate of a modernized civil service system would rest on the creation of "professionalized personnel divisions" in each department that would be "directed to carry on the work of personnel assignment, training and administration on a merit basis in each such unit." These divisions would be subordinate to a central personnel agency, or "cog," as Ordway referred to it. This cog, he said, would "become a service agency to the departmental units instead of an ornery policeman with a rubber club to be waved at ignorant or recalcitrant departments."[20] While others supported the creation of departmental personnel offices, they questioned the ability of the Civil Service Commission to recruit a capable workforce.

Many on the committee favored a new personnel structure that would eliminate the Civil Service Commission. Herbert Emmerich of the Brownlow Committee complained that the commission had become divorced from the operating departments and had therefore lost touch with agency needs. Because commissioners had privileged the "quantitative factor," he said, "[p]ractically no difference is allowed in rating an application for variations in the quality of experience. Five years of outstanding and brilliant work at Harvard Business or Wharton School may count for less than ten years of mediocre time-serving at an inferior institution, in qualifying an economist." Similarly, he noted, in-service promotions too often went to those with the longest service rather than those who had proven ability to assume new duties. "Time and again," he complained, "this retards the progress of extraordinarily gifted young career men, and frequently discourages them out of the service."[21]

As a result of this tension between operating departments and the commission, many personnel reformers found the commission had been relegated to the role of policing, rather than staffing, the executive branch. Consequently, the commission was often put in the position of denying department officials what they desired. According to Leonard White, this antagonism undermined the credibility of the commission and prevented it from undertaking "constructive leadership in developing and extending techniques of personnel management." Like Emmerich, he favored some decentralization. Under his recommendations, agency personnel divisions would be strengthened so that the most progressive personnel managers in the federal bureaucracy could "plan and develop forward-looking personnel methods for approval by the President, and subsequent to such approval for their introduction in the respective agencies." The committee's answer to an ineffective Civil Service Commission would be to place more authority with departmental personnel officers as well as with a single administrator responsible to the president.[22]

Overall, the committee's work reflected an executive orientation toward management and revealed the friction so prevalent in New Deal politics between those who favored a traditional decentralized power structure and those who were now convinced that the federal government needed more centralized planning. With the reputation of democratic institutions damaged by the Great Depression, many American citizens were encouraged to debate the nature and structure of authority in their new, highly organized society. Political events in Europe similarly influenced the outlook of reformers. Some public administrators expressed ambivalence about centralized power, especially in the context of the rise of fascism.[23] Others, like Brownlow, reversed this argument by maintaining that the best possible way to make the U.S. government more effective, and thus save democracy, would be to strengthen the executive. According to one scholar, the Brownlow Committee considered its mission to be of "decisive importance to the survival of democracy as a political system in the face of totalitarian threats throughout the world." Foes of the president's plan charged that the president was becoming what he professed to despise: a dictator. Ultimately Congress expressed its ambivalence about this issue by voting down the president's personnel reform legislation in 1937.[24]

When the Brownlow Committee's legislative proposals failed, Roosevelt used his executive power. On June 24, 1938, he signed Executive Order 7916, extending the merit system and directing executive department and independent agency heads to "establish . . . a division of personnel supervision and management, at the head of which shall be appointed a director of personnel qualified by training and experience." In addition, the order created the Council of Personnel Administration to assist the president in spreading the merit system and coordinating departmental personnel functions. Roosevelt named Frederick Davenport, head of NIPA, as chair of the council. Ordway called the order "as great a landmark in federal personnel progress as was the Pendleton Act itself."[25]

Ordway also recognized, however, that government departments and bureaus had long operated as fiefdoms, and he feared that the presiding lords would undermine efforts to create separate and specialized personnel bureaus within agencies. Thus, he wrote, personnel managers would have to make a strong effort to ensure the implementation of "the *principle* and spirit of professionalized personnel units in each department."[26]

The task of defining the "principle and spirit of professional personnel units," however, pushed to the surface tensions between a competitive, merit-based civil service and the caste bureaucracy. Few standards existed for the appointment and creation of personnel officers and offices. How much "training and experience," department heads wondered, made a personnel director "qualified"? Thus, the spirit of professional personnel management lacked definition.

As an occupation, personnel administration was bolstered by Executive Order 7916, but the debate over caste made acquisition of professional credentials problematic. Federal personnel specialists found that they had to walk a fine line between advocating elitism and promoting professionalism. Indeed, the professionalization of management reflected a larger debate about the structure of the civil service. The Algers firmly believed that a merit-based civil service meant that individual applicants would qualify for appointment on the basis of an examination *and* that once in, individuals with talent would have an opportunity to climb the ladder to success. To believers, the fusion of merit and upward mobility made the civil service system democratic, for any worthy person could rise, regardless of "class" or "status." Yet these champions of the merit system ignored the fact that ladders suggested hierarchy and thus signified inequity. Their belief in upward mobility implied a desire to have elite positions vested with authority to control the behavior and activities of those occupying lower positions. Personnel specialists were disturbed not by the existence of a hierarchy but by the means through which people obtained top positions.

While personnel managers supported the existence of a hierarchy, they were also anxious about their own place in that hierarchy. Some personnel administrators worried that their positions did not carry enough authority. Thus, some began to call for a more professional orientation to their craft. Resting their power on a knowledge base and credentials outside the organization, they believed, would more tightly secure their positions. By mandating the creation of specialized positions to carry out personnel functions, Executive Order 7916 greatly assisted personnel managers in their struggle toward job and economic security, political recognition, and professional status. Ultimately, the quasi-professionals and elites earned the support of the Algers in their pursuit of professionalism by transforming the debate over caste into one concerning class. They emphasized the need to separate personnel managers from clerical workers on the organizational chart.

Program development offered personnel managers the best opportunity to acquire authority in the organization. Under the president's order, personnel directors were charged with controlling the administration of efficiency ratings and the development of grievance procedures. For example, William Bowen, personnel director at the Railroad Retirement Board, aggressively used his position to devise new evaluation procedures. He explained that he was experimenting with programs used by his former employer, Western Electric. Under his plan, the research and analysis section of the personnel office aided him in forming work committees composed of rating supervisors. These committees then generated rating criteria for different classes of employees. After employees received their ratings, they were to meet with supervisors. A year later, Bowen declared his experiment a success.[27]

Other directors demonstrated their managerial skills by writing agency grievance procedures. This issue fused organizational and professional authority. For example, during the 1930s, two pioneers in government personnel administration, William Stockberger and Paul Appleby of the Department of Agriculture, began fashioning an agencywide personnel policy. Their plan included elaborate procedures for employees with grievances. When they unveiled Memorandum 753 in 1938, they argued that it would aid employees by standardizing the process for dealing with work-related conflicts. In fact, however, the memorandum enhanced the role of the personnel office but left employees with virtually no power to correct inequities. The process required employees to take complaints up the chain of command from immediate supervisor to bureau chief and, if necessary, department administrator. At each level, the employee had the option to appeal. If employees were dissatisfied by the department head's ruling, they were given the opportunity to go before an appeal board whose decision carried only the force of a recommendation. Employee input on the policy itself, moreover, was limited to suggestions on statements already drawn up by personnel managers and department officials. Department officials, while accommodating on some issues, also dictated the final version, a statement that provided for some employee input but still left decision-making authority with department elites.[28]

Despite this hierarchical structure, personnel managers trumpeted their ability to give equal voice to employees and supervisors. Stockberger's successor, Roy Hendrickson, hailed Memorandum 753 as a democratic document that brought together "the ideas and suggestions of bureau chiefs, business managers, personnel officers, national and local employee unions, and unaffiliated employees." Hendrickson believed it was his role as the neutral negotiator to foster cooperation between employees and department officials. After revising the memorandum two years later, he said that "in employing the democratic process of consultation with administrators, employees and employee representatives, we find that there are no great differences of viewpoint in developing a personnel policy and procedure of this kind."[29] By overseeing the standardization and implementation of grievance procedures, however, personnel officers laid claim to elite staff positions and reinforced the agency's hierarchy.

By the late 1930s, personnel specialists began to downplay technical tasks such as job classification and to highlight program development. This, they believed, would broaden their authority and separate them from their previous paper-processing (and clerical) image.[30] They paid increasing attention to the issue of employee relations and, with the support and encouragement of an elite cadre of administrators, personnel managers began to fashion an image as labor relations specialists. This was especially critical, for by the late 1930s unionization of civil servants concerned personnel managers. Nearly all personnel administrators perceived it as a threat to their authority. This external threat, ironically, helped them close ranks and establish a cohesive identity. Labor specialists Clarence J. Hicks and William Leiserson encouraged personnel managers to get involved in labor relations. In the late 1920s, Hicks proclaimed, no one thought of labor relations as a profession. Now that it was considered one, he noted, "the qualifications and professional standards of men getting into personnel work are important." Leiserson warned personnel directors either to become "labor relations managers" or to learn to work with a boss who was one.[31]

Even so, a year after the president issued Executive Order 7916, personnel administrators continued to derive much of their authority from their departmental positions rather than from their access to professional knowledge. Within the corridors of their departments, personnel administrators were accorded the discretion to establish and implement personnel programs. They trained supervisors in the official canons of personnel administration, classified jobs, administered the efficiency rating program, and coordinated hiring and transfers with the commission. Davenport applauded the directors' aggressive pursuit of organizational authority, hoping that some of that energy could be translated into professional power.

On the eve of the war, Davenport and his council staff were poised to do just that. Davenport called for the implementation of a government-wide "human relations" policy that would address the unionization of government employees and enhance productivity. His approach seemed successful, for, according to Ordway Tead, personnel managers were beginning to recognize the importance of balancing and reconciling the aims of "production and personality."[32]

Human relations strategies promised to elevate the status of personnel managers as labor arbitrators. Developed by Elton Mayo in the 1920s, human relations called upon managers to use social science knowledge— particularly sociology, psychology, and anthropology—as a means of diagnosing worker pathologies, deemed to be the root of inefficiency.[33]

Because human relations experts believed that personal interaction and emotional involvement were essential to achieving harmonious labor relations and, hence, high production levels, they urged supervisors to don the hats of scientific psychoanalyst and nurturing counselor. Personnel managers in the Agriculture Department, for instance, linked morale not only to "good salaries, reasonable hours, . . . and job tenure," but also to the "imponderables of human relations—attitudes, omissions, commissions, suspicions, personalities, ambitions, and fears." To foster labor–management cooperation, the department's personnel office implored supervisors to recognize that employees had "feelings," and to understand that "what [an employee] thinks . . . may be determined by a complex of mental patterns only tenuously related to the real situation." Hence, personnel officers warned, "the real situation is not so important as what [the employee] thinks the real situation is." Because "the observed facts are filtered through mental stereotypes and a host of relevant, near relevant, and irrelevant experiences," supervisors would have to learn about each employee's personal life. Only then could supervisors successfully discern the difference between "fancied" and "real" grievances.[34]

Personnel managers labored to learn the difference between "fancied" and "real" grievances—indeed, to practice the art of human relations—for both professional and ideological reasons. First, this approach bolstered the professional authority of personnel managers and distanced them from low-level workers. The popularity of human relations in the corporate world and the social sciences it drew upon made those who embraced it appear objective and sophisticated.

Second, public personnel administrators found human relations an appealing strategy because it encouraged a more "personal" approach to management that promoted the idea that the bureaucracy was an organism consisting of human beings, not a machine run by automatons. According to Luther Gulick, "[r]eorganization is not a mechanical task, but a human task, because Government is not a machine, but a living organism."[35] Personnel administrators wanted to recognize the individuals who worked in this organism as a contrast to the faceless collective they associated with authoritarian regimes. Even in the labyrinth of the federal bureaucracy, individualism was to triumph.

Similarly, this philosophy appeared attractive because it stressed employee participation in decision-making—an activity consistent with American democracy, which was then under attack from European fascism. Personnel administrators perceived themselves as frontline warriors in the campaign against this system of governance. According to Frederick Davenport, "[t]he up-to-date philosophy of the personnel office is the philosophy of the democratic process." Public personnel managers agreed that they were to teach office supervisors that autocratic methods of management were intolerable. "Supervision," as one personnel specialist claimed, "must be democratic if it is to serve a democratic society." Another specialist observed that "democratic internal administration," unlike the "*fuhrer prinzip*," represented the "modern way" for "civilized society."[36] During and after the war, managers heartily supported suggestion systems, employee councils, and grievance procedures as a means of securing employees a voice in the system.

Many of the personnel administrators entering government during the late 1930s and early 1940s shared a commitment to New Deal liberalism and a desire to promote a more pluralistic management system. As educational standards for managers rose, a growing cadre of ambitious and idealistic personnel administrators moved from municipal and state reform organizations into federal government positions. With their advanced degrees, these managers seized the opportunity to apply their knowledge. For them, human relations also promised to create a more liberal and just bureaucratic system.[37]

These administrators often had strong ties to Social Gospel traditions. Davenport, for example, was a former Methodist minister who had crusaded for various moral reforms before moving into academics. He also became an active member of the Progressive Party, and ran for lieutenant governor of New York in 1912. Similarly, Arthur Flemming, appointed by Roosevelt as civil service commissioner in 1939, had strong ties to the Methodist Church and remained active in church affairs throughout his life. Kenneth O. Warner, the progressive personnel director of the Office of Price Administration, was the son of a Methodist home missionary. For these public administrators, liberal politics and support for nonpartisan administration were an extension not simply of their secular academic training but also of deep convictions regarding the moral superiority of democratic government.

These progressive, professionally oriented managers tended to support employee unionization and union participation in agency management. Members of the Brownlow Committee, for example, recommended that the government establish a labor relations policy modeled on the Wagner Act. In their draft policy, they stipulated that employees had the right to organize; that administrators had to recognize and negotiate with employees on issues such as working conditions, hours, and pay; and that the government should establish a Federal Service Personnel Relations Board, similar in functions and purpose to the National Labor Relations Board. At the Office of Price Administration, Warner helped establish an employee relations division and encouraged union participation.[38]

But this more liberal orientation was often moderated by a pervasive fear that a democratic bureaucracy would be dysfunctional. Indeed, the Roosevelt administration felt that these schemes would have to be balanced with the need for an efficient and accountable federal bureaucracy. If the civil service was not productive and effective, personnel administrators worried, democracy would be discredited.[39] "The European dictators," asserted Ordway, "taunt us with the inefficiency of our governmental administration."[40] To ensure the survival of democracy, administrators would need a personnel system that promoted both cooperation and efficiency.

Under this ideology, independent and unlimited employee input into administrative personnel policy-making, such as collective bargaining and striking, would have to be tempered. Administrators claimed that excessive employee power was "anti-democratic," for it established a civil service unaccountable to the public. In explaining why the principle of collective bargaining could not be "transplanted" into the federal government, Roosevelt emphasized accountability. Because the "whole people" acting through Congress represented the "employer," government workers could not enter into binding agreements with administrators or engage in "militant tactics" that might damage the public welfare.[41] Ultimately, personnel administrators used human relations to justify an administrative hierarchy that benefited the status quo. While purporting to be more democratic, managers were in effect becoming more authoritarian. While giving workers more input, they refused to give workers more power.

Democratic rhetoric therefore masked the hierarchical nature of the state's labor relations system. Just as the aim of welfare capitalism in the 1920s was "to attach individual workers to the corporate system by ties of self-interested 'loyalty' and frank dependence," public sector human relations was designed to encourage civil servants to obey elite agency administrators and elected officials.[42] Even though Hendrickson's personnel newsletter in the Department of Agriculture described an organization in soothing words, the structure he outlined was clearly one of domination and subordination: "[organization is] the complicated series of channels— through which authority *flows* from the top to the bottom, and through which, *if management likes*, information and suggestions flow from the bottom to the top."[43] In maintaining control over the flow of information and suggestions, managers retained control over the flow of power.

"[A]s I understand it," council chair Davenport stated, "[democracy] represents two things, the common sense of the mass, which under certain methods shall finally control, but also it represents leadership of intelligent and honest people." Hence, he added, democratic societies needed to pick the "right" kind of people to do the "business" of government.[44] Along with other elites, Davenport was revitalizing a strand of Progressive thought that maintained that leadership in a democracy rested on the shoulders of an educated elite, albeit with the consent of the governed.[45] Even though personnel managers promoted participation, they were advocating civil *service* to democracy, not civil *equality* within the bureaucracy.

The war against a fascist regime powerfully legitimated the democratic ideology espoused by the personnel managers. A relatively rigid system of hierarchy existed in the federal government; indeed, personnel managers believed clear lines of authority to be most efficient. But they were able to use human relations to balance the necessity of consolidated power with the desire for democratic participation, and thus to calm their audience's fear of totalitarianism. Centralized authority would be developed with the "consultation of employees themselves."[46]

Yet by emphasizing worker participation and the evaluation of worker behavior, personnel managers simultaneously masked and enhanced a hierarchical personnel structure often based on race and gender. During World War II, federal administrators recruited thousands of women and minorities to process the paper and administer the programs produced by the government's war machine.[47] This demographic shift in the workforce channeled the expression of human relations down paths that often reinforced a sexual and racial division of labor.

When personality became linked to productivity, management experts obtained the right to evaluate and define appropriate personality traits for government workers, including women. One government training manual for secretaries distinguished between the "bad" secretary, "Ruth," who was irritable, difficult, and brusque, and "Jane," the "good" secretary, who was soft, accommodating, and conciliatory. In detailing the best way to "get along" in the office and with one's boss, the manual instructed the secretary to refrain from appearing so efficient "as to seem managerial to her supervisor, for most men put bossy women in the same class with rattlesnakes." Managers perceived women as office subordinates who should be committed to the group effort. Without such an effort, said one management writer, "personal ambitions and jealousies [would] grow like weeds" and destroy democratic principles.[48] Women were to nurture and serve democracy at its lowest levels.

One contemporary article about women and office promotions warned women about "an all too common disease" known as "executivitis." This "disease" afflicted self-absorbed women who displayed an eagerness to advance. One executive failed to reach the top ranks because of one "fatal flaw": her blatant ambition. Subordinates, said the author, labeled her a "dictator" because she wanted to "dominate and control." She was not alone, however. "Executivitis" attacked "women with particular frequency and virulence" because female executives suffered from deep insecurities about their position in the organizational hierarchy. Accordingly, those women who demonstrated individual initiative and ambition threatened democratic principles, and were criticized and categorized as dysfunctional workers unfit for leadership roles.[49]

African Americans were excluded not only from leadership roles but also from human relations strategies. On the surface, this seemed to exempt them from the potentially harmful consequences of applied psychology. But personnel managers still relied upon social scientific theories to manage race relations and justify exclusionary policies. They developed a crude sociological explanation for separatism, arguing that white workers would not tolerate integration. As Agricultural Department administrator Paul Appleby remarked, "[s]o many whites would refuse to work under the supervision of a negro that this fact—important to the underlying job of administration—simply must be recognized." One supervisor asserted that white people had a right "to state their preferences" with regard to the hiring and integration of black employees.[50] Although agency managers did not formally evaluate African Americans under the rubric of human relations and routinely denied black workers participation in agency management, managers used social scientific language to defend discriminatory acts.

The social scientific language employed by counselors and personnel officials to evaluate employees legitimated stereotypes and reinforced preexisting sexual and racial divisions of labor. Human relations also professionalized personnel management, fortified democratic values, discouraged collective action among lower-level employees, and obscured the degree to which supervisors and elite administrators authoritatively ruled over a growing pink-collar workforce.

Government administrators perceived themselves as teachers of the democratic way. Their mission was to spread the gospel of democratic management. But democratic theories of leadership and authority were based upon a series of unstable, and contested, oppositions. At various times, civil servants contrasted democracy to elitism (and aristocratic values); to highly centralized and authoritarian structures like fascism; and to impersonal machines. While lower-level workers and Alger administrators worried about the creation of a "caste"-based civil service during the New Deal years, this fear soon gave way to new concerns. By the end of the 1930s, the threat was no longer elitism in the form of an aristocratic caste, but authoritarianism in the form of impersonal, machinelike institutions that denied individuals liberty. During the 1930s and 1940s, Roosevelt labored to balance these opposing principles with respect to presidential authority. But his struggle was only a small part of a larger battle waged within the executive branch over the meaning and exercise of power in a democratic state.

In the 1940s those in positions of power worried about the deadening conformity perpetuated by authoritarian regimes. By creating a more "personal" labor system, they believed, they would preserve the individualism associated with democratic societies. But in doing so, bureaucrats and elected officials implemented management theories and structures that reinscribed hierarchical power within the federal government.

Ideology therefore played a crucial role in the internal formation of the American administrative state. It framed debates over power within the organization, including the struggle for professional status. Not only did personnel managers creatively use the state's organizational power to professionalize themselves, but they also learned to appropriate a variety of political discourses to enhance their status. They widened their authority and created internal networks to protect their influence.

Stephen Skowronek, among other scholars, has detailed the series of external forces that led to the emergence of administrative power at the turn of the twentieth century.[51] However, by midcentury, internal forces, as much as external pressures, helped to expand the capabilities of the administrative state. Personnel managers and the system they devised helped the sate expand its resources and enhance its autonomy. The creation of a career service enabled the state to nurture its own policies and programs. It provided what Theda Skocpol claimed was a necessary underpinning of state power: "a prestigious and status conscious career civil service with predictable access to key executive posts." Similarly, during World War II, the state began to present its personnel system as superior and used its expanded war authority to implement new personnel policies in private companies holding government contracts.[52]

This expansion of personnel power was not necessarily permanent. Managers found that the political ideologies upon which they based their authority were themselves in a continual state of flux. Moreover, their control over a distinct academic body of knowledge remained weak. Both of these factors made it difficult for managers to become fully autonomous professionals. They largely remained professionals dependent on organizational power. Because of this, each generation has had to renegotiate its power on the basis of prevailing ideologies.

For the first two generations of personnel managers, human relations promised some measure of professional status and some measure of democracy. To some progressive managers, it offered a true alternative to hierarchy and suggested that management could be more nurturing, more cooperative, and less authoritarian. A conservative resurgence associated with the Cold War and anticommunism, however, undermined these more liberal interpretations.

Despite the efforts of personnel administrators to stabilize and democratize their professional authority, the compatibility of professionalism and democracy remained questionable. Human relations superficially resolved this tension, but even this strategy failed to promote a more democratic labor–management system and was eventually contested. These disputes over power intensified during the Cold War, as conservative managers used a fear of communism to root out those who challenged their autonomy and authority. In response, lower-level civil servants began a renewed effort in the postwar era for union recognition. Americans hence continued to wrestle over the competing cultural values associated with professionalism, bureaucracy, and democracy. Indeed, personnel managers' effort to personalize the administrative state at midcentury reflected an escalating debate in America over the meaning of individualism and equality in an organizational society. Subsequent social and political movements would alter the terms, but not the substance, of the debate. Nevertheless, the successful expansion of state power at midcentury would raise the stakes for all those affected by this ongoing struggle.

NOTES

1. Kenneth Davis, *FDR: The Beckoning of Destiny, 1882–1928* (New York: G. P. Putnam's, 1972), p. 86.

2. Alan Lawson, "The Cultural Legacy of the New Deal," in Harvard Sitkoff, ed., *Fifty Years Later: The New Deal Evaluated* (New York: McGraw-Hill, 1985), p. 156.

3. Leffingwell to Burlingham, 5/25/36, Papers of the National Civil Service Reform League (NCSRL), Acc. 7947, Box 86, 1936, Misc. Correspondence, A to M, American Heritage Center (AHC), Laramie, Wyoming.

4. Morgenthau to Gulick, 1/16/34, RG 56, Office of Secretary, Box 90, Personnel (General), 1933–1956, National Archives and Records Administration (NARA), Washington, D.C. The concern with recruiting the best "men" was reiterated in the commission's final report. *Federal Employee* 20 (Feb. 1935).

This concern with the credentials of government workers was a relatively recent development in the 1930s. From the nineteenth into the early twentieth century, government jobs were stigmatized. The general public perceived them as dull and "unsuited for men of ambition." Olivier Zunz, *Making America Corporate, 1870–1920* (Chicago: University of Chicago Press, 1990), p. 39. Cindy Sondik Aron has made a similar point, although she elaborated that many men entering government employ perceived it as a means of advancing their careers and of acquiring middle-class status. Cindy Sondik Aron, *Ladies and Gentlemen of the Civil Service: Middle-Class Workers in Victorian America* (New York: Oxford University Press, 1987), pp. 25–39.

5. Although Louis Brownlow, the head of the committee, felt that the study should focus primarily on altering the structure of government as a means of strengthening the president's hand in executive management, he later agreed to a

broader study that included agency personnel practices. Barry D. Karl, *Executive Reorganization and Reform in the New Deal: The Genesis of Administrative Management, 1900–1939* (Cambridge, Mass.: Harvard University Press, 1963); Kenneth Davis, *FDR: Into the Storm, 1937–1940* (New York: Random House, 1993), pp. 23–24; Delano to Chair, 10/30/35; Notes on a Conference on a Study of Over-all Management in the Federal Government, 12/16/35; Emmerich to Elliott et al., 4/28/36, all three in President's Committee on Administrative Management, A-II-22, Box 1, Franklin D. Roosevelt Library (FDRL); Davenport to Brownlow, 10/21/37, Papers of Frederick Davenport, NIPA Correspondence, Box 8, Aug.–Dec. 1937, Syracuse University Archives (SUA).

6. The National Institute of Public Affairs favored recruitment outside the service. It began its controversial college intern program in 1935. Collier to Davenport, 7/12/38, Davenport Papers, NIPA Correspondence, Box 8, July–Dec. 1938, SUA; *Washington Post*, 5/29/38, B1.

7. See, for example, "Union Activities," *Personnel Administration* 1 (Mar. 1939): 9. On the suggestion that the U.S. executive branch have an elite corps of administrators (loosely modeled on the British civil service corps), see Paul P. Van Riper, *History of the United States Civil Service* (Evanston, Ill.: Row, Peterson, 1958), p. 326–332.

8. *Washington Post*, 2/15/39, 26. Steward to Rhudy, 4/8/37, NCSRL, Acc. 7947, Box 91 (5000.2), 1937, National Federation of Federal Employees, AHC.

9. Mitchell, telephone call, 1/2/39, OF 2, Civil Service Commission, Jan.–May 1939, FDRL; Baker to Davenport, 7/29/40, Davenport Papers, NIPA Correspondence, Box 23, July–Sept. 1940, SUA. One Civil Service Commission member had expressed his support in 1934 for the creation of a distinguished career service. He also objected to the practice of giving relief workers jobs similar to those of regular career civil servants, stating that this would denigrate the work done by civil servants and make the service a "haven" for the unemployed. Commissioner to FDR, 10/17/34, Davenport Papers, NIPA Correspondence, Box 18, Oct. 1935, SUA.

10. Miller to Smith, 2/19/40, Davenport Papers, NIPA Correspondence, Box 23, Jan.–Mar. 1940, SUA; *Washington Evening Star*, 11/9/35, A18.

11. See, for example, Harris to Elliot et al., 4/28/36, President's Committee on Administrative Management, A-II-22, Box 1, FDRL. The merit reform movement split during the 1920s as practitioners of personnel management tried to distance themselves from the "propagandizing" of reform groups like the National Civil Service Reform League. See, for example, "Some Trends in Public Personnel Administration," *Public Personnel Studies* 7 (Nov. 1929): 157.

12. On professionalism, see Barbara Ehrenreich and John Ehrenreich, "The Professional-Managerial Class," in Pat Walker, ed., *Between Labor and Capital* (Boston: South End Press, 1979); Margali Sarfatti Larson, *The Rise of Professionalism: A Sociological Analysis* (Berkeley: University of California Press, 1977); and Andrew Abbott, *The System of Professions: An Essay on the Division of*

Expert Labor (Chicago: University of Chicago Press, 1988). On the work of professionals in organizations and the restrictions placed upon their autonomy, see W. Richard Scott, "Professional Employees in a Bureaucratic Structure: Social Work," in Amitai Etzioni, ed., *The Semi-Professions and Their Organization: Teachers, Nurses, Social Workers* (New York: Free Press, 1969); G. Harries-Jenkins, "Professionals in Organizations," in J. A. Jackson, ed., *Professions and Professionals* (Cambridge: Cambridge University Press, 1970); and Don K. Price, "The Profession of Government Service," in Nathan O. Hatch, ed., *The Professions in American History* (Notre Dame, Ind.: University of Notre Dame Press, 1988).

13. In his theoretical examination of communication within large organizations, Dennis Mumby has illuminated the mechanism through which Horatio Alger stories can "manage" the contradiction that organizations face between the reality of their hierarchical, authoritarian structures and the high value placed on equality in the larger culture. Dennis Mumby, *Communication and Power in Organizations: Discourse, Ideology and Domination* (Norwood, N.J.: Ablex, 1988), pp. 16–19, 101–125.

For background on all the personnel directors, refer to Scott Hart's 1939 "Federal Diary" columns in the *Washington Post* and U.S. House of Representatives, Committee on Appropriations, *Independent Offices Appropriation Bill for 1941. Part 1*, 76th Cong., 3d sess., pp. 989–1007.

14. *Washington Post*, 3/5/39, sec. 6, p. 10.

15. See *Washington Post*, 6/25/39, sec. 6, p. 13; 5/28/39, sec. 6, p. 8; 3/12/39, sec. 6, p. 6; 6/4/39, sec. 6, p. 11; 5/7/39, sec. 6, p. 2. Most of the Algers had little formal education; several had attended only grade school. Switzer, for instance, had completed one year of high school when he began his messenger job in 1904. Nevertheless, all these administrators were ambitious members of the firstborn generation of optimistic Progressives, and they used their white-collar government jobs to further their education. Of the thirteen personnel directors in 1939 who had risen through the civil service ranks, nine had engaged in course or degree work while employed in the government. Five of the nine had received Bachelor of Laws degrees (usually taken from National University or Georgetown University) during their civil service tenure. And, while two of the thirteen—McNamara and Edwin Ballinger (Treasury)—did not receive degrees, they did take law classes at George Washington University and Ben Franklin University, respectively. Law graduates Piozet and Francis Brassor (of the Securities and Exchange Commission), moreover, had gone on to receive their Master of Laws degrees.

16. Sociologist Amitai Etzioni has made a critical distinction between administrative and professional authority. The former is based upon one's position in the hierarchy; the latter is founded upon competence and control over a distinct body of knowledge. Etzioni, *The Semi-Professions*, pp. x–xiii.

17. David Gordon, Richard Edwards, and Michael Reich, *Segmented Work, Divided Workers: The Historical Transformation of Labor in the United States*

(Cambridge: Cambridge University Press, 1982). On the "proletarianization" of clerical work in the twentieth century, see Harry Braverman, *Labor and Monopoly Capital: The Degradation of Work in the Twentieth Century* (New York: Monthly Review Press, 1979).

18. Jürgen Kocka has argued that relative to Germans, Americans at the turn of the century did not differentiate clearly between blue- and white-collar work. Zunz, on other hand, has claimed that a distinct collar line was evident (although he does concede that it was blurred in some areas) during this period. His study is perhaps more narrow than Kocka's because he examines only employees of America's large corporations, presumably more elite than their white-collar counterparts in less "glamorous" businesses. I claim that the segmentation of the workforce was very evident to personnel administrators in the 1930s. They had witnessed significant shifts in the occupational status of government work as increasing numbers of women entered clerical positions. See Jürgen Kocka, *White Collar Workers in America, 1890–1940: A Social–Political History in International Perspective*, trans. Maura Kealey (London: Sage Publications, 1980), pp. 123–125; and Zunz, *Making America Corporate*, pp. 126–148.

19. See, for example, Karl, *Executive Reorganization*, pp. 25–36, 166–210; Davis, *FDR: Into the Storm*, pp. 19–28, 32–37.

20. Ordway, "Minimum Requisite Civil Service Legislation," 2/38; Emmerich to Harris, 2/26/38, both in President's Committee on Administrative Management, E-XVII-16, Box 12, FDRL; *Washington Post*, 6/25/38, p. 1 and 6/29/38, p. 1; Ordway to Johnson, 2/15/37, NCSRL, Acc. 7947, Box 90 (3000), 1937, U.S. Civil Service Commission, AHC.

21. Emmerich, "Integrating Federal Personnel Service with Operations," n.d., EXII-3, Box 11; Tentative Plan for a Study of Personnel Management, May 8, 1936, 4/28/36, A-II-22, Box 1, both in President's Committee on Administrative Management, FDRL.

22. White memo, n.d., President's Committee on Administrative Management, EXII-4, Box 11, FDRL; President's Committee on Administrative Management, *Report of the Committee with Studies of Administrative Management in the Federal Government* (Washington, D.C.: U.S. Government Printing Office, 1937), pp. 101–102, 105–107.

23. William Leuchtenburg, *Franklin D. Roosevelt and the New Deal, 1932–1940* (New York: Harper & Row, 1963), pp. 148–166, 340–345; William Graebner, *The Engineering Consent: Democracy and Authority in Twentieth Century America* (Madison: University of Wisconsin Press, 1987), pp. 91–109; Edward A. Purcell, Jr., *The Crisis of Democratic Theory: Scientific Naturalism and the Problem of Value* (Lexington: University Press of Kentucky, 1973), pp. 117–138; John P. Diggens, "Flirtation with Fascism: American Pragmatic Liberals and Mussolini's Italy," *American Historical Review* 71 (Jan. 1966): 487–506.

24. Davis, *FDR: Into the Storm*, pp. 21–23, quote from p. 21; see also Davenport to Brownlow, 10/21/37, Davenport Papers, NIPA Correspondence, Box 8,

Aug.–Dec. 1937, SUA. For a critical view of the president's administrative reform program, see Gary Dean Best, *Pride, Prejudice, and Politics: Roosevelt vs. Recovery, 1933–1938* (New York: Praeger, 1991), pp. 143, 152–153, 165–167; and, for a more favorable appraisal, Frank Friedel, *Franklin D. Roosevelt: A Rendezvous with Destiny* (Boston: Little, Brown, 1990), pp. 273–280.

25. Executive Order 7916, 7/24/38; Ordway, "Meaning of the Executive Orders of June 24, 1938," n.d., NCSRL, Acc. 7947, Box 97 (2000.1), 1938, Executive Orders, AHC.

When Roosevelt extended the merit system, he temporarily exempted some professional positions. He then created the special Committee on Civil Service Improvement in 1939, chaired by Supreme Court Justice Stanley Reed, to create a "blueprint of principles and methods to be followed in procuring the highest type of men and women for the Government service." The president and his close advisers wanted to recruit worthy candidates, but did not always feel that the Civil Service Commission was capable of this task. According to critics of the plan, creating parallel recruiting systems threatened to establish a two-tier career service: a classified service of clerks to be funneled through the Civil Service Commission and an elite group of professionals selected under a separate system of rules. To those who entered the civil service as messengers or low-level clerks, these reforms promised to build a stratified career service of favored recruits and struggling staffers whose promotional possibilities were severely limited. *Washington Post*, 3/12/39, p. B5.

26. Ordway to Johnson, 2/15/37, NCSRL, Acc. 7947, Box 90 (3000), 1937, U.S. Civil Service Commission, AHC. The Civil Service Commission urged the creation of exams for personnel directors as a means of elevating their status within their departments. Commissioners argued that this might weaken some of the resistance from bureau chiefs and department heads who were not eager to relinquish control of personnel functions. Commissioners to Roosevelt, 1/10/38, OF 2, Civil Service Commission, Jan.–May 1938, FDRL.

27. 50th Council Meeting, 3/28/40, Box 5; 92nd Council Meeting, 3/6/41, Box 9, both in RG 146, Federal Personnel Council (FPC) Meetings, NARA; *Washington Post*, 7/16/39, p. 6

28. For a copy of the policy, see *Federal Employee* 23 (June 1938): 10. On the process followed, see, for example, Wallace to Carmody, 7/20/39, RG 16, Office of Secretary, Box 3059, Personnel, July–Oct. 1939, NARA.

29. *Personnel Bulletin* (May 1940): 1–5, copy in RG 16, Office of Secretary, Box 129, Personnel, Mar. 13–Aug. 22, 1940, NARA; *Government Standard* 23 (May 10, 1940): 1. Hendrickson noted that he consulted so many groups that the memorandum went through twenty-three drafts. 26th Council Meeting, 9/13/39, RG 146, FPC Meetings, Box 3, NARA.

30. See, for example, Milton J. Esman, "The Organization of Personnel Administration in a Sample of Federal Agencies" (Ph.D. diss., Princeton University, 1942), pp. 6–7, 242–243.

31. 33rd Council Meeting, 11/22/39, Box 4; 96th Meeting, 4/11/41, Box 10, both in RG 146, FPC Meetings, NARA.

32. Tead, "The New Trends in Characterizing Personnel Management," rec'vd. 4/3/43, RG 146, FPC Project Files, Box 1, C43-16, Personnel Director, Place of, NARA.

33. On Mayo and the human relations school of management, see Richard Gillespie, *Manufacturing Knowledge: A History of the Hawthorne Experiments* (Cambridge: Cambridge University Press, 1991). Stephen Waring follows human relations forward into the 1940s and 1950s in *Taylorism Transformed: Scientific Management Theory Since 1945* (Chapel Hill: University of North Carolina Press, 1991).

34. Hendrickson, "Employee Relations," 5/6/40, RG 16, Office of Secretary, Box 875, Personnel (2 of 5), Feb. 1–May 31, 1943, NARA.

35. As quoted in Davis, *FDR: Into the Storm*, p. 23n.

36. Frederick Davenport, "The Personnel Office and the Full Use of Manpower," *Personnel Administration* 5 (Jan. 1943): 3; Bradford White, "Article Abstracts: 'Social Theory Involved in Supervision,' " *Public Personnel Review* 5 (Oct. 1944): 256; Reining to Clapp, 11/8/37, Davenport Papers, NIPA Correspondence, Box 21, Oct.–Dec. 1937, SUA. For an overview of this prolonged crisis of democracy, see Purcell, *Crisis of Democratic Theory*, esp. chs. 6 and 7.

37. For a larger discussion of administrative reformers and their commitment to industrial democracy, see Howell John Harris, "Industrial Democracy and Liberal Capitalism, 1890–1925," and Ronald W. Schatz, "From Commons to Dunlop: Rethinking the Field and Theory of Industrial Relations," both in Nelson Lichtenstein and Howell John Harris, eds., *Industrial Democracy in America: The Ambiguous Promise* (Cambridge: Cambridge University Press, 1993). On attempts to infuse the bureaucracy with liberalism, see Sidney Milkis, *The President and the Parties: The Transformation of the American Party System Since the New Deal* (New York: Oxford University Press, 1993), pp. 132–134.

38. "Right to Organize and Negotiate: Conciliation and Adjustment of Disputes," President's Committee on Administrative Management, EXIII-I, Box 11, Draft of a Bill on Rights of Federal Employees to Organize, etc., FDRL; Kenneth O. Warner, phone interview with author, May 22, 1995.

39. Jürgen Habermas has written extensively about the "legitimacy" of modern states. He has noted that states require mass loyalty in order to authenticate and execute administrative decisions. An "input crisis" occurs when the state fails to accrue a necessary level of mass loyalty to make decisions; an "output crisis" ensues when the state becomes totally inefficient. In the 1930s, public officials worried that an ineffective bureaucracy would undermine the mass support needed to make and enforce decisions. Similarly, Andrew Abbott has contended that professionals gain legitimacy by promoting values held in their culture. In this instance, personnel administrators trumpeted efficiency and accountability, both deemed worthy ideals in post-Progressive America. Jürgen Habermas, "What

Does a Crisis Mean Today? Legitimation Problems in Late Capitalism," *Social Research* 51 (Summer 1984): 51–54; Abbott, *The System of Professions*, p. 184.

40. Ordway to Reining, 3/25/41, Davenport Papers, NIPA Correspondence, Box 23, Jan.–Apr. 1941, SUA.

41. Roosevelt to Steward, 8/16/37, OF 252, Government Employees, 1937, FDRL.

42. Howell John Harris, *The Right to Manage: Industrial Relations Policies of American Business in the 1940s* (Madison: University of Wisconsin Press, 1982), p. 169.

43. *Personnel Bulletin* (July 1940): 1, copy in RG 16, Office of Secretary, Box 129, Personnel 3, *Bulletin of Personnel Administration* (Correspondence re:), NARA. Emphasis added.

44. 104th Council Meeting, 6/5/41, RG 146, FPC Meetings, Box 10, NARA.

45. Diggens and Purcell date this perception to the period between World War I and the New Deal. I contend that it was not thoroughly discredited in the 1930s, although people like Ordway and Davenport defended their position in a slightly different manner than did intellectuals of that period. They reasoned that because the educational system was "democratic," by extension the process of selecting administrative leaders from college and universities was also democratic. Diggens, "Flirtation with Fascism," pp. 490–491; Purcell, *Crisis of Democratic Theory*, pp. 106–107, 117–127.

46. Employee Relations Committee Minutes, 5/16/45, RG 146, FPC Project Files, Box 48, P485-1 (cont.), Effective Relationships with Organized Employee Groups, 8/1/49, NARA.

47. From 1939 to 1945, the proportion of women working for the federal government increased from 40 percent to 60 percent. War agencies often had even higher percentages. In the Office of Price Administration, for example, women constituted 74.1 percent of the workforce. U.S. Department of Labor, Women's Bureau, *Women in the Federal Service, 1923–1947*, Part I. *Trends in Employment*, Bulletin no. 230-1 (Washington, D.C.: U.S. Government Printing Office, 1949), pp. 19, 29, 35.

48. U.S. Civil Service Commission, "Secretarial Practice" (1942), copy in Papers of William McReynolds, Box 3, Committee on Administrative Personnel—II, FDRL; "Democratic Attitudes Test, *Independent Woman* (June 1945): 165–166.

49. Louise Snyder Johnson, "Are You Polishing off Those Rough Spots?" *Independent Woman* (Jan. 1947): 28.

50. Appleby to Baldwin, 2/16/37, RG 16, Office of Secretary, Box 2606, Personnel [Jan.–July] [3 of 3], NARA; Steen to Cramer, 3/31/42, RG 228, Complaints Against Government Agencies, Box 103, Fair Employment Practices, US CSC, Steen, Anna J., NARA.

51. Stephen Skowronek, *Building a New American State: The Expansion of National Administrative Capacities, 1877–1920* (Cambridge: Cambridge University Press, 1982).

52. Theda Skocpol, "Bringing the State Back In: Strategies and Analysis in Current Research," in Peter Evans, Dietrich Rueschemeyer, and Theda Skocpol, eds., *Bringing the State Back In* (Cambridge: Cambridge University Press, 1985), p. 12; James N. Baron, Frank R. Dobbin, and P. Devereaux Jennings, "War and Peace: The Evolution of Modern Personnel Administration in U.S. Industry," *Journal of American Sociology* 92 (Sept. 1986): 350–383.

4

When Henry Met Franklin

Martin Halpern

In the film *Annie!*, Little Orphan Annie persuades the obstreperous business tycoon Oliver P. Warbucks to meet with President Franklin Roosevelt. As one of the forgotten people of whom FDR spoke, Annie is a Roosevelt supporter who has been inspired by the president's hopeful message. Due to Annie's presence at the meeting, FDR is able to persuade Warbucks to join in singing the optimistic and humanistic song "Tomorrow." The greedy businessperson is clearly on his way toward a moral transformation. The coupling of Roosevelt's charm and the appeal of the needy, as represented by Annie, is irresistible. Of course, compared with Ebenezer Scrooge, Warbucks suffers little on his way to redemption.

Annie!, of course, is fiction, and a fantasy at that. In fact, it's a revisionist fantasy. Harold Gray's comic strip "Little Orphan Annie" was anti–New Deal. In one strip, for example, the self-reliant Annie says, "I never thought I'd *rather* be in a 'home' . . . but that was 'fore I knew there could be anybody like Mrs. Bleating-Hart. . . . But I don't want to be a 'public charge' if I can help it! At least here I'm earning my way and not livin' off o' taxpayers!" Sounding very much like Henry Ford, the comic strip self-made millionaire individualist Oliver Warbucks proclaims, "I see nothing so unusual in sharing our profits with our workers—when our business makes money I feel all those connected with it should make money. . . . I think [our workers] . . . are entitled to a piece of the profits—the bigger our profits—the bigger their wages." It is of pivotal importance, however, that this generosity emanates from the benevolence and wisdom of the business owner Warbucks, and not from protests by what he characterizes as "sore-headed" workers or their unions or regulations of a caring government. Indeed, Gray's Oliver Warbucks died in 1944 because he could not continue to live under the New Deal regime. After FDR died, Gray brought Warbucks back to life.[1]

Interestingly, the anti–New Deal comic strip was Henry Ford's favorite.[2] Neither the comic strip Warbucks nor the real-life Henry Ford was likely to be taken in by the collectivistic notion that government should take responsibility for helping the needy to survive and live decent lives when the private economy failed to provide employment at decent wages for all who needed work. Nevertheless, there *was* a real-world meeting between Roosevelt and Ford on which some pinned hopes that one or the other of these two famous individuals would be transformed. Five years after FDR assumed office, he had his first meeting as president with the country's most famous industrialist. On April 27, 1938, Ford and Roosevelt met for a two-hour luncheon conference. Attending the meeting with Ford were his son Edsel and his publicist, William J. Cameron. Also present were G. Hall Roosevelt, the president's brother-in-law, and Marriner S. Eccles, governor of the Federal Reserve Board. Hall Roosevelt, Eleanor Roosevelt's brother and comptroller of the city of Detroit when Frank Murphy was mayor, had arranged the meeting. Hall's effectiveness as an intermediary to Ford may have been due to the fact that he was then an employee of the Ford Commercial Credit Company, an auto financing firm.[3] By the summer of 1938, moreover, Hall "had become antagonistic" to Murphy, Michigan's New Deal governor.[4]

This chapter will address the following questions: What brought Ford, the antiunion exponent of individualist self-reliance, and Roosevelt, architect of New Deal programs of government's social responsibility and advocate of a new acceptance of trade unionism in American political life, together on April 27, 1938? What were the hopes and fears of observers? What was the significance of the meeting in the context of the overall relationship between these two influential figures?

WHY DID FDR WANT TO MEET WITH FORD?

The FDR–Ford meeting took place after FDR had been substantially weakened by the fight over his proposal to pack the Supreme Court, the formation of an anti–New Deal coalition of Republicans and conservative Democrats in Congress, and, most important, the onset of a severe recession. Sales of industrial products slumped dramatically, layoffs mounted, and the unions' bargaining power ebbed. By mid-April 1938, employment in the Detroit area had declined from 250,000 to 70,500. The plunge was especially severe at the Ford Motor Company, where employment was down to 11,500 from a normal level of 87,000.[5] The recession created political problems for the Roosevelt administration, which could not escape responsibility for the bad economic news. It threatened to undermine the basis of the administration's popularity.

Although the initial signs of a business downturn were evident as early as August 1937 and a major stock market sell-off occurred in October, the Roosevelt administration was unsure what actions to take to counteract the situation. Indeed, later analysts attribute a major share of the blame for the recession to a cutback in federal funding as the administration sought to balance the budget. Other factors were a tightening of the money supply by the Federal Reserve and a withdrawal of $2 billion in consumer purchasing power due to the initiation of regressive Social Security tax payments. A common conception at the time was that businesspeople were holding back on investing. Liberals within the administration thought that there was a strike by capital against the administration. The president himself "was convinced that the situation was at least partially the result of a business conspiracy . . . against him." In a mirror-image version of the latter analysis, Roosevelt's conservative advisers thought the problem underlying the economy was lack of business confidence and argued for a return to an NRA-style business–government cooperation as the road to recovery. Weakened by the Court-packing battle, Roosevelt for several months vacillated between the advice of liberals to increase social spending and attack monopoly practices, and the advice of conservatives to continue with the budget-balancing approach and establish an entente with business.[6]

In the closing days of 1937, administration liberals took the offensive. In a December 26 radio address, Assistant Attorney General Robert Jackson, head of the Justice Department's Antitrust Division, blamed the recession on monopoly pricing practices. Jackson maintained that there was a "strike of capital" against New Deal reform. In a December 30 national radio network address, Secretary of the Interior Harold Ickes attacked the "big business fascism" of the Fords and others of America's Sixty Families.[7]

The Jackson and Ickes speeches gained extensive press coverage. When a reporter asked Roosevelt on December 31, "Do you agree with what those two gentlemen have been saying?" FDR responded by reciting a parable about "a President by the name of Theodore Roosevelt" who had called some individuals " 'malefactors of great wealth' " and was charged with calling all people of great wealth "malefactors"—"which, of course," FDR declaimed, "had absolutely nothing to do with what he had actually said." The frustrated reporter's rejoinder, "Mr. Ickes and Mr. Jackson were much more specific, Mr. President," elicited laughter but no follow-up comment from the president. When another reporter tried to pin him down—"Does that mean that you say that Mr. Ford and General Motors and the others who are named are responsible for the Depression?"—FDR demurred, "Oh, I think we will leave it to the parable."[8]

At the next Cabinet meeting, FDR jokingly gave the two officials credit for a January 14 meeting with Alfred Sloan of General Motors and Ernest Weir of Bethlehem Steel: "Do you know that this conference would not have been possible if it had not been for the speeches of Bob Jackson and Harold Ickes? Prior to the speeches, these businessmen refused even to come in to talk to me. After the speeches they were only too glad to come in. One of them said this morning: 'But for God's sake call off that man Ickes.' "[9]

Despite the joking, FDR's meetings with business executives were a response to his conservative advisers' entreaties. In a politically precarious position, he was keeping his options open. Ford was an atypical and idiosyncratic businessperson, but one who had a substantial public following. Roosevelt had been able to win all sorts of allies through a combination of his personal charm and the appeal of the power of the presidency. Perhaps even as strange a duck as Henry Ford could be won over.

WHY DID FORD WANT TO MEET WITH FDR?

Prior to the 1938 meeting, Ford had rejected appeals to meet with the president. Although he occasionally had said nice things about FDR and had exchanged birthday greetings with him,[10] his criticisms of the president were more frequent. Roosevelt, in turn, offered criticisms of the auto magnate. Ford campaigned for Hoover in 1932; FDR responded by charging that "the Republican campaign management and people like Henry Ford . . . are guilty of spreading the gospel of fear."[11] Although most business leaders supported the administration's National Recovery Administration (NRA), Ford pointedly refused to sign the auto industry code. Ford was worried—unnecessarily, to be sure—that Section 7(A) of the National Industrial Recovery Act (NIRA) was a threat to the open shop and that "every detail of our operation can be placed under control of a committee one-third of whom are politicians and one-third of whom are labor leaders." Of the

NRA's Blue Eagle, Ford told Ernest Liebold, his personal secretary, "Hell, that Roosevelt buzzard! I wouldn't put it on the car."[12]

NRA head Hugh Johnson inaugurated a federal government boycott of Ford cars, a policy that FDR publicly supported. After several months, the federal government relaxed the ban. During the more than yearlong dispute, Charles Edison, son of Ford's friend Thomas Edison, and James Couzens, Ford's former business partner, sought unsuccessfully to arrange a meeting between Ford and FDR to resolve the NRA dispute. Although Ford wrote to Edison that he had "deep respect" for Roosevelt "personally and as President," and believed that FDR had "an earnest and religious desire to do everything possible to ease the situation of this country," he refused to respond to the president's wish that Ford meet "to talk this over with him." Eventually, Edsel and Eleanor Ford visited the president in Warm Springs, Georgia, on November 24, 1934; the elder Ford telegraphed that he and his wife, Clara, were unable to visit because of the state of Clara's health. Cameron recalled that it was he who "wrote this refusal." Edsel's visit "was just a graceful out for Mr. Ford. For some reason he didn't want to go."[13]

Several important Ford officials recalled Ford's essential hostility to Roosevelt. Cameron remembered Ford's very negative reaction to Roosevelt's inaugural address and maintained, "I doubt that he ever trusted Mr. Roosevelt."[14] Liebold stated that Ford disliked the new president's actions in the banking crisis and "had a very personal reaction" to Roosevelt's criticism of "economic royalists." The icing on the cake, according to Liebold's 1951 reminiscences, came "when we found that he [FDR] was of Jewish ancestry."[15] Harry Bennett said simply, "Mr. Ford hated Roosevelt."[16]

Perhaps Ford was willing to meet with Roosevelt in April 1938 because of FDR's new political vulnerability and the fact that this was one in a series of meetings in which, as his conservative advisers wished, the president was seeking economic guidance from business leaders. In addition, Ford may have been willing to meet because his supporters had waged a nationwide campaign for such a get-together. This campaign developed in reaction to the attacks on Ford by Ickes and other administration liberals.[17] Early in January 1938, the Ford–Dearborn post of the Veterans of Foreign Wars complained to the president that "their neighbor and benefactor" had been "unduly criticized and defamed by high members" of his administration. The VFW post called on the president to eliminate any opposition to the "sound industrial principles and policies of Henry Ford."[18] To assure that their entreaty would receive attention from the president, the group sent copies of their communication to members of Congress and the Dearborn press.

A more extensive campaign on Ford's behalf was organized by the Dearborn Pioneers Club, which described itself as "a 70 member noonday luncheon group." Motivated by the attacks on Ford by members of FDR's "official family," the club circulated petitions praising Ford as "one of the best friends that the working man has had." The club's petition claimed that attacks on Ford were causing discord, and thus slowing the recovery; it called on the president to settle labor-management differences equitably and "stop demoralizing and demolishing propaganda." The club's initiative became a national campaign, with a claimed total of 540,000 signatures from over 7,000 cities and towns. Although the petitions reflected the existence of a substantial pro-Ford sentiment, the president and his wife also were sent complaints that in some instances employees were being forced to sign the petitions.

When Republican Representative George Dondero asked the president if he would meet with representatives of the club to receive the petitions, he reported that most of the signatures came from businesspeople. When no meeting was forthcoming, the petitions were mailed to the president. In an accompanying letter, club president Arthur Ternes assured the president that neither the Ford Motor Company nor the Republican party was involved in the campaign, and that he and the club secretary had voted Democratic in the last three presidential elections. This campaign received considerable press coverage and culminated with Ternes's dedication to Henry Ford at a public celebration in Dearborn of Henry and Clara Ford's fiftieth wedding anniversary. Acknowledging that the attacks on Ford had ceased, Ternes hoped the petitions would help the president "better determine the esteem with which Mr. Ford is held throughout the nation," and he expressed optimism about the forthcoming meeting between Ford and Roosevelt.[19]

Although, when interviewed years later, Cameron pooh-poohed the Dearborn Pioneers Club campaign, he sounded the same themes in an address to a Chamber of Commerce dinner in Bay City, Michigan, on April 19. "Government can help now," he said of the recession, "by keeping still, by putting a gag on Ickes and Jackson, by ceasing to act as God over forces of nature, and by ceasing to pass punitive legislation."[20]

While these specific 1938 events set the stage for Ford's willingness to visit FDR, it must be acknowledged that there is no "smoking gun" to Ford's thinking. A person of actions rather than words, Ford tended to produce verbalizations that were often unclear. He was regarded as "emotional" by his son Edsel, "inconsistent" by labor adviser Harry Bennett, and a shy person afraid of his cultural and educational "inferiority" by public relations spokesperson Cameron. "He lived on the fringes of the community all the time," Cameron explained, "physically and intellectually."[21] Because of Ford's penchant for saying peculiar and sometimes incomprehensible things in public, company officials accompanied him when he spoke to reporters and advised reporters on what Ford really meant and what the company preferred be kept out of the papers. Cameron played this role with such frequency that it was said that he seemed able to read Ford's mind.[22]

To the nonmind-reading scholar, there remains an element of uncertainty about what Ford hoped to accomplish in visiting the president. *Detroit News* reporter Jay Hayden had good access to the company but was unsure of Ford's goal. He asked, "Is Ford . . . coming in the hope of finding a basis for compromise of his differences with the President or will he stand pat and use the White House as a sounding board for accentuating the conflict?"[23] Ford's public comments about his acceptance of Roosevelt's invitation contributed to the doubts about his purpose. Interviewed outside the Wayside Inn in Boston on April 21, Ford said: "I'm going to let him look at somebody who is not coming to tell him how to run the country. I'm not going to give him advice." Referring to the fact that he had known the president when the latter was assistant secretary of the navy, Ford declared: "I'm going to renew an old acquaintanceship of years' standing. I am going to give the President a chance to look at somebody who doesn't want anything."[24]

IMPACT OF THE *MORGAN* DECISION

Although Ford's antagonism to FDR stemmed in large part from FDR's labor policies, the company was relying on the courts, not the presidential meeting, for help in this area. Just two days before the FDR–Ford meeting, the company received favorable news on the legal front. After extensive and well-publicized hearings on the company's violation of workers' rights by such actions as the beating of unionists at the Battle of the Overpass, the National Labor Relations Board (NLRB) had found the company guilty of unfair labor practices and ordered it to cease such practices on December 23, 1937. The Supreme Court's decision in the *Morgan v. U.S.* case, however, gave Ford an opportunity to bring the enforcement process to a standstill for over a year. Although the *Morgan* case involved the Department of Agriculture and the Packers and Stockyards Act, the Court's finding that "Those who are brought into contest with the Government in a quasi-judicial proceeding aimed at the control of their activities are entitled to be fairly advised of what the Government proposes and to be heard upon its proposal before it issues its final command" applied equally to the NLRB and the Wagner Act.

Since there had been no intermediate report in the Detroit case, Ford attorney Frederick Wood, representing the litigants in both the *Morgan* and the *Schechter Poultry Corp.* v. *U.S.* cases, went on the offensive on April 27. He sought a delay in the Circuit Court of Appeals hearing on Ford's appeal of the NLRB decision so that he could take depositions on how the NLRB made its decision and whether the members were influenced in their decision by CIO or Roosevelt administration figures. In response to the Ford offensive, the NLRB retreated on May 2, 1938, asking the Circuit Court of Appeals to allow it to withdraw its decision so that it could issue an intermediate report. The legal maneuvering became increasingly complex. Suffice it to say that a comparable decision and order were finally issued on August 9, 1939, more than nineteen months after the initial order.[25]

HOPES AND FEARS FOR THE MEETING

With the labor policy context in flux in April 1938, it is understandable that there were both hopes and fears about the meeting. CIO unionists, liberals, and leftists were worried. Although industrial unionism had established a base in such leading companies as General Motors, Chrysler, United States Steel, and General Electric in 1937, it was far from clear in 1938 if it would become a permanent part of the American scene. An important section of American industry, including such companies as Bethlehem Steel and Westinghouse as well as Ford, resisted any change from the old order of labor relations in their factories. Henry Ford personally symbolized this antiunionism because of his fame, wealth, and publicly stated determination to never accept unionization by his employees. Ford's anti-Semitic record at a time when fascism was on the march also made him anathema to many. United Auto Workers (UAW) executive board member Irvan Cary wired the president to call attention to Ford's "absolute refusal to abide [by] the Wagner Act at his assembly plant at Long Beach, California," and to report that the "entire West Coast labor front [is] anxiously awaiting outcome of tomorrow's conference." A Detroit Ford employee wrote to FDR that his meeting with Ford "is sure playing with fire. . . . Every time any of the employees mention anything about Law the big bosses tell them that you are working for the Ford Motor Com[pany] and that Ford makes his own Laws."[26]

Although his antiunion practices made him anathema to industrial unionists and their liberal allies, Henry Ford drew support from anti–New
Deal, pro-business Republicans as well as from many other Americans who
saw Ford as an antiestablishment figure. The Ford Motor Company's $5 per
day wage policy of 1914, Ford's low price policy, and his conflicts with
bankers had won him a significant public following. There had even been
a significant Ford for President boom in 1923. To Americans untroubled by
his recent right-wing and antilabor proclivities, Ford symbolized the small
town and rural virtues of individualism, hard work, and piety. While many
of Ford's supporters may have been pleased at the prospect of a meeting
between their idol and the president, there were also letters and telegrams
sent to Ford at the White House, "begging Mr. Ford not to be beguiled into
surrender of his individualistic ideas."[27]

In the press, there was speculation that FDR might ask Ford to inaugurate
an annual wage as a way of contributing to the recovery and renewing the
tradition of labor reform established more than twenty years earlier with
the $5 a day wage policy. If Ford initiated such a policy, other auto
companies might follow suit. General Motors was considering such an
innovation because the Social Security Act provided an exemption of the 3
percent payroll tax for employers who guaranteed workers 1,200 hours of
work per year.[28] Among those who were hopeful about the annual wage
possibility was *Detroit News* correspondent Blair Moody (later appointed
to the U.S. Senate by Democratic Governor G. Mennen Williams). Moody
wrote: "One of the tragedies of the present situation is that two men with
the vision of Roosevelt and Ford—both New Dealers in the best sense of
the word—cannot get together on the national problem instead of sticking
their tongues out at each other at a distance." Those who were not New
Dealers "in the best sense," in Moody's view, were Roosevelt's "one-sided
NLRB and "the high-handed autocracy of Henry's little army."[29]

WHAT ACTUALLY TRANSPIRED AT THE MEETING?

What actually transpired at the meeting became a source of controversy
in the days following the event. Apparently, it was a pleasant lunch.
Cameron recalled that Roosevelt "used . . . all" his charm that day, telling
Ford, "I'm so glad to see you. My mother was so pleased to know that you
were coming. She said, 'Franklin, I'm so glad that you're going to see Mr.
Ford because Mr. Ford is not only a great man, he's a good man.' " However,
there was no meeting of the minds on the principal topic discussed:
government economic policy. Roosevelt outlined his pump-priming plans

and Eccles explained the logic behind government deficit spending. Ford was unmoved. In parting, Ford told Roosevelt, "You know, Mr. President, before you leave this job, you're not going to have many friends, and then I'll be your friend." Emerging from the meeting, the Ford party adhered to the etiquette of allowing the White House to report on meetings with the president. As an unofficial White House adviser, Hall Roosevelt felt free to make some vague positive remarks: "There was nothing that smacked of commercialism in any way, and very little economics was discussed. In fact, it reminded me very much of a family conversation at Wayside Inn." Stephen Early, FDR's secretary, announced that "there would be no statement now or later concerning the conference."[30]

Following the White House meeting, the Ford party headed by train to New York, where Henry was scheduled to give a speech to the Bureau of Advertising of the American Newspaper Publishers Association. En route to New York, Ford spoke with *Detroit News* reporter Hayden and *Detroit Free Press* reporter Clifford Prevost. Having an early deadline, Prevost took down Ford's words and filed his story. Hayden's later deadline permitted him to get Cameron's interpretation of Ford's words. Cameron went with Hayden to the *New York Times*, where Hayden typed up the story. Apparently, Cameron knew Ford's thinking better than Ford knew it. Ford blew up when he read Prevost's account and barred him from the company. Actually, the problem with Prevost's story was that it included some questionable statements by Ford that the latter presumably found embarrassing.[31]

The two news accounts made it evident that there was no meeting of the minds between FDR and Ford. Prevost reported that "Ford was obviously of the opinion that President Roosevelt has no plan for solving [the] present depression." Hayden reported Ford as saying: "If finance would get out of government and government would get out of business everything would go again. . . . If government will just get out of the way and give natural American enterprise a free wing it will do the job." In a similarly conservative formulation, Prevost quoted Ford as saying: "The Government should be the policeman to exercise only that power necessary to maintain an orderly method of living." Ford expressed his opposition to the annual wage idea and to the president's notion that the automobile industry should plan its production to reduce the recessionary impact of big swings in auto sales. He agreed with Roosevelt that decentralization of industry was desirable but saw no role for the government in this process.

According to Hayden, Ford's "praise of Mr. Roosevelt was confined to one point. 'I believe he is entitled to great credit for rousing the people to think. . . . There is more public interest in national problems today than ever before.' " That this was a dubious compliment was evident when Ford added: "The American people basically are sound and they will right the situation for themselves as soon as they come to understand it." Ford expressed enthusiasm for one politician, the anti–New Deal vice president, John Nance Garner, and repeated his strange idea that "some of the men in Wall Street" were "responsible for much of the labor strife so prevalent in the country," by which he meant that unions were somehow controlled by financiers as part of their effort to gain control of all manufacturing and marketing operations.[32]

The main difference between the two stories is that Prevost reported that "Ford clashed frequently" with Eccles at the meeting and took positions at the meeting for reducing government spending and against increasing the debt.[33] In response to these comments, Roosevelt intimates gave "a broad and amused hint . . . that . . . Ford . . . didn't think up his good speeches until long after he was through visiting President Roosevelt." Noting that Ford's audience "didn't consist of clairvoyants," FDR's unnamed spokespersons said they did not know what was going on in Ford's mind until they read the news accounts of his interview. The president was said to have read Ford's statements "with mingled surprise and amusement." Eccles publicly maintained that "Mr. Ford didn't clash with me. I guess he said he didn't agree, and shook his head in dissent. But I'm not aware of any wordy clash having taken place." Although most news accounts were favorable to Ford, the *New York Post* suggested that "the aged multimillionaire motor maker . . . seems to have got mixed up about what he actually said and what he thought later he should have said."[34]

A column by Joseph Alsop and Robert Kintner disputed the charge that Ford was thinking up good arguments only after the meeting. Relying on an unnamed source, they reported that the president asked Ford what plans he had to bring about recovery. Ford replied, "I haven't any and I don't think you have either." Ford was said to have disagreed with the president's idea of a quota on auto production and to have asserted that, by aiding the CIO, the president was really aiding the large bankers. The columnists reported that Ford disagreed with Eccles's ideas on deficit spending, among other topics, with statements such as "The less this country spends, the quicker the recovery."[35]

Irritated by the stories putting him in a bad light, Eccles issued a statement on May 3 elaborating on his role in the meeting and criticizing the "uniformly false" reports that he and Ford "discussed and differed" with respect to governmental policy. He insisted that his role in the meeting, apart from "purely incidental conversation," was to provide Edsel Ford and Cameron with two quotations dealing with England's debt in the nineteenth century and the maldistribution of income in the United States in the late 1920s. Henry Ford was "inspecting some of the White House rooms" while Eccles presented the quotations to his companions.[36]

AFTERMATH OF THE MEETING

While in New York, Ford met with a large group of reporters at his hotel the day after his meeting with the president. Questioned by several reporters in his hotel room, Ford complained, "People are looking for a leader. They ought to be their own leaders, but they're looking for a leader. And they've got a leader who is putting something over on them, and they deserve it." When reporters sought to pin Ford down on whether he was talking about Roosevelt, the auto magnate refused to say. The *New York Times* reporter concluded that Ford probably was not talking about FDR because, earlier in the interview, Ford said of the president: "You never heard me say anything against him, did you?" The *New York Times* report of the Ford interview noted that Ford then lowered his voice and said, " 'What's the use. . . . What's the use? He's like the rest of us, trying to do the best he can. Don't you think so?' "[37]

That evening Ford attended the newspaper publishers' banquet at the Waldorf-Astoria. Unfortunately for his hosts, he had changed his mind about delivering one of that evening's three speeches. No one who knew Ford would have been surprised. Ford production head Charles Sorensen recalled that Ford "could not make a speech. His few attempts to do so were pitiful." When a group of dealers presented him with a windmill, Ford "was called on to make a speech," executive H. C. Doss remembered. "He stood up and said something like 'good morning,' waved his hand to us, and that was all." Sorensen recounts a similar incident in which Ford attempted a spur-of-the-moment speech to plow salespeople: "Mr. Ford didn't say more than a dozen words. He was so confused, no one could understand him. He turned to me, mumbled something, and walked out of the room." After the latter incident, Ford said he'd never try to speak in public again.

Why, then, did Ford accept the invitation to speak to the newspaper publishers? Perhaps his love of favorable publicity led him to agree to speak, but as the moment drew near, Ford's fear took over. Cameron recalled, "I often wonder how I lived through some of these things. There was always the tension of not knowing what was going to happen. . . . Finally I induced him to say something." The publishers, Cameron told Ford, "were in the same trouble that he was. They were important. . . ." Ford finally agreed, and gave a speech variously reported as twenty-three, twenty-four, twenty-seven, or thirty words: "Mr. Toastmaster, and gentlemen, we are all on the spot. Stick to your guns, and I will help you, with the assistance of my son, all I can. Thank you." When he sat down, the toastmaster remarked that it had been a long time since Ford had given a speech. Ford replied that it would be the last time.[38]

FDR's only comment to the press about his visit with Ford was that he "was interested to see what the press said about it." When he was asked to comment on Ford's speech to the editors, the president replied, as he often did, "I have only read the headlines." The quick reporter's comeback, "That is all there was to it," elicited laughter but no further comment from FDR.[39]

REACTIONS TO THE MEETING

Newspaper commentaries after the meeting, like those before it, were favorably inclined to Ford's position. Labor partisans expressed their dismay. The day after the Ford–FDR meeting, former Ford employee Marjorie Vincent wrote to the president: "If the interview you had with Henry Ford is as purported in the newspapers, real New Dealers feel that to have given the prestige to a man such as he is known to be, by having him to a White House conference was a mistake." Vincent credited James Couzens, Ford's former partner, for the wage policy and any past "humanitarian motives" in the company. Henry Ford, on the other hand, was "the most selfish, self-centered man alive." Vincent hoped Roosevelt would do something to "offset . . . the vicious propaganda" resulting from his meeting with Ford.[40]

Confessing his "fears and trepidations that you would accomplish the impossible and make Henry a human being," George Knott passed along the humorous resolution of his United Mine Workers local union:

> Whereas the President of the United States met with Henry
> Ford for the purpose of changing his mind and
> Whereas this was to all intents and purpose[s] a waste of
> time, therefor[e] be it resolved
> That the President of these United States shall in the
> future, by some scientific means ascertain beforehand
> whether his guests have a mind.[41]

Pleased that Ford made no move in Roosevelt's direction, conservatives and far right groups were upbeat in the wake of the meeting. A week after the Ford–FDR meeting, 400 Nazis of the German-American Bund in the

Yorkville section of New York City cheered "wildly" when a speaker proposed Ford as a candidate for president. Roosevelt, on the other hand, was ridiculed as the "Charlie McCarthy of the White House."[42]

WHY NO MEETING OF THE MINDS?

There was no meeting of the minds between Ford and Roosevelt, no change in their essentially antagonistic positions. Although Roosevelt wanted business support, what he wanted was business support for his leadership, not a 1920s-model business–government partnership in which business needs were the fulcrum of government policy. FDR thus welcomed an April 26, 1938, statement of business leaders pledging cooperation with the administration and continued with his new leftward tilt, which involved increasing funds for housing and welfare and a determined campaign to pass a wages and hours bill. Although Roosevelt had made occasional gestures to antilabor critics in 1937 and 1938, he generally offered strong support to the embattled NLRB and expressed a sympathetic attitude to the position of organized labor. Ford, meanwhile, maintained his stance at the opposite end of the political spectrum, which involved both a conservative philosophical framework and a determined policy of blocking unionization of the company.

In retrospect, the failure of the Ford–FDR meeting to produce a significant change in direction by either protagonist seems to have been an inevitable result of the two principals' philosophical and class orientations. FDR's orientation toward the working class and poor involved no socialist commitment, to be sure, but it did involve a substantial revision of the U.S. political system to grant a greater stake, and even some power, to the people at the bottom. FDR was a leader of upper-class origin who included service to the needy as part of his vision. Ford was a leader of middle-class origin who became wealthy and thought that pursuing his personal interests would mean personal success for himself and would be good for others.

Although Ford's antagonism to unionism and FDR were typical of the business community, the depth of the social crisis of the 1930s and the strength of the desire for change by working people led some employers toward new ways of thinking. Interestingly, the need for new business approaches was so great that Ford's only child, Edsel, who became president of the Ford Motor Company in 1918, was among those who wished for a new direction. If Henry Ford, just three months shy of his seventy-fifth birthday in April 1938, had stepped aside, the results of the White House get-together likely would have been positive.

The president had a different and warmer relationship with Edsel Ford than with Henry Ford. In 1928, shortly after FDR purchased Warm Springs and established the Warm Springs Foundation, Edsel and Eleanor Ford made a donation of $25,000 to enclose the pool at Warm Springs so that it could be used year round. FDR wrote to his mother about the *"fine* cheque" Edsel sent him for the foundation and noted: "The Edsel Fords were with the Piersons for a week and I liked them both very much."[43] In 1938, Edsel served as treasurer for the Detroit Committee for the President's Birthday Ball for the Benefit of the Sufferers from Infantile Paralysis.[44] In January 1938, with other auto industry officials, he attended a White House conference with FDR aimed at discouraging "high pressure" selling of autos.[45] Among those with whom Edsel served on the President's Birthday Ball were Michigan Governor Frank Murphy and Abner Larned, head of the Works Progress Administration (WPA) in Michigan. Edsel was present at the farewell party for Murphy after his 1938 electoral defeat and subsequent appointment as U.S. attorney general. After Henry Ford made his statement about building 1,000 planes a day in May 1940, Ickes noted in his diary that Edsel told Secretary of the Treasury Henry Morgenthau "that sometimes his father got 'emotional' and that it was up to him [Edsel] to make good. Morgenthau was satisfied that Edsel Ford wants to cooperate to the fullest extent possible."[46]

Edsel's humanistic and cooperative impulses had little impact on company policy, however. Although Edsel was president of the company, Henry retained control and often overrode his son's decisions to the point of publicly humiliating him.

In the years following the 1938 meeting, the differences between FDR and Ford grew. Ford's foreign policy orientation was isolationist and anti-British, whereas FDR was pro-British and increasingly interventionist. Ford continued to defy the National Labor Relations Act while Roosevelt played a critical role in preventing the act from being crippled by amendments. As the economy improved, organized labor rebuilt and eventually prepared a new campaign to organize Ford Motor Company. By the time the union campaign got under way, the defense program had reached massive proportions and there were new calls for restricting labor in the name of the defense effort. Ford began to receive large contracts for producing defense items, which the union protested. The union called for a consumer boycott of Ford cars and federal government denial of government contracts to Ford and other labor law violators, on the grounds that such contracts aided the company in its illegal activities. The union argued, moreover, that Ford was not a reliable producer because it failed to deal equitably with its employees.

The union campaign began to produce results. Sidney Hillman, codirector of the National Defense Advisory Commission and the Office of Production Management, argued the union's case within the councils of government and FDR himself began to raise the question with other members of the administration. Finally, on April 1, 1941, the union shut down Ford's River Rouge complex, site of two-thirds of Ford's production activity. Ford charged the strike was a Communist plot to disrupt defense production. FDR and Michigan's Democratic Governor Van Wagoner gave Ford no aid. Instead, they sought to persuade the company to bargain with the union and agree to an NLRB election. The company capitulated to the pressure. On May 21, 1941, 70 percent of Ford workers voted for the UAW. One month later, the company and the union signed their first contract. At the last moment, Henry Ford threatened to carry out his earlier promise to shut down the factory rather than go forward with a new relationship with his employees. His wife threatened to leave him if he pursued this course, and Ford decided to accept the new situation. There was not a fundamental change in his outlook, however. The company's labor relations policies remained chaotic and would be put on a new footing only after Edsel Ford's premature death in 1943 and the cessation of Henry Ford's active involvement in the company following a second stroke. Edsel's son, Henry Ford II, defeated those in the company who would carry on in the old way in 1945.[47]

The New Deal approach to labor relations had become consolidated in major areas of the industrial economy. By then, however, Franklin Roosevelt was dead. Postwar hopes for a resurgent New Deal were dashed by the eruption of the Cold War and by a renewed big business offensive to enact restrictive labor legislation with no FDR in the White House to help stem the tide.

NOTES

1. Robert C. Harvey, *The Art of the Funnies: An Aesthetic History* (Jackson: University of Mississippi Press, 1994), 99–104. Emphasis in original.

2. David L. Lewis, *The Public Image of Henry Ford* (Detroit: Wayne State University Press, 1976), 538 n17.

3. Clipping, *Washington Star*, May 2, 1938, Acc. 984, Reel 25, Ford Motor Company Archives, Dearborn, Mich. (hereafter FMCA).

4. *New York Times*, April 28, 1938, p. 1; Sidney Fine, *Frank Murphy: The New Deal Years* (Ann Arbor: University of Michigan Press, 1984), 486–88.

5. Report of UAW Research Department on Employment in Greater Detroit, April 18–23, 1938, UAW Executive Board Minutes, Addes Coll., Box 6, Archives of Labor History and Urban Affairs, Wayne State University.

6. Kenneth S. Davis, *FDR: Into the Storm 1937–1940* (New York: Random House, 1993), 237–42.

7. William Leuchtenburg, *Franklin D. Roosevelt and the New Deal* (New York: Harper & Row, 1963), 246–48.

8. *Complete Presidential Press Conferences of Franklin D. Roosevelt* (New York: Da Capo Press, 1972), 10: 439–41.

9. Harold L. Ickes, *The Secret Diary of Harold L. Ickes: The Inside Struggle, 1936–39* (New York: Simon & Schuster, 1954), II: 295.

10. Birthday greetings can be found in Acc. 1, Boxes 3 and 64, and Acc. 23, Box 7, FMCA.

11. *The Public Papers and Addresses of Franklin D. Roosevelt*, 13 vols. (New York: Random House, 1938–1950), 1: 795.

12. As quoted in Sidney Fine, "The Ford Motor Company and the N.R.A.," *Business History Review* 32 (Winter 1958): 360–62.

13. Ibid., 362–71; Reminiscences of William J. Cameron, 240, FMCA.

14. Reminiscences of William J. Cameron, 147, FMCA.

15. Reminiscences of E. G. Liebold, 1337, 1393–94, 1406, FMCA.

16. Harry Bennett, *We Never Called Him Henry* (New York: Fawcett, 1951), 120.

17. Clipping, "Ford Attacks Bring Protest," Federal Mediation and Conciliation Service (FMCS), Case #199-1461, National Archives.

18. Gordon G. Moore to FDR, January 8, 1938, and attached Resolution OF 3217, FDR Library.

19. Clipping, "Two Mile Petition—Longest in the World—Honors Henry Ford," April 12, 1938, Acc. 984, Reel 25, FMCA; Arthur A. Ternes to FDR, April 23, 1938, and attached petition, Anonymous, Chicago, March 8, 1938, and George A. Dondero, March 24, 1938, all in OF 3217, FDR Library; Clipping, "Ford Attack Brings Protest," n.d., Mildred V. Smith to Mrs. Roosevelt, March 18, 1938, Walter Williams to FDR, and Wyman Silcox to FDR, April 3, 1938, all in FMCS, Case #199-1463, National Archives.

20. Clipping, *Detroit Free Press*, April 20, 1938, Ford Clipping File, Acc. 984, Reel 25, FMCA.

21. Reminiscences of William J. Cameron, 115–16, 137, 191, FMCA.

22. Reminiscences of William J. Cameron, 155, FMCA; Clipping, "The Commentator," *Detroit News*, April 29, 1938, Acc. 984, Reel 25, FMCA.

23. Hayden also expressed uncertainty about whether FDR was seeking to compose his differences with Ford or to put Ford on the spot. Hayden was probably trying to provide a balanced article, raising questions about both sides. There seems little doubt that FDR was not trying to put Ford on the spot. Clipping, *Detroit News*, April 23, 1938, Clipping File, Acc. 984, Reel 25, FMCA.

24. Clippings, April 21, 1938, Acc. 984, Reel 25, FMCA; *Newsweek*, May 2, 1938, p. 10.

25. *In re Ford Motor Co. and UAW*, 14 NLRB 346 (1939); James A. Gross, *The Reshaping of the National Labor Relations Board* (Albany: State University of New York Press, 1981), 30–39.

26. Irvan J. Cary to the President, April 26, 1938, Truly Ford Employees to the President, April 25, 1938, both in OF 3217, FDR Library.

27. *New York Times*, April 28, 1938. See also Reminiscences of William J. Cameron, 151, FMCA.

28. Clipping, *Detroit Times*, April 25, 1938, Acc. 984, Reel 25, FMCA; Alfred P. Sloan, Jr., *My Years at General Motors* (New York: McFadden-Bartell, 1965), 404.

29. Blair Moody to Laurence Lenhardt, April 6, 1938, Blair Moody Papers, Michigan Historical Collection, Bentley Library, Ann Arbor.

30. Reminiscences of William J. Cameron, 150–52, FMCA.

31. Robert Lacey, *Ford, the Men and the Machine* (Boston: Little, Brown, 1986), 384–86.

32. *New York Times*, April 28, 1938, pp. 1, 3; Clipping, *St. Louis Post-Dispatch*, April 28, 1938, OF 3217, FDR Library; Clipping, *Detroit Free Press*, April 28, 1938, Acc. 984, Reel 25, FMCA; *Time*, May 9, 1938, p. 10.

33. Clipping, *Detroit Free Press*, April 28, 1938, Acc. 984, Reel 25, FMCA.

34. Clippings, *New York News*, April 29, 1938, *New York Post*, April 29, 1938, both in Acc. 984, Reel 25, FMCA.

35. Clipping, *Washington Star*, May 2, 1938, Acc. 984, Reel 25, FMCA.

36. Clippings, *Baltimore Sun*, May 4, 1938, and UPI, May 4, 1938, both in Acc. 984, Reel 25, FMCA.

37. *New York Times*, April 29, 1938, p. 14.

38. Charles Sorensen, *My Forty Years with Ford* (New York: W. W. Norton, 1956), 27–29; Reminiscences of H. C. Doss, 55, FMCA; Reminiscences of William J. Cameron, 153–54, FMCA; *Time*, May 9, 1938, p. 1; Clipping, UPI dispatch, April 29, 1938; Clipping, *Detroit Times*, April 28, 1938; Clipping, *New York News*, April 29, 1938; Clipping, *New York Post*, April 29, 1938, all in Acc. 984, Reel 25, FMCA. After an analysis of the company's extensive clipping books, David L. Lewis concluded that "Ford spoke to groups unfamiliar to him only sixteen times in his life." *Public Image of Henry Ford*, 64.

39. *Complete Presidential Press Conferences of Franklin D. Roosevelt*, 11: 398–99.

40. Marjorie E. Vincent to FDR, April 28, 1938, OF 3217, FDR Library.

41. George Knott to FDR, May 2, 1938, OF 3217, FDR Library.

42. Clipping, *New York Advance*, May 5, 1938, Acc. 984, Reel 25, FMCA. Although that Yorkville paper called the participants in this gathering "pro-Nazi," the Bund was a Nazi organization. Ronald H. Baylor, *Neighbors in Conflict* (2d ed.; Urbana: University of Illinois Press, 1988), 60–62.

Its leader was Fritz Kuhn, a Ford Motor Company employee from 1928 to 1937. Lewis, *Public Image of Henry Ford*, 152.

43. Nathan Miller, *FDR: An Intimate History* (Garden City, N.Y.: Doubleday, 1983), 212; Edsel Ford to FDR, March 15, 1928, and FDR to Mama, March 17, 1928, both in Elliot Roosevelt, ed., *F.D.R.: His Personal Letters, 1905–1928* (New York: Duell, Sloan & Pearce, 1948), 634–45.

44. Abner E. Larned to Frank Murphy, December 30, 1937, Frank Murphy Papers, Box 19, Michigan Historical Collection.

45. *New York Times*, January 22, 1938, p. 1; Clipping, "Magnate Who Has Fought New Deal to Give No Advice," AP dispatch, April 21, 1938, both in Acc. 984, Reel 25, FMCA.

46. Abner E. Larned to Frank Murphy, December 30, 1937, Frank Murphy Papers, Box 19, Michigan Historical Collection; Sidney Fine, *Frank Murphy: The New Deal Years* (Ann Arbor: University of Michigan Press, 1984), 27–28; Ickes, *The Secret Diary*, III: 197.

47. Sorensen, *My Forty Years with Ford*, 268–71; Allan Nevins and Frank Ernest Hill, *Ford: Decline and Rebirth, 1933–1962* (New York: Scribner, 1963), 252–69.

5

The Utility of Newness: State Managers and the Creation of Civil Works

Michael Lewis

Over the past fifteen years, a debate has arisen in political sociology over the source of power in the development of policy. In this debate two views have emerged. Supporters of the first view contend that political struggles are essential contests between social and economic classes. In this view the state is nothing more than an arena in which conflicts over basic social and economic interests are fought. It is further asserted by society-centered theorists that, due to their control of the economic forces of society, elites will usually win these political battles.[1]

In contrast to the society-centered view, Theda Skocpol and others argue that "states may be sites of official autonomous action, not reducible to the demands or preferences of any social group(s)."[2] State autonomy theorists assert that state managers often have agendas separate from those of economic elites. Further, the existing structure of the state may affect policy by determining what is politically practical or possible.

Although much has been written on this subject (or perhaps because of it), there is still no clear consensus on what a state must do to become "relatively autonomous."[3] While I do not intend to address this issue completely in the course of this chapter, I would like to offer one possible circumstance as a clear example of an autonomous state. If by "autonomy" we mean that the state is capable of something more than reflecting the interests of various societal elites, then one way of demonstrating autonomy is to detail a case in which state managers pursue their own interests, even when these are antithetical to those of societal elites.

To do this, two things are necessary. First, it must be demonstrated that no elites were involved in the decision-making process. This, by itself, is not enough, since it has been widely argued that state managers can, and often do, take elite preferences into account when creating policy, even if elites are not present.[4] Thus, to establish the autonomy of the state, it must be shown that state officials ignored the expressed wishes of elites when developing a policy.

The description of a case in which this type of autonomy occurs is one goal of this chapter. The other goal is to examine one cause of this autonomy, the newness of the policy. By "newness" I mean that the policy under discussion is distinctive in one or more significant ways from any previous attempt to deal with the same issue. The creation of policy innovations gives the state an initial advantage in shaping a program. If they are able to move quickly enough, or if elites are distracted by other issues, then state managers may be able to create a policy that is against elites' wishes without elites' getting involved.

Speed by itself does not guarantee state autonomy in policy development. Other policies developed during the New Deal illustrate this clearly.[5] It is only when it is combined with newness that speed will lead to state autonomy.

To discuss both of these issues further, this chapter will examine the case of the Civil Works Administration (CWA). Created through an executive order of President Roosevelt, the CWA was a large-scale work relief program that employed 4 million people during the winter of 1933–1934. Its director, Harry Hopkins, saw it as a departure from previous government efforts (the Federal Emergency Relief Administration and the Public Works Administration) that had concentrated primarily on dispensing relief. Instead, Hopkins envisioned the CWA as an emergency employment corporation that would provide not relief but jobs.

In this spirit, the CWA hired workers on the basis of their skill rather than their financial need, and paid them wages equal to those offered in private industry. Further, to avoid meddling by local officials who were reluctant to go along with the program, the CWA was federally funded and administered. Once the CWA began in November 1933, it immediately drew criticism from business leaders and social workers. These groups, working together, were able to stop the CWA after only five months. When a new work relief program, the WPA, was started in 1935, it conformed to the desires of both business and social work.[6]

HISTORICAL BACKGROUND

The story of relief policy in the United States is a long and complex one that has been well documented in other places.[7] My purpose in this section is to establish that nothing like the CWA existed prior to the Great Depression. To do this, I will focus on two areas. These are the federal government's refusal to finance or administer relief (in contrast to the CWA, which was a federal program) and the use of work relief solely as a punitive measure rather than a way to employ the poor.

Prior to the twentieth century, relief was broken into two types, private charity and state or locally funded assistance. Private charities generally worked with needy families who had homes but were not able to support themselves completely. In these cases an overseer would give the family an allowance, or arrange to pay its grocery bills or rent. Public assistance was confined to those who were permanently disabled or were otherwise unable to care for themselves. Throughout this period the primary method of relief was indoor relief, that is, the placing of individuals in a county almshouse where they could be cared for.

After the turn of the century, the reform spirit of the Progressive movement began to lead to a shift in outlook on relief. Social workers and statistical researchers such as Lawrence Veiller produced studies of tenement crowding, and Robert Hunter spoke for many when he wrote that "social evils must be remedied and certain social wrongs must be put right."[8]

This new concern with unemployment also piqued the interest of technological experts, most notably engineers and economists. Influenced by Frederick Winslow Taylor's ideas on scientific management, these technicians began to argue that disorders in the industrial system created "labor turnovers" that put men out of work.[9] Equipped with these new explanations for unemployment, two groups—social workers and social engineers—began to seek new methods of relief.

Social Work and Relief

The early part of the twentieth century saw the development of social work as a profession. The central part of this process was the increasing importance of casework, which was an attempt by social workers to base treatment upon the collection and interpretation of social evidence gathered through the application of a means test. As Lubove notes, "In the early twentieth century social work had no distinctive focus. It was a compound of casework, settlement work, institutional and agency administration, and social reform. . . . By the early 1920s, casework had emerged as the nuclear skill, shaping the public image of social work."[10]

Social Engineering and Relief

While social workers concentrated on meeting the needs of individual clients with funding from private charities, a growing group of technicians and experts moved from factories and universities to the public arena. The impetus for this move came from two sources. The first of these was the work of Frank J. Goodnow. In a series of studies Goodnow proposed the separation of governmental ends and means. Questions of ends were within the realm of politics and legislation, whereas the means were in the realm of administration. Although the former were fraught with partisanship, the latter, according to Goodnow, could be treated impartially and scientifically.[11]

The other source of reformers was disciples of Progressive engineer Frederick W. Taylor, who argued for the ideal of rationalized public administration as an alternative to the corruption of machine politics. Initially, Taylor's work focused on time and motion studies for assembly line workers, but as his ideas developed, Taylor and others began thinking of the "ultimate applicability of Scientific Management principles and ideas, not only to every industrial activity but to every conceivable human activity."[12]

The most pressing concern for both university-trained public administrators and those who came from the Taylorite tradition was efficiency in all areas of society. "All that is necessary," wrote Charles Steinmetz of General Electric, "is to extend methods of economic efficiency from the individual industrial corporation to the national organism as a whole."[13]

As Steinmetz suggests, business leaders also were involved in the Taylorite movement. Having spent much of their professional lives concerned with factory efficiency, it was an easy shift for many of them to make. Haber writes that as the Taylorite movement grew, "members of the human engineering department of General Electric, statisticians from DuPont, and plant managers from AT&T began to take part in Taylor Society activities."[14]

The drive for societal efficiency led to a new way of viewing unemployment. In contrast to social workers, who concerned themselves with the individual, "social engineers" looked at the society as a whole, and argued that unemployment was largely a situation of inefficiently used man-power.[15] What was necessary was a public works program to employ those out of work until they find jobs in private industry.

Although their ideas had been tried by several cities, social engineers received their greatest opportunity during the postwar recession of 1921. As demands for relief came from the population, Secretary of Commerce Herbert Hoover initiated the Conference on Unemployment. Many of the advisers Hoover brought to Washington "emphasized rationalization of government and of society according to the rules discovered by social scientists, with attention particularly to corporate planning and . . . Taylorism efficiency."[16]

The conference's recommendations for relief included the suggestion that private industry undertake repairs and improvements, as well as the necessity of increasing government public works projects. However, it limited the federal government's role by noting that "primary responsibility must rest with local governments" for both funding and administration.[17] Ultimately, several states and localities experimented with public works on a small scale. One of the effects of these programs was to give experience to public administrators who later worked in the federal government during the New Deal. Among these were CWA planner Aubrey Williams, as well as Robert Kelso, Arch Mandel, and Pierce Williams who became CWA field representatives.

On the eve of the Great Depression, both social workers and social engineers had well-developed views of relief. Nevertheless, neither had been able to gain increased control of public relief. Social workers, adhering closely to the casework method, were still operating largely through private funding. Social engineers and businessmen were interested in public works, but these plans were adopted on only a small scale, and not on the national level. In the early stages of the depression, both groups would have an opportunity to increase their control over the administration of relief.

The Great Depression

When the Great Depression struck in 1929, the ground broken by social workers and social engineers had not changed the fact that public assistance was funded almost exclusively at the state and local levels. Katz documents the situation quite well: "In constant dollars, public welfare expenses, fueled especially by mothers' pensions, increased 168 percent between 1903 and 1928. Still, per capita spending on welfare by government remained low.

Between 1913 and 1929, per capita federal spending rose from $.09 to $.25; state spending from $.78 to $1.85; and city spending from $1.65 to $3.12."[18]

By October 1930, Hoover realized that the federal government had to become involved in emergency relief. As the nation prepared to face its second winter of the depression, Hoover created the President's Emergency Committee for Employment (PECE). Only a small number of social workers participated in PECE, compared with the collection of public administrators and efficiency experts, most of whom had participated in the 1921 Conference on Unemployment. Among this group were several people who were influential in the CWA, including Robert Kelso, Rowland Haynes, and Arch Mandel.

Hoover hoped that PECE would serve as a "moral leader for coordinated action," but that it would not involve the federal government directly in handing out relief.[19] When PECE's studies revealed that exhausted local funds had created "a vicious cycle of municipal bankruptcy and human suffering," PECE director Colonel Arthur Woods urged federal action.[20] In a message to Congress he called for accelerated public works as well as advanced planning of federal projects, so as to ward off future economic catastrophes. Ultimately, Hoover rejected these proposals, and PECE was disbanded in April 1931, a step that frustrated many social engineers who felt it was a necessary organization.

The TERA

The unwillingness of Hoover to send federal funding for relief forced states to bear the brunt of the burden. By far the most effective of these efforts occurred in New York, where Franklin D. Roosevelt was governor. New York's Temporary Emergency Relief Administration (TERA) warrants special attention because its director, Harry Hopkins, later became the driving force behind the CWA.

Hopkins had been in social work for close to two decades when he received the TERA appointment. He began his work in this area during the recession of 1914–1915, when he worked as a relief agent for the AICP's (Association for Improving the Condition of the Poor) Bureau of Family Rehabilitation and Relief. At this time he became aware of the necessity to provide jobs, not just case files, for the unemployed. When he took control of the TERA in September 1931, Hopkins established a dual system of relief. The first part consisted of home relief, for which payment would be in kind (groceries, clothes) but no cash. Although local relief officials were still in charge of home relief distribution, Harry Hopkins and the TERA board controlled the amount of relief money each locality would receive. Whenever a city or county applied for or sought to renew a TERA grant, its welfare personnel were subject to review by the TERA board. Using this as leverage, Hopkins insisted on "the need for competent people, with experience and training . . . and defended the policy of bringing social workers from the private agencies to the aid of the public departments."[21]

The other half of the TERA consisted of a work relief program administered at the state level. While this represented a departure from previous types of relief and reflected Hopkins's preference for giving the unemployed jobs, Hopkins still felt it had limitations. As Bremer explains:

> Hopkins could not candidly support the illusion that work relief duplicated the normal job situation. Recipients were still investigated and placed on relief rolls, from which they were drawn for work. Moreover, their wages were not really wages, because they were paid according to a "budgetary deficiency" standard instituted by the TERA: casework investigators geared their earnings to estimates of each family's needs. Their working conditions, including their hours of work, also remained below standards set in private industry, and the work they did frequently lacked social usefulness.[22]

As word of the TERA spread, other states attempted to emulate it. This allowed other administrators to experiment with work relief, some of whom (such as Aubrey Williams in Texas and Alan Johnstone in South Carolina) would eventually join Hopkins in creating the CWA. The TERA also increased Roosevelt's popularity among the unemployed, because it made him seem like someone who would take bold action to alleviate the suffering caused by the depression.

The election of Roosevelt to the presidency gave people new hope. Social workers across the country had seen the prominent role played by their counterparts in the TERA, and hoped they would be given similar posts at the national level. Social engineers were impressed with Roosevelt's willingness to spend money for relief, and were hopeful of persuading him to begin a national public works program. All groups, regardless of their particular wishes, were aware that with Roosevelt in the White House, it was time to experiment with relief on a national level.

The FERA

Roosevelt's first 100 days in office resulted in breakthrough legislation in a number of areas. One of these was poor relief. The Federal Emergency

Relief Act of May 1933 marked the first time the federal government accepted direct responsibility for assisting the jobless. The newly created Federal Emergency Relief Administration (FERA) received $500 million to distribute to the states to help with the relief load. This sum was to be distributed in two different ways.

Half of the $500 million was given out on a matching basis, with states contributing $3 for every $1 of federal funding they received. The other $250 million was used for grants to the states without any matching stipulation. In this way, states that had used all their funds could still receive federal aid. The distribution of the remaining $250 million was at the discretion of the director of the FERA.[23]

For this post, Roosevelt chose the director of the New York State TERA, Harry Hopkins. Since he had played a prominent role in the TERA, social workers anticipated the expansion of casework procedures on a nationwide scale. Hopkins understood these goals, and initially turned to C. M. Bookman, former president of the American Association of Social Workers, for advice on how to run the FERA.[24]

As he allocated FERA money to the states, Hopkins required the employment of social workers to dispense these funds at the county level. Schwartz discusses the dilemma Hopkins faced when making this decision. "Although disdainful of case work techniques, he still preferred the integrity of dedicated professionals to ensure that relief went to those in need and to protect the FERA against political interference."[25]

Social workers applied the means test and drew up minimum budget standards just as they had done in the TERA. Using lists of essential family items, local prices, and family size and income as guides, investigators made certain that budget assistance equaled a family's budget deficit, if that portion could be made available from FERA funds. Social workers were understandably pleased with the FERA; Hopkins, however, did not share their enthusiasm. He continued to consider the dole a temporary expedient, and began searching for a more creative response to unemployment.[26]

Once the FERA was begun, Hopkins began to bring to Washington a group of professionals who would aid him in the establishment of a different type of federal relief program. The corps that Hopkins assembled ushered in a new way of dealing with relief. Instead of graduates from social work school, they were public administration experts and social engineers who, like Hopkins, had moved beyond neighborhood agencies and casework to rationalized fund-raising and systematic disbursement based on technical expertise.

On Hopkins's staff were Robert Kelso, who had administrated relief in Boston and St. Louis and had published several books, including *The Science of Public Welfare*; Rowland Haynes, who had directed the Cleveland Recreation Council and Welfare Association; Louis Brownlow, director of the Public Administration Clearing House; Frank Bane, the former head of the American Public Welfare Association and the former Virginia commissioner of public welfare; Aubrey Williams, head of the Wisconsin State Conference of Social Work and director of the Texas Relief Commission; and Jacob Baker, head of the Emergency Exchange Association, which enlisted scientific management experts to direct the cooperative production of goods and rendering of services by New York City's unemployed.[27]

All of these men shared Hopkins's preference for work relief as the primary method of aiding the poor. Williams was especially clear on this point. "Whenever possible," he told the Wisconsin Relief Executive Committee, "relief shall be in the form of wages for work done."[28]

The initial goal of Hopkins's federal staff was to upgrade work relief within the FERA. Among their concerns was the fact that social workers still applied the means test to applicants for work relief. A worker qualified as long as his or her personal resources could not provide the necessities of life. The use of a means test, rather than hiring based on ability, led to unskilled labor, which further limited the types of projects that could be undertaken. Further, in order to ensure that any given worker did not get paid more than he or she needed, work schedules were often staggered. This led to less continuity than was necessary on many local projects, and ultimately caused their abandonment.[29] FERA statistician Corrington Gill found that FERA work relief "left much to be desired."[30] Hopkins agreed that drastic changes would be needed in the relief system.

BUSINESS VIEWS ON RELIEF

This viewpoint did not go unchallenged. Many business leaders expressed concerns with New Deal relief policy. Some saw unemployment as a form of laziness that would only be encouraged by federal relief. The president of the National Association of Manufacturers made this point clearly when he argued, "Many of those who are most boisterous now in clamor for work have either struck on the jobs they had or don't want to work at all."[31]

Other business leaders objected not to relief but to the further government encroachment into the economy that would result from it. As Henry Ford put it, "Government should stick to the strict function of governing. Let them let business alone."[32] Merle Thorpe, editor of *Nation's Business*, concurred: "Either state enterprise must give ground or private enterprise must succumb."[33]

Not only did government relief programs compete with private industry, they also created a federal deficit. Businessmen warned that one inevitable result of such policies was destruction of business confidence. Merle Thorpe argued, "Where political uncertainty is the rule, businessmen cannot make long term contracts; they cannot plan ahead; they cannot expand."[34] This lack of business growth, it was argued, would keep business from hiring workers, and would ultimately prolong the depression.

Despite their concern over the increasing amount being spent on unemployment relief, business elites did not organize and actively promote these arguments when the CWA was being discussed by members of the Roosevelt administration. The reason for this lack of political maneuvering around the unemployment issue was twofold. First, business elites were more concerned with the newly created National Recovery Administration, which promised to have a more direct impact on them than did any relief bill.

Further, the existence of the Public Works Administration (PWA), which was already engaged in large-scale public works, combined with the FERA, which was giving direct relief to many other unemployed people, seemed to be the end of Roosevelt's relief policy. Since elites were not expecting further work in this area, they were caught off guard by the introduction of a new relief plan. The other reason for elites' lack of interference as the CWA was being created was that business elites had no alternative plan, short of cutting unemployment relief altogether, to offer Roosevelt.

THE CREATION OF THE CWA

Dissatisfied with FERA work relief, several of Hopkins's assistants began searching for a different type of relief agency. Jacob Baker, director of the FERA work division, and his assistant Arthur Goldschmidt were the first to develop a plan for borrowing money, probably from the (PWA). This money could be used to finance a number of work programs under the planning and direction of the federal government.[35]

At about the same time, FERA field representative Aubrey Williams began looking for a solution to the work relief problem. In a memo to Hopkins, "On the Reemployment of the Unemployed," Williams outlined his plan. He started by arguing that the current relief funds given to clients were inadequate. He calculated that, on average, a family received 50 cents a day worth of relief. "What this means is obvious," Williams wrote. "At its best ($1.20 a day in Massachusetts), it provides a minimum maintenance in food and shelter. At its average (50 cents a day) it means inadequate food, indecent and deplorable housing and desperately inadequate living all along the line. In the lower brackets (16 cents a day in Oklahoma), it means slow starvation."[36]

Williams also discussed the plight of those not on the relief rolls. "There are approximately four million heads of families who are receiving no benefit from FERA. They are too proud to ask for relief. . . . They are electing to allow their children to go hungry and exist in a state of destitution rather than accept relief. . . . Relief as such should be abolished."[37]

In place of the system of direct relief, Williams suggested a program that "would do away with relief as such to all employable unemployed persons and put in its stead a system of employment in which men would be paid a daily wage for performing work."[38]

Williams proposed combining public works programs with relief programs in the creation of a "middle-ground agency that will lift the status of relief to an employment level" by eliminating the means test. At the same time, the proposed program would avoid the elaborate red tape and tight spending of public works by "moving public works arrangements to a direct government conducted affair" in which the federal government was the contractor under an "Emergency Employment Corporation."[39]

Still somewhat hesitant, Hopkins traveled to the Midwest, where he met with Frank Bane, director of the American Welfare Association; Louis Brownlow, director of the Public Administration Clearing House; and Robert Hutchins, president of the University of Chicago. All three agreed the plan was sound, but wondered about the support it would receive from PWA director Ickes, who would have to be sold on the plan if PWA funds were to be used.[40]

Upon his return to Washington, before meeting with the president, Hopkins scheduled a conference with PWA director Ickes. Following Jacob Baker's suggestion, Hopkins tried to get much more than he thought the new program would need, thinking that he could always bargain down from there. He wound up receiving a guarantee for $400 million from the PWA director.

With this money assured, Hopkins presented the plan to Roosevelt on Thursday, November 2. After hearing an overview of the plan, Roosevelt asked how many jobs would have to be provided; Hopkins said about 4 million. "Let's see," said Roosevelt. "Four million people—that means roughly four hundred million dollars."[41] Hopkins told him about his meeting with Ickes, and the guarantee of PWA funds he had received. Convinced of the program's soundness, Roosevelt ordered Hopkins to start immediately. Hopkins recalled later, "Before I could opine how long it would take, he told me 'Thirty Days!' Well, I didn't see any sense in saying forty or forty-five. . . . I knew it was just a little way to the Union Station, and I could go back to New York. So I said, 'All right.' "[42] Facing the task of providing jobs for 4 million people within thirty days, Hopkins and those advisers familiar with the new program met virtually around the clock to hammer out the details.

Agreeing they had little time to put the program together and get each state to cooperate, Hopkins and his staff made the CWA not only a federally funded relief program but the first federally administered one as well. Hopkins, rather than the governors, appointed all state civil works administrators, and they remained accountable only to Hopkins or his field representatives.[43]

To recruit workers for the new program, Hopkins turned to the newly created United States Employment Service (USES). Since it was a bureau within the Department of Labor, the USES gave Hopkins two benefits. The first was its ability to organize and process workers quickly, a necessity because the CWA was to begin in a month. Second, and more important, the USES allowed the CWA to avoid use of the means test in the hiring of its workers. As Hopkins stated, "These fellows have to be hired and fired like everybody else on a contract job."[44]

With hiring practices settled, the CWA staff had to address the issue of wages. Since the CWA's funding came initially from the PWA, Hopkins adopted the PWA wage scale. This scheme divided the country into three zones that corresponded roughly to the prevailing wage rates in each area. Minimum wages for skilled labor were $1.00, $1.10, and $1.20 in the southern, central and northern regions, respectively; unskilled workers received $.40, $.45, and $.50 an hour. In addition, CWA set special rates for white-collar employees at $12.00, $15.00, and $18.00 a week for the southern, central, and northern regions. Each CWA jobholder could work up to thirty hours a week; white-collar workers could put in as many as thirty-nine hours.[45]

Although these rates followed suggested floors established by the NRA, many businesses did not follow these recommendations. The result, then, was that CWA wages were often higher than the prevailing wages in private industry. This was especially true where employers were not members of the NRA. As these wage discrepancies became apparent, business leaders would come together to protest and demand an end to the CWA.

A final area of concern for the CWA staff was the types of projects that would be done by the new program. Unlike the PWA, which subcontracted to private firms, the CWA operated by "force account," where the federal government did the planning of all projects. "If you contract this stuff out, you will never get these fellows to work,"[46] declared Hopkins, in comparing his new agency with the slow-starting PWA.

The CWA staff envisioned their projects as middle-range public works, different from those done by the PWA. As Jacob Baker described it, "the CWA is not doing any work on airports. The bulk of the work [done by CWA workers] will be clearing, grading, and ditching."[47] In addition, CWA workers helped construct parks and playgrounds, water mains, and sewer extensions.[48]

By November 15, 1933, the CWA was far enough along that Hopkins could meet with relief administrators from across the country and go over the preliminaries of the program. The CWA was ready to start up.

FROM CWA TO WPA

Although the focus of this chapter has been on the creation of the CWA, it is necessary to go beyond this and examine the reactions of business and social work to the CWA. By demonstrating the displeasure with the CWA expressed by both business and social workers, we can reaffirm the lack of input these two groups had in its creation. Put another way, had business and social work been more involved in the creation of the CWA, it likely would have resulted in a program that was more suited to their policy interests. With this in mind, I will briefly sketch the concerns voiced by business and social workers regarding the CWA, and then look at the differences between the CWA and the Works Progress Administration (WPA), in which both business and social workers had a much greater influence.

Despite its enormous popularity with the unemployed, the CWA had aroused opposition from other groups, most notably the business community. Some expressed hostility to the program on the grounds that it was aiding "unworthy" people who did not deserve relief of any kind. One businessman stated, "My observation so far leads me to believe that the majority of those they term 'unemployed' are those that have never cared to work and are now taking the opportunity of this CWA because they can get by for the most part on the job without working and use the money on Saturday night to get drunk with."[49]

Others complained that this large, well-paying public employment program seemed to be competing directly with private industry. With the majority of CWA projects in light construction, complaints most often came from builders who found themselves left out. The Pittsburgh Builders

Exchange complained that "general contractors and subcontractors have had little to do in the past three years and then you set up a construction program which continues to leave them on the outside."[50] The Chicago Plumbing Contractors Association cried that the CWA "had put the master plumber out of business,"[51] and an Illinois paving contractor complained that his work "had been eliminated by the CWA."[52]

Manufacturers also protested CWA wage rates, which they claimed enticed workers away from their factories. "We have no objection to anyone leaving our employ in order to improve themselves," protested a steel executive, "but it does seem unfortunate that we should lose men from industry because they are able to obtain higher hourly rates on welfare projects."[53] Another employer suggested, "Had this CWA work been put out at about $.35 an hour it would have given outside employers some chance."[54]

While small businessmen complained that the CWA was hurting them personally, leaders of big business concentrated on the effect CWA had on the federal budget. Their argument centered on "the tremendous additional expense involved in work relief as against home relief for materials, supplies, and supervision."[55] Business leaders felt that this excessive spending would lead to a situation in which "the soundness of the nation's financial structure will be jeopardized by a debt burden which is excessive."[56]

The ending of the CWA was aided not only by these complaints from business but also by the unwillingness of social workers to defend the program. Their antipathy was a result of CWA hiring procedures that replaced the means test with hiring based on skill alone. Many social workers were concerned that there would be "local reactions, now that jobs are supplanting doles, to a continuance of adequate investigation and service to the families on relief rolls."[57] Other social workers worried that their position of leadership in federal relief was being supplanted by the new program. Kurtz wondered, "Will these [relief] standards be maintained and advanced? Will the FERA continue to exercise leadership it has shown in this field to date, despite the Civil Works program?"[58]

With mounting pressure from business to end the CWA, and with no support for the plan from social workers, Roosevelt made the decision to end the program in April 1934, after only five months of operation.

THE WPA

By 1935, Roosevelt was again forced to rethink his stance on work relief. The rise of populist movements led by Huey Long, Father Charles Coughlin, and Dr. Francis Townsend indicated a shift of the populace in favor of, among other things, a more extended welfare policy. Roosevelt's response to this was the Works Progress Administration (WPA), a program designed solely around work relief as the CWA had been.

Despite this superficial resemblance to its predecessor, the WPA reflected the reactions of business and social workers to the initial program. For example, although the WPA began in Washington, it functioned through a network of state offices; thus the federal government lost control over the execution of projects. Further, the WPA replaced the USES hiring system used in the CWA with decisions made by social caseworkers who determined eligibility for employment through the means test. Finally, the WPA wage rates reflected the concern of businessmen that work relief not compete with private industry. Wages ranged from $19 a month for unskilled workers in the south to $94 for professional employees in the north. In addition, the WPA imposed maximum hours on all projects to ensure that wages would not equal those in private industry.[59] The WPA became a testimony to the limits of work relief in the New Deal.

CONCLUSION

This chapter has attempted to show two things. First, the creation of the CWA was a case of state autonomy, and second, that this autonomy was rooted in the newness of the CWA program. With regard to the autonomy of the state, it has been shown that the state managers who devised this policy were lifelong civil servants, and that there were no consultations with business leaders or social workers during the development of the CWA. Further, the CWA plan went against the expressed wishes of elites by putting government directly in competition with business, and by eliminating social workers from the implementation of the program.

This kind of state autonomy interpretation is not without its critics. Among the most persuasive is Domhoff, who notes that state managers and business elites often share an ideological orientation. He argues that "the power elite is the leadership group of a capitalist class that is also a social upper class, and the interests of that social class are more general . . . than mere 'business' interests."[60] In this class he includes corporate lawyers, policy experts, investment bankers, and politicians. Given this similar social position and shared interests, state autonomy cannot be proven simply by demonstrating that business elites were not involved in the creation of a policy.

Although I agree with Domhoff's critique in general, I do not believe it is appropriate in the case of the CWA. This is not to argue that opponents of the CWA, particularly business, did not agree at all with the ideological orientation of the program. However, it is equally clear that the parts of the CWA program to which business did object were seen to be so detrimental to their cause that neither business nor social work could let the CWA continue. Put another way, it is difficult to envision the CWA turning out the way it did had business or social workers been involved in its initial planning. This, I believe, makes the CWA a clear instance of state autonomy.

With regard to newness, the CWA was distinct from any previous work relief plan. The goal of making the CWA an emergency employment corporation rather than a relief program led to a federally funded and administered program that hired workers on the basis of skill and paid them wages that were equal to those offered by private industry. As such, the CWA differed dramatically from work relief prior to the depression, which was used only for punitive purposes, and differed from early depression relief policy that was locally administered and given out on the basis of needs of the client.

NOTES

1. See, for example, G. William Domhoff, "Corporate Liberal Theory and the Social Security Act," *Politics and Society* 15 (Winter 1986): 297–330; Jill S. Quadagno, "Welfare Capitalism and the Social Security Act of 1935," *American Sociological Review* 49 (October 1984): 632–647.

2. Ann S. Orloff and Theda Skocpol, "Why Not Equal Protection: Explaining the Politics of Public Social Spending in Britain, 1900–1911, and the United States, 1880's–1920," *American Sociological Review* 49 (December 1984): 726–750.

3. Many writers in this debate use this phrase. See, for example, Theda Skocpol and Kenneth Finegold, "State Capacity and Economic Intervention in the Early New Deal," *Political Science Quarterly* 97 (Summer 1982): 259.

4. See, for example, G. William Domhoff, *The Power Elite and the State* (New York: De Gruyter Press), 1990; J. Craig Jenkins and Barbara Brents, "Social Protest, Hegemonic Competition and Social Reform: A Political Struggle Interpretation of the Origins of the American Welfare State," *American Sociological Review* 54 (1989): 891–909; Quadagno, "Welfare Capitalism and the Social Security Act of 1935."

5. Perhaps the best example of a quickly developed policy that was controlled by societal elites is the Emergency Banking Act, which was written and passed through Congress in eight days. The best discussions of bankers' influence on this legislation are Robert McElvaine, *The Great Depression* (New York: Times Books, 1984), pp. 139–142; Arthur M. Schlesinger, Jr., *The Coming of the New Deal* (Boston: Houghton Mifflin, 1959), pp. 4–10.

6. The story of the CWA is told in detail in Bonnie Fox Schwartz, *The Civil Works Administration* (Princeton: Princeton University Press, 1984); Forest A. Walker, *The Civil Works Administration* (New York: Garland, 1979).

7. See, for example, Michael Katz, *In the Shadow of the Poorhouse* (New York: Basic Books, 1986); Roy Lubove, *The Professional Altruist* (Cambridge, Mass.: Atheneum, 1965); Walter I. Trattner, *From Poor Law to Welfare State* (New York: Free Press, 1974).

8. Lubove, *Professional Altruist*, p. 9.

9. For a more complete discussion of Taylor and his ideas, see Samuel Haber, *Efficiency and Uplift* (Chicago: University of Chicago Press, 1964).

10. Lubove, *Professional Altruist*, p. 119.

11. Frank J. Goodnow, *Politics and Administration: A Study in Government* (New York: Macmillan, 1900).

12. Haber, *Efficiency and Uplift*, p. 107.

13. Charles Steinmetz, "Industrial Efficiency and Political Waste," *Harper's* (November 1916): 926.

14. Haber, *Efficiency and Uplift*, p. 163.

15. The term "social engineer" is taken from Herbert Hoover, who, as secretary of commerce, initiated the 1921 Conference on Unemployment to deal with this "technical problem that could be solved by socially responsible engineers." See Carolyn Grin, "The Unemployment Conference of 1921: An Experiment in National Cooperative Planning," *Mid-America* 55 (April 1973): 83–97.

16. Ibid., p. 84.

17. Ibid., p. 86.

18. Katz, *Shadow of the Poorhouse*, p. 208.

19. E. P. Hayes, *Activities of the President's Emergency Committee for Employment: October 7, 1930–August 19, 1931* (Concord, N.H.: Rumford Press, 1936).

20. Edward Ainsworth Williams, *Federal Aid for Relief* (New York: Columbia University Press, 1939), pp. 27–29.

21. William W. Bremer, *Depression Winters; New York Social Workers and the New Deal* (Philadelphia: Temple University Press, 1984), p. 82.

22. Ibid., pp. 122–123.

23. William Leuchtenburg, *Franklin D. Roosevelt and the New Deal* (New York: Harper & Row, 1963), p. 120.

24. JoAnna Colcord, "Social Work and the First Federal Relief Programs," *NCSW Proceedings* (Chicago: University of Chicago Press, 1943), pp. 384–394; *Fortune* 12 (July 1935): 59; Russell H. Kurtz, "On the Governor's Doorsteps," *Survey* 62 (October 1933): 344–345.

25. Schwartz, *Civil Works Administration*, p. 30.

26. Aubrey Williams, "A Year of Relief," *NCSW Proceedings* (Chicago: University of Chicago Press, 1934), p. 158; Russell H. Kurtz, "Two Months of the New Deal in Federal Relief," *Survey* 69 (August 1933): 284–290; Gordon Hamil-

ton, "Case Work Responsibility in the Unemployment Relief Agency," *The Family* 15 (July 1934): 135–141.

27. Schwartz, *Civil Works Administration*, pp. 28–30.

28. John A. Salmond, *A Southern Rebel: The Life and Times of Aubrey Wills Williams* (Chapel Hill: University of North Carolina Press, 1983), p. 32.

29. Arthur Edward Burns and Peyton Kerr, "Survey of Work Relief Wage Policies," *American Economic Review* 27 (December 1937): 711–713.

30. Corrington Gill, "The Civil Works Administration," *Municipal Yearbook* (1937): 420.

31. Arthur M. Schlesinger, Jr., *The Crisis of the Old Order* (Boston: Houghton Mifflin, 1957), p. 178.

32. Ibid.

33. Ibid.

34. Merle Thorpe, "Work Relief," *Nation's Business* 22 (May 1934): 11.

35. Walker, *Civil Works Administration*, p. 29.

36. Aubrey Williams to Harry Hopkins, "On the Reemployment of the Unemployed," October 30, 1933, Civil Administration Papers (CWA), Box 64, p. 8, National Archives (hereafter cited as NA).

37. Ibid.

38. Ibid., p. 10.

39. Ibid., p. 12.

40. Louis Brownlow, *A Passion for Anonymity* (Chicago: University of Chicago Press, 1958), p. 286.

41. Robert Sherwood, *Roosevelt and Hopkins: An Intimate History* (New York: Harper & Row, 1948), p. 51.

42. Walker, *Civil Works Administration*, pp. 34–35.

43. Harry Hopkins to State Administrators, "Rules and Regulations Number 1," November 11, 1933, CWA, Box 73, NA.

44. Schwartz, *Civil Works Administration*, p. 43.

45. Gill, "Civil Works Administration," p. 422.

46. Schwartz, *Civil Works Administration*, p. 45.

47. Jacob Baker to Henry Hunt (PWA), December 13, 1933, CWA, Box 40, NA.

48. Harry Hopkins, "Civil Works Administration, Rules and Regulations Number 3," November 15, 1933, CWA, Box 40, NA; Gill, "Civil Works Administration," pp. 425–426.

49. Jack Whiten to (Georgia Governor) Eugene Talmadge, December 10, 1933, CWA, Box 126, NA.

50. Pittsburgh Builders Exchange to (Pennsylvania CWA Administrator) Eric Bidle, January 16, 1934, CWA, Box 40, NA.

51. Chicago Plumbing Contractors Association to Harry Hopkins, March 6, 1934, CWA, Box 13, NA.

52. Harvey K. Rhoades to Harry Hopkins, March 13, 1934, CWA, Box 13, NA.

53. Ludlum Steel Company to Harry Hopkins, January 29, 1934, CWA, Box 32, NA.

54. Nick Caspers to (NRA Director) Hugh Johnson, February 2, 1934, CWA, Box 124, NA.

55. Winthrop D. Aldrich, "The Financing of Unemployment Relief," *Vital Speeches of the Day* 1 (December 1934): 178–179.

56. American Liberty League, *The Legislative Situation* (Washington, D.C.: American Liberty League, 1935), p. 4.

57. Russell H. Kurtz, "Relief from Relief," *Survey* 69 (December 1933): 405.

58. Ibid.

59. Donald S. Howard, *The WPA and Federal Relief Policy* (New York: Russell Sage Foundation, 1943), 173–266.

60. Domhoff, *The Power Elite and the State*, p. 39.

6

"Plenty at Our Doorstep": FDR on the Causes and Cures of the Great Depression

James F. Pontuso

Franklin Roosevelt began his presidency by quieting the nation's alarm. "So first of all, let me assert my firm belief that the only thing we have to fear is fear itself," he professed to an audience made anxious by the worst economic cataclysm since the rise of the industrial age. A less known, but perhaps more controversial, element of his first inaugural address was the statement that "I shall ask the Congress for the one remaining instrument to meet the crisis—broad Executive power to wage a war against the emergency, as great as the power that would be given to me if we were in fact invaded by a foreign foe."[1] The remark made even his wife, Eleanor, fearful "because when Franklin got to that part of his speech when he said it might become necessary for him to assume powers ordinarily granted to a President in war time, he received his biggest demonstration."[2]

To many, Roosevelt's statement and his later assertion of executive power during the New Deal marked a turning point in the duty and stature of the presidency. Prior to Roosevelt, it is argued by scholars such as James Sterling Young, the presidency was weak and subordinate; except in times of military crisis, presidents were hardly more than errand boys for the lawmaking branch. The Constitution granted few actual powers to the chief executive. When a president had to act quickly and decisively without a congressional mandate, he did so solely on the strength of his personality.[3]

Roosevelt's years in office changed all that. His "extraordinary leadership in expanding the federal government to meet the demands of . . . the Great Depression and . . . the Second World War" created the "modern presidency."[4]

David Nichols insists that the modern presidency is mostly a myth. According to Nichols, all of the elements of what is called the modern presidency were present at the creation of the office, including initiating and forwarding legislation in Congress, overseeing the administration of government, directing the nation in foreign relations, and acting as the people's representative—the so-called rhetorical presidency. What changed under Roosevelt, Nichols maintains, was the scope and responsibilities of the national government: "The truth behind the myth of the modern Presidency is that recent Presidents do more than previous Presidents, but that is traceable to the simple fact that modern American government as a whole does more. It is the broader change in the extent of government action, not a change in the constitutional balance of power among the branches, that provides some legitimacy to the myth of the modern Presidency."[5]

Both proponents and detractors of the "modern presidency" thesis agree that Roosevelt altered the role of the national government. Why did Roosevelt bring about such a massive shift in the function of government? To most the answer is obvious: the Great Depression. There is no doubt that the Great Depression frightened people. Nothing like it had ever been seen: a worldwide economic panic with millions of people unable to find work. Yet, there is more to the story. We cannot fully understand the New Deal and the long-lasting transformation of government it brought unless we comprehend what Roosevelt thought caused the Great Depression. In other words, we must look to Roosevelt's interpretation of the origins of the depression to become fully aware of the creation of the social welfare state.

Most commentators argue that Roosevelt was a moderate and that he took a pragmatic approach to reform. Roosevelt himself said, when asked about his political philosophy, "Philosophy? I am a Christian and a Democrat—that is all."[6] Arthur M. Schlesinger's three-volume biography goes to great lengths to show that although Roosevelt was a reformer and a pragmatist, he had no clear-cut vision of what actions to take in order to stem the downward economic spiral.[7] For example, during the 1932 campaign, the Democratic platform insisted on a balanced federal budget rather than the lavish government expenditures later adopted under the tutelage of John Maynard Keynes.[8] As one commentator explains, "Roosevelt's search for measures to bring about recovery from the depression was not very successful. By the spring of 1932 he had not worked anything more than a few general ideas. . . . One thing was certain, however: a workable recovery plan would have started with stimulation of consumption . . . , while underlying his whole attitude was a willingness to experiment with any proposals that seemed sensible."[9] However, while it is true that Roosevelt undertook "bold, persistent experimentation" because he was uncertain about how to cure the depression, it is also clear that he had a well-defined understanding of the causes of the collapse.[10] He believed that the very strength of the free market was the source of its malaise. Like some giant cresting wave, capitalism had crashed under its own inner dynamic, and Roosevelt feared that it would sweep away freedom and democracy in its rushing undertow.

CAUSES OF THE GREAT DEPRESSION

For most of its history the United States accepted what is generally called free-market capitalism. The role of the government was to apply the rule of law so that the competing business and labor interests could interact on a more or less equitable footing. "The business of America" really was "business," as Calvin Coolidge expressed it. Indeed, prior to the Great Depression, and even after it, of course, the "American success story" was attributed to the ability of individuals to invent, invest, buy, sell, own, and labor without interference from the government. Since the New Deal, it has become somewhat customary to portray defenders of the market system as hard-hearted capitalists, oblivious to the cares of the common man. But as the overwhelming victories at the polls of the pro-business Republican Party attests, the majority of Americans believed that they benefited from economic liberty as much as they did from civil and religious freedom. It is important to realize that Republicans also wanted increased wealth and individual prosperity; the debate over the proper arrangement of the economy has always been a fight over the best means to achieve those ends. Of course, there were dissenters. The Progressive movement attacked the corruption and greed of the newly developing urban and industrial life. To the Progressives the most egregious example of the perversion of American ideals was the rise of monopolies. Progressives wanted to break up the monopolies and, despite their name, return to a model of small business competition.

Prior to the depression, Roosevelt, too, had been a Progressive. In a speech comparing his hero Thomas Jefferson to his political mentor, Woodrow Wilson, Roosevelt echoed the principal fear of the Progressives: the perversion of individual liberty through the concentration of economic power. "Where Jefferson had feared the encroachment of political power on the lives of individuals, Wilson knew that the new power was financial."[11] But the Great Depression made Roosevelt rethink his position. He still saw the concentration of economic power as dangerous, but distrusted competition as well. He doubted whether market forces, left untended, could actually sustain prosperity. He expressed skepticism of economic theory that suggested continued growth of industry would ensure widespread prosperity.[12]

In 1932, Roosevelt continued to criticize monopolistic business and speculated that with unabated concentration of economic power, by the end of the twentieth century industry would be "controlled by a dozen corporations, and run by perhaps a hundred men . . . plainly we are steering a steady course toward economic oligarchy, if we are not there already."[13] Like the Progressives of an earlier age, Roosevelt thought that monopolies squeezed out the little man and he boldly declared; "equality of opportunity as we have known it no longer exists." Although he acknowledged that under capitalism individuals still had the opportunity to pursue business ventures, in reality, given the power of corporations, the average person "starts under a handicap."[14]

Roosevelt came to doubt the efficacy of an economy made up of small entrepreneurs and businesses. Such a system allowed the little man to compete, but that competition itself turned out to be socially harmful. Roosevelt maintained that this system resulted in wasted resources, unnecessary duplication of facilities, numerous commercial failures—much of which could have been avoided "by greater foresight and by a larger measure of social planning."[15]

Just after Roosevelt's election in 1932, his "brain trust" released a statement that reflected this new thinking on competition. It rejected

> the traditional Wilson–Brandeis philosophy that if America could once more become a nation of small proprietors, of corner grocers, smithies under spreading chestnut trees, we could solve the problems of American life. We agreed that the heart of our difficulty was the anarchy of concentrated economic power. . . . We believed that any attempt to atomize big business must destroy . . . a higher standard of living. . . . Competition, as such was not inherently virtuous . . . competition created as many abuses as it prevented.[16]

Rather than commending the entrepreneurial spirit that had been the hallmark of the expansion of the American economy, Roosevelt saw the overly eager industrialist as an "unethical competitor" and "reckless promoter" who had effectively brought the law of the jungle into civilized society. FDR explained that the only force capable of controlling this destructive force and ensuring the public good was a strong government.[17] Liberty had turned into license, or at least license of the few who were denying freedom to all the rest.

Not only did economic centralization close the door to economic opportunity, according to Roosevelt, more importantly, it created a maldistribution of wealth. The rich had too much money, even to spend on luxuries; the poor had too little, even to purchase necessities. The result was not just inequity, but an odd economic condition in which consumers could not consume what they produced. Supply outstripped demand. Furthermore, since the rich had an overabundance of money, they continued to invest their profits in plants, which only served to create more excess. Roosevelt explained that prior to the Great Depression, while the costs of production declined, consumers saw none of the benefits. Instead, the wealthy became wealthier and the working people were left behind.[18]

For Roosevelt the Great Depression was merely a symptom of the general failure of capitalism. Capitalism collapsed not because it had strayed from its optimal path but, rather, because its very strengths caused its weakness. In fulfilling its highest or best course, capitalism produced goods quickly, cheaply, and efficiently. This was so because corporations were compelled to compete with their rivals. In order to produce more goods at a lower cost, the owners introduced ever more complex technologies and simultaneously kept wages flat. The result was a market glutted with too many goods. When companies could not sell their merchandise, they warehoused inventory, then lowered prices, and finally laid off employees. As people became unemployed, the demand for goods dropped even further, resulting in more layoffs, more plant closings, and, of course, less demand for what was being produced. There was a tumbling effect in the economy that eventually led to collapse. Although, in Roosevelt's words, "plenty is at our doorstep," most could not afford to purchase it.

The primary cause of the Great Depression, for Roosevelt, was overproduction. The most powerful impulse of free-market capitalism was to produce more, always more. Therefore, it was necessary to rethink the very foundations of the free-market system. Hence, Roosevelt called for a reappraisal of America's traditional stance toward its economic system. The capitalists who built more railroads and plants were "as likely to be a danger as a help." The nation did not require more natural resources and did not need more goods to be produced. The new economic realities called for controlling "underconsumption," adjusting production to consumption, and distributing wealth more equitably. "The day of the enlightened administration" had come.[19]

Market forces could not be counted on to correct the ills of the nation, for competition would result in more speculation, more investment, more productive capacity, and more unemployment.[20]

THE CURES FOR THE GREAT DEPRESSION

At the beginning of the twentieth century, most people in the West accepted that civilization was at the dawn of a more prosperous and enlightened age. Europe and the United States had enjoyed a relatively long period of peace, and it appeared that the scourge of war had retreated in the face of a more human and tolerant attitude toward mankind. New scientific discoveries were announced nearly every day. New technologies were introduced that revolutionized the way people lived. The opportunity for economic advancement seemed unlimited. The shock and horrors of World War I dampened much of this optimism. Nevertheless, many people were still hopeful that the war had been a temporary deviation from the road of progress; for them, the 1920s were a return to normalcy.

The Great Depression was more than just an economic crisis. It was a challenge to the belief in progress, prosperity, individual effort as a means to advancement, and free democratic government. Indeed, as Arnold Toynbee wrote at the time, there was real doubt whether Western civilization would survive: "In 1931, men and women all over the world were seriously considering and frankly discussing the possibility that the Western system of society might break down and cease to exist."[21] Furthermore, the liberal democratic governments appeared less capable of dealing with economic dislocation than were the Communist regime in the Soviet Union, the fascist dictatorships in Italy and later in Germany, or the autocratic states in Latin America. Although we know now that their prosperity was as much propaganda as successful policy, many in the public believed that freedom and democracy might be overwhelmed. Even in the United States people talked openly of revolution and what to do if one occurred. Some thought that the "Reds will run the country—or maybe the Fascists. Unless, of course, Roosevelt does something." Reinhold Niebuhr wrote that "capitalism was dying," and that "it ought to die."[22] Father Charles Coughlin exclaimed to a congressional committee, "I think by 1933, unless something is done, you will see a revolution in this country." Huey Long, the other great populist leader of the depression years, wanted to share the nation's wealth through a radical policy of redistribution that would make "ev'ry man a king."[23]

Roosevelt's first act upon taking office was to call a "bank holiday," a measure taken to forestall a run on depository reserves. The new president closed the banks under his executive authority and sent a bill to Congress asking for legislative approval. So potent was the fear engendered by the depression that the usually deliberative House passed the measure in less than an hour and the Senate took less than half a day. "Vote! Vote!" echoed from the floor during the brief debate. "The House is burning down," said the impatient Bertrand H. Snell, Republican floor leader, "and the President of the United States says this is the way to put out the fire."[24]

With fear, desperation, and talk of revolution looming in the background, Roosevelt reasoned that only a major shift in government's relationship to the economy could salvage the American way of life. Government could "obviate revolution" by acting more vigorously to forestall the root causes of misery. FDR likened poverty to a disease and declared that it was far better to focus on prevention than to wait for society to become ill.[25] "I believe," the president maintained, "that we are at the threshold of a fundamental change in our popular economic thought, that in the future we are going to think less about the producer and more about the consumer."[26] FDR further maintained that the concentration of economic power had created a kind of tyranny that could only be eradicated by a strong government.[27]

At first, Roosevelt attempted to coordinate production, distribution, and consumption through the voluntary "agreements" of the National Recovery Act (NRA). The act was ruled unconstitutional by the Supreme Court. Despite his attack on the "Nine Old Men," Roosevelt had lost confidence in the NRA by the time the Court ruled. When businesses acted in unison under the provisions of the bill, they in effect became a trust, limiting competition and pocketing high profits. Although Roosevelt had believed that high prices were necessary to invigorate industry, thereby restoring jobs and wages, he saw that this "bold experiment" had resulted in price-fixing. By 1938 he had lost faith in industrial cooperation as a viable policy. He reverted to the Progressive notion that competition was good because it ensured lower prices.[28] On the other hand, he worried that low prices could lead to more business closures. The principle of adjusting production to consumption remained active in the New Deal's agriculture programs, where subsidies and price supports were instituted to support the family farm. One critic said of Roosevelt's wavering on this issue that the "basic faults in the congeries of the administration's economic policies sprang from Roosevelt's refusal to make a choice between the philosophy of Concentration and Control and the philosophy of Enforced Atomization."[29]

Much more successful and long lasting was Roosevelt's graduated income tax. He favored this course not simply for reasons of equity. He did argue that the rich benefited more from society and therefore ought to bear a greater share of the burden. But the most important reason for redistributing wealth, according to Roosevelt, was to take money out of the speculators' hands, thereby decreasing production, and to enlarge the buying power of the populace, thereby increasing demand. The problem, FDR theorized, was not a lack of capital, but rather the inability of many working people to buy goods and services.[30] Roosevelt believed in demand-side economics. He might have accepted that a rising tide lifted all the ships, but he was not certain that the free market, left to itself, would move in the direction of shore. The government had to ensure that citizens could afford to buy what their labor produced. Prosperity, he suggested, should be "uniform" so that all groups in society could purchase what they need.[31]

Whether or not Roosevelt ever fully understood Keynes's principles is unclear, but he came to the conclusion, perhaps by trial and error, that deficit spending and expanding the money supply, the primary tools of Keynes's macroeconomics, could serve to increase demand by putting money in people's hands. Moreover, deficit spending was used for government jobs programs, such as the Civilian Conservation Corps and the Works Progress Administration, which could be steered toward helping the most needy citizens.

None of Roosevelt's policies seemed to have much of an effect. Well into his second term, the depression continued only somewhat abated. Although he remained personally popular, his policies were losing much of their support. The pragmatist in Roosevelt understood that his agenda might be abandoned for lack of results if it did not get a firm hold in the minds of the people. Moreover, Roosevelt dismissed the idea of adopting a more radical solution to the nation's economic plight because any "paternalistic system which tries to provide for security for everybody from above only calls for an impossible task," and because the regimentation such a program would entail was "utterly uncongenial to the spirit of our people." It was late in the 1930s that he began to emphasize what was arguably his boldest and farthest-reaching strategy. He attempted to rise above disputes concerning policy and emphasize something on which virtually all Americans could agree when he said that progress in a democratic system could be impeded about disagreement over means, even when society shares certain ends.[32]

On what do most Americans agree? They agree on the protection of their rights. In order to advance his program for recovery, Roosevelt changed the definition of rights. "The task of statesmanship has always been the re-definition of these rights in terms of a changing and growing social order. New conditions impose new requirements upon Government and those who conduct Government."[33] To the freedom *of* speech and the freedom *of* religion he added freedom *from* want and freedom *from* fear.[34] The new rights were not specific in their content, as religion and speech were. They were to be defined by the ever-changing desires of the people for well-being. The new rights could be put forward by individuals as claims or demands on the government. The new rights made the government responsible not just for the safety of the nation, or even for the health of the economy, but also for the security of every citizen. Roosevelt foresaw that he could promote his cure for capitalism's ills without having to become too specific about details. He could create an expectation in the people that the government must stand as a bulwark against economic disaster and personal failure. It must establish and maintain a social safety net—the welfare state.

The best way for the government to satisfy people's needs was, ironically, not to follow their every wish. Rather, the people would supply the ends by dictating to the rulers what they desired, and the government would contrive the means to satisfy those ends. It would employ experts who would administer the programs on the basis of the latest scientific and technological knowledge. It would be government of the people and for the people, but not necessarily by the people.

The presidency, too, would have to change. Although Roosevelt is famous for putting together a winning electoral coalition, he did not think that the executive needed to play the various factions against one another. As the Brownlow Commission Report suggests, the New Deal was dependent on centralization of decision-making in the White House as a mechanism for both formulating policy and carrying it out. Perhaps Nichols is correct to argue that all of Roosevelt's actions had precedents in earlier presidents, but surely Roosevelt greatly increased the scope of those actions. It is an axiom that differences in degree become differences in kind. Moreover, Roosevelt also changed the expectation of what a president should be. We might say that prior to Roosevelt, presidents served to preserve and protect the nation; after Roosevelt, they undertook to preserve and provide for the people.

CONCLUSION

Franklin Roosevelt believed that the economic disaster of the Great Depression was an inevitable outgrowth of capitalism. Capitalism could not be reformed by restoring it to its proper workings. Exactly when it was working properly, the drive to compete inherent in the free market could not help but squander resources, concentrate wealth, restrict opportunity, and overproduce goods. If strong actions were not taken to overcome the depression and forestall future crisis, free and democratic government would vanish. The cure for economic calamity was for the government to take on the role of manager. Its power over the whole society had to be increased in order to administer the nation's riches in a manner that would not lead once again to the economic anarchy that had precipitated the depression. In this Roosevelt acted as founder of sorts, for he saw that "the task of Government in its relations to business is to assist the development of an economic declaration of rights, an economic constitutional order."[35] While he was unsure exactly what might be called for in the new order, he did perceive clearly that the structure of the government had to change, and along with it, the responsibilities, authority, and expectations placed on the presidency.

John Kenneth Galbraith argued that Roosevelt's policies have been responsible for creating the extensive middle class in the United States. New Deal measures boosted the buying power of many groups in the nation, especially wage earners and farmers. By distributing wealth, the welfare state corrected the imbalance inherent in free-market capitalism.[36] Yet, it is more persuasive that the large middle class in America is the result of economic expansion. Since the Great Depression, the gross domestic product in the United States has grown nearly 1000 percent. New factories, new industries, and new technologies have increased the productivity of workers without economic disaster. New inventions, such as the computer, have changed the way we live. It is difficult not to conclude, with the wisdom of hindsight, that Roosevelt was wrong about the causes of the depression. The free market had not reached the outer limits of its useful productive capacity. No politician and few experts or citizens would argue in the 1990s, as Roosevelt did in the 1930s, that the nation has enough factories to meet all of its economic needs—and perhaps even more.[37]

We are more likely now to agree with Herbert Hoover's criticism of Roosevelt than with Roosevelt's assessment of our economic plight. Hoover "challenged the whole idea that we have ended the advance of America, that this country has reached the zenith of its power, the height of its development." He argued that progress is "due to the scientific research, the opening of new inventions, new flashes of light from the intelligence of our people." He predicted that there "are a thousand inventions for comfort in the lockers of science and invention which have not come to light."[38] Moreover, liberal democracy is triumphant. It is not threatened, as Roosevelt believed it was.

Partly due to his leadership, it has defeated all serious challenges to its way of life. Even the worst despots pay lip service to it tenets. It has prevailed in part because of its ability to satisfy the material needs of its citizens.

If Roosevelt was incorrect about the origins of the Great Depression, why has the welfare state survived? First, Roosevelt was successful in changing people's expectations toward government. Government became not the enemy of liberty but the guarantor of people's economic rights. When problems arise, many expect the government to solve them. Second, once a program is initiated, it develops its own constituency, making its elimination—or even substantial cutbacks—extremely difficult. Finally, the very wealth created by the free-market system makes overt poverty in any segment of society unacceptable to most Americans. There is a broad consensus that providing some sort of a social safety net is a fundamental task of government.

Despite having been proven wrong about the weakness of the free market, Roosevelt would no doubt be pleased to look back on the years since the Great Depression. Democracy has flourished, there is no "paternalistic system" that guides the economy. Yet, the harsher aspects of capitalism have been softened. Few citizens are ill clothed, ill housed, or ill fed. The government is much stronger than it once was, and therefore is more able to meet any future crises that might befall the nation. And the presidency that Roosevelt helped establish is the center of the country's political life.

NOTES

1. Franklin D. Roosevelt, "First Inaugural" (March 1932), in *The Public Papers and Addresses of Franklin D. Roosevelt*, Vol. II (New York: Random House, 1938), pp. 11, 15. See also Arthur M. Schlesinger, *The Crisis of the Old Order* (Boston: Houghton Mifflin, 1957), p. 8; and Thomas H. Greer, *What Roosevelt Thought: The Social and Political Ideas of Franklin Roosevelt* (East Lansing: Michigan State University Press, 1958).

2. Quoted in Arthur M. Schlesinger, Jr., *The Coming of the New Deal* (Boston: Houghton Mifflin, 1958), p. 1.

3. James Sterling Young, *The Washington Community* (New York: Columbia University Press, 1966).

4. Sidney M. Milkis and Michael Nelson, *The American Presidency: Origins and Development, 1776–1990* (Washington, D.C.: Congressional Quarterly Press, 1990), p. 259. See also Philip Abbot, *The Exemplary Presidency* (Amherst: University of Massachusetts Press, 1990).

5. David K. Nichols, *The Myth of the Modern Presidency* (University Park: Pennsylvania State University Press, 1994), p. 7.

6. Quoted in Schlesinger, *The Coming of the New Deal*, 585.

7. Arthur M. Schlesinger, Jr., *The Politics of Upheaval* (Boston: Houghton Mifflin, 1960), pp. 647–659. See also Ted Morgan, *FDR: A Biography* (New York: Simon and Schuster, 1985), pp. 413–441.

8. Although Roosevelt knew Keynes, evidently he never fully appreciated the finer points of the economist's theories. Nevertheless, he agreed with the "demand-side" principles espoused by Keynes. These ideas became the backbone of welfare state economics until the 1980s. See Howard Zinn, ed., *New Deal Thought* (Indianapolis: Bobbs-Merrill, 1966), pp. 403–404.

9. Daniel Fusfeld, *The Economic Thought of Franklin D. Roosevelt and the Origins of the New Deal* (New York: Columbia University Press, 1956), p. 206.

10. "Address at Oglethorpe University," *Public Papers and Addresses*, I, 646.

11. "Commonwealth Club Address," *Public Papers and Addresses*, I, 749.

12. "Address at Oglethorpe University," *Public Papers and Addresses*, I, 643.

13. "Commonwealth Club Address," *Public Papers and Addresses*, I, 751.

14. Ibid., 750–751.

15. "Address at Oglethorpe University," *Public Papers and Addresses*, I, 642.

16. Raymond Moley, *After Seven Years* (New York: Harper and Brothers, 1939), pp. 23–24.

17. "Commonwealth Club Address," *Public Papers and Addresses*, I, 755.

18. "A New Deal for the American People," *Public Papers and Addresses*, I, 650–651.

19. "Commonwealth Club Address," *Public Papers and Addresses*, I, 751–752.

20. Schlesinger explains that the "tenets of the First New Deal were that the technological revolution had rendered bigness inevitable; that competition could no longer be relied on to protect social interests; that large units were an opportunity to be seized rather than a danger to be fought; and that the formula for stability in the new society must be combination and cooperation under enlarged federal authority. This meant the creation of new institutions, public and private, to do what competition had once done (or was supposed to have done) in the way of balancing the economy—institutions which might well alter the existing pattern of individual economic decision, especially on investment, production, and price." Moreover, the "depression introduced special elements . . . a sobering sense that the age of economic expansion had come to an end. The First New Deal thus tended to see the problem of institutional reorganization not in the context of economic growth which the New Nationalism [of Theodore Roosevelt] had carelessly assumed but in the context of what became known as 'economic maturity.' " Schlesinger, *The Coming of the New Deal*, 179–180.

21. Arnold J. Toynbee, *Survey of International Affairs: 1931* (London: Oxford University Press, 1932), p. 1.

22. Schlesinger, *The Crisis of the Old Order*, 4–5.

23. Schlesinger, *The Politics of Upheaval*, 17, 66.

24. James MacGregor Burns, *Roosevelt: The Lion and the Fox* (New York: Harcourt Brace Jovanovich, 1956), p. 167.

25. "The Philosophy of Social Justice Through Social Action," *Public Papers and Addresses*, I, 773; Schlesinger, *The Politics of Upheaval*, 648.

26. "Address at Oglethorpe University, *Public Papers and Addresses*, I, 645.

27. "Acceptance of the Renomination for the Presidency" (1936), *Public Papers and Addresses*, V, 231.

28. "Recommendation to Congress to Curb Monopolies and the Concentration of Economic Power," *Public Papers and Addresses*, VII, 305–332.

29. Moley, *After Seven Years*, 367.

30. "Address at Oglethorpe University," *Public Papers and Addresses*, I, 645.

31. "Commonwealth Club Address," *Public Papers and Addresses*, I, 752.

32. "Address to the Young Democratic Clubs of America," *Public Papers and Addresses,* IV, 343.

33. "Commonwealth Club Address," *Public Papers and Addresses*, I, 753.

34. "Address to International Student Assembly," *Public Papers and Addresses*, XI, 354.

35. "Commonwealth Club Address," *Public Papers and Addresses*, I, 752.

36. John Kenneth Galbraith, *American Capitalism* (Boston: Houghton Mifflin, 1952).

37. "Address at Oglethorpe University," *Public Papers and Addresses*, I, 645.

38. Herbert Hoover, *The Memoirs of Herbert Hoover* (New York: Macmillan, 1952), p. 252.

PART II

Leadership and Presidential Powers

7

FDR's Party Leadership: Origins and Legacy

Sean J. Savage

The thesis of this chapter is that Franklin D. Roosevelt had always been committed to making the Democratic Party a distinctly liberal majority party in national politics. This chapter favorably judges Roosevelt's party leadership according to how well he was able to unite, expand, and liberalize the Democratic Party, in light of the fact that he had to operate within the inherently factious, decentralized political system of American federalism. Roosevelt was confident that by identifying the Democratic Party with the New Deal's ideology and policy agenda espousing federal intervention to reform the economy and broaden the distribution of wealth, he could not only unite the previously conflicting Northern and Southern wings of the party but also attract liberally inclined Republicans, independents, and third party members into the Democratic Party.

Since its publication in 1956, James MacGregor Burns's classic work on Roosevelt and the New Deal, *Roosevelt: The Lion and the Fox*, has been widely accepted as an authoritative text on the party politics of the New Deal era. According to Burns, Roosevelt, unlike Jefferson and Jackson, initially did not try to redefine the Democratic Party in terms of new voting blocs and interest groups adhering to a new, distinct political philosophy and policy agenda.[1] Burns suggests that Roosevelt relied too much on his personal popularity with the voters for his political success, and failed to develop and implement a long-term strategy to build a consistently liberal Democratic Party able to maintain its majority status. He intimates that only in 1935 did Roosevelt make the transition from a relatively moderate, nonideological "power broker" of conflicting interests to a more liberal party leader in order to placate the populist criticism of the New Deal represented by the Long, Coughlin, and Townsend movements and to assure his reelection in 1936.[2] In short, Burns concludes that Roosevelt was a passive captive, not an active shaper, of the forces within his political environment.[3]

In two later works, *Presidential Government* (1965) and *The Deadlock of Democracy: Four-Party Politics in America* (1963), Burns assesses Roosevelt's leadership of the Democratic Party according to his own concept of successful presidential leadership of a major party. Burns's concept of the ideal party leader is Britain's prime minister, who is able to effectively mobilize and discipline his party in Parliament in order to pass his legislation.[4] Using the prime minister's strong, centralized party leadership as his way of comparing and evaluating the party leadership of several American presidents, Burns concludes that only Thomas Jefferson's party leadership was truly successful, in that it was the only one that approximated a prime minister's control of his party's legislators and success in getting his bills passed.[5]

Measured by Burns's admiration for Jefferson and the British parliamentary system, all of the other presidents evaluated are portrayed as being unsuccessful party leaders, in varying degrees, because of their own political flaws and because of forces and structures within the American political system that thwart strong party leadership. Burns refers to the American political system as the Madisonian system because it diffuses and decentralizes power in both governmental authority and party politics.[6] Within this federalist, factious power structure, strong, centralized presidential leadership of a party, especially within Congress, is very difficult to achieve and maintain.

This fragmentation of power and the president's difficulty in achieving such leadership are exacerbated by the fact that the American political system really contains four parties, according to Burns. Each of the two major parties consists of two "parties"—one in Congress and one in the presidency.[7] Burns concludes *The Deadlock of Democracy: Four-Party Politics in America* by proposing reforms to make the president a stronger party leader by basically making the American political system more like a parliamentary system, especially in regard to the president's ability to unite and discipline his party and the executive–legislative relationship to policy-making.[8]

Burns admits, therefore, that he has high standards in evaluating the party leadership of Roosevelt and other presidents. He fails to recognize, though, that he is being unrealistic in classifying Roosevelt as a successful party leader only if he had achieved the type of disciplined, centralized control of his party that a prime minister can exercise. While faulting Roosevelt for not inducing a realignment of the two parties according to clear ideological distinctions, Burns concedes that "in assessing Roosevelt's role as party leader we must keep in mind the enormous effort and the huge political risks that party realignment would have required."[9]

E. E. Schattschneider argues that "the authors of the Constitution set up an elaborate division and balance of powers within an intricate governmental structure designed to make parties ineffective."[10] Besides being mindful of the decentralized, antiparty nature of the American constitutional order while evaluating Roosevelt's party leadership, this chapter will also assess his performance according to the following question: Was the Democratic Party a larger, stronger, and more distinctly liberal party by 1945 than it had been in 1932? By assessing Roosevelt's party leadership during his presidency according to these criteria, the thesis of this chapter contends that Franklin D. Roosevelt was mostly successful not only in making the Democratic Party stronger, larger, and more electorally successful but also in making it more liberal through its advocacy of greater federal intervention to solve social and economic problems. In explaining how the New Deal transformed the American party system by establishing the Democratic Party as the majority party, Everett C. Ladd, Jr., and Charles D. Hadley concluded that, as a result of the New Deal's influence on the Democrats' ideology and policy agenda, there emerged among the voters "a perception rather widely held that the Democracy under FDR . . . spoke effectively to the salient concerns and problems defining a social and political era."[11]

In his analysis of changes within the Democratic Party from 1932 to 1945, Otis L. Graham, Jr., criticizes Burns for expecting Roosevelt to have spent an inordinate amount of time and attention on his role as party leader. Graham argues that "it ought to be clear how great a commitment of presidential time, energy, and political capital is implied in Burns' vision of real party leadership."[12] Because Roosevelt was forced to concentrate on two back-to-back crises, the Great Depression and World War II, it is unreasonable to expect him to have made the transformation of the Democratic Party his top priority as president. Despite Roosevelt's focus on these more important responsibilities and the reverses that he suffered as a party leader, Graham concludes that Roosevelt had mostly succeeded in making the Democratic Party larger, stronger, and more liberal. "As an institution the party had been expected to recruit able leaders, nominate them to office, mobilize a majority, win elections, and enjoy power. This the party accomplished, beyond its fondest dreams."[13]

Besides arguing that Roosevelt was more successful in his role as a party leader than Burns claims, it can also be asserted that Roosevelt had a stronger ideological commitment to making the Democratic Party a vehicle for liberal ideas and public policy goals than Burns suggests in his power-broker thesis.[14] The power-broker thesis portrays Roosevelt as a non ideological conciliator of conflicting economic interests during the first two years of his presidency. Consequently, Burns's thesis holds that Roosevelt shifted to the left in his rhetoric, policies, and coalition-building efforts only in order to appease leftist discontent with the early New Deal.[15]

When one examines the ideological influences on Roosevelt prior to his presidency, however, it appears that he had always been committed to making the Democratic Party more liberal in its ideology and policy objectives, and that the early New Deal was not a betrayal of or a contradiction to this commitment. Roosevelt's commitment to liberalism in both public policy and the reformation of the Democratic Party had been firmly established in his political career prior to 1932. His family background, religious activities, and mentor relationships with Endicott Peabody, Theodore Roosevelt, and Woodrow Wilson instilled an ideological commitment to public service and progressive reform within him. Thus, he first sought to make the New York Democratic Party a liberal, reformist party equally attractive to urban and rural voters through a consensus-building economic policy agenda. From 1921 until 1932, Roosevelt sought to unite the conflicting Northern and Southern wings behind a unifying policy agenda that addressed their economic grievances and interests.

James L. Sundquist and Arthur M. Schlesinger, Jr., agree that Roosevelt's liberal ideology would not have been abruptly suspended during the first two years of his presidency.[16] Instead, Roosevelt's desire to seek the cooperation of business by suspending antitrust laws through NRA codes can be attributed to his experimental, innovative approach. He tried to stimulate economic recovery in this cooperative manner and did not reject or suspend his liberalism.[17] Furthermore, Roosevelt's use of the New Deal policy agenda during his first term, especially the public works projects, union rights, and agricultural subsidies, enabled him to unite, expand, and liberalize the Democratic Party by addressing a diversity of economic interests and grievances. With a sharp increase in the number of appointed bureaucratic jobs, Roosevelt's novel approach to patronage distribution not only rewarded party regulars for their campaign contributions and services but also used "ideological patronage" in order to co-opt academics into the increasingly liberal Democratic Party.

Roosevelt's leadership, therefore, of both the Democratic Party and public policy initiatives throughout his presidency reveals greater ideological continuity than discontinuity. In his 1988 book *Corporatism and the Rule of Law*, Donald Brand cogently refutes Burns's power-broker thesis. He argues that Roosevelt did not suspend his liberalism during the early New Deal. "Roosevelt entered his presidency with a clear, principled commitment to progressive reform. . . . In contrast to the political broker . . . Roosevelt was committed to reform for the sake of social justice, and he did not shy away from the political conflict that such reforms might entail."[18] Furthermore, Brand convincingly rejects Burns's perception of the first New Deal as the reflection of a cautious, nonideological power-broker approach. "The first New Deal is the radical New Deal. It was during the first New Deal that the state acted forcefully to subordinate private power, not simply by regulating private organizations, but by more ambitiously attempting to bring about an organizational and ethical revolution that would transform trade associations and trade unions into institutions serving public rather than private interests."[19]

In order to understand why Roosevelt wanted to make the Democratic Party not only larger and stronger but also more liberal in its ideology and policy agenda, one must understand the content, extent, and limit of Roosevelt's liberalism. The most important aspect of his liberalism was his concept of the proper role of government in the economy. As the scholarship indicates, Roosevelt evolved ideologically from progressivism to liberalism. Morton Frisch distinguishes progressivism from liberalism in his study of Roosevelt's political thought.[20] Progressivism, especially the philosophy exemplified by Woodrow Wilson's New Freedom platform in 1912, feared and distrusted both big business and a big national government.[21] New Freedom progressivism stressed vigorous trust-busting to improve competition among businesses and prevent monopoly.[22]

Conversely, New Nationalist progressivism, articulated by Herbert Croly and Theodore Roosevelt, wanted an expanded federal government to cooperate with big business in forming a corporate welfare state to provide economic security for all Americans. The New Nationalist progressives believed that bigness in economic activities was both inevitable and desirable because constant technological change centralized and consolidated business activities. Thus, government must become large enough and powerful enough to ensure that this inexorable process would provide a more bountiful and secure economic life for the average citizen and would not threaten the public interest.

The New Freedom progressives, by contrast, opposed federal social welfare programs because they believed "that a big paternalistic government would inevitably be controlled by big business."[23] In his campaign for the New York State Senate in 1910, Roosevelt clearly personified New Freedom progressivism as he stressed economy in state government and the need to destroy machine control of both parties.[24] By his second term in the state senate, though, Roosevelt became a strong supporter of social welfare and labor reform legislation.[25] He had begun to make the transition from New Freedom progressivism, with its fear of expanded, centralized governmental power, to liberalism, with its belief in using federal intervention by an enlarged national government to solve social and economic problems.[26]

Although Roosevelt used the words "progressive" and "liberal" synonymously during the 1920s, he mostly used the word "liberal" alone to describe his and his party's philosophy and policies during his presidency.[27] When he accepted the Democratic nomination for governor of New York in 1928, Roosevelt stated his determination to pursue liberal policies: "[T]he growing feeling of responsibility toward those who need the protection of the State, call for ceaseless improvement . . . of . . . the whole body politic which we call Government." The culmination of his evolution from progressivism to liberalism would become more evident during his governorship with its emphasis on social welfare programs, prison reform, farm aid, and state-sponsored electrification of rural areas.[28]

Despite Al Smith's characterization of Governor Roosevelt's forest conservation proposal as "Socialistic," Roosevelt was certainly not a socialist or a Communist.[29] He was a capitalist who accepted the right to own private property and earn profits from it.[30] But Roosevelt also believed that government has the responsibility to make sure that the operations and practices of businessmen do not produce social injustices and economic problems, and that capitalism and democracy could not endure if many citizens were hungry, homeless, and jobless. The rights and liberties that the federal government is obligated to protect would now include the economic security of the individual.[31]

He stated that whereas the "liberal party" understood the government had a responsibility to ensure the social and economic well-being of "the average person," the "conservative party" did not.[32] Thus, Roosevelt and the Democratic Party intended the New Deal to reform capitalism so that it would provide a more abundant and secure economic life for the average

American. As early as 1934, he stated that the New Deal intended to go beyond merely ensuring economic "subsistence" for all and would entail a more fulfilling life beyond economics.[33]

Besides seeking to protect the public interest from threats by private interests, Roosevelt's liberalism expressed a belief that government should ensure not only that citizens have the liberty to achieve personal fulfillment beyond economic security but also that they have the tangible opportunities to do so through government efforts in culture and education. There is evidence to suggest that through the New Deal, Roosevelt sought to develop a society in which every citizen could satisfy his or her basic economic needs while also having opportunities, promoted or even provided by government, to fulfill himself or herself intellectually or culturally. In short, as Thomas Greer explained in *What Roosevelt Thought* (1958), Roosevelt hoped that the New Deal would lay the foundation for an Aristotelian "good society." In such a society, government policies would enable citizens to become happier, more fulfilled individuals who could develop talents and enjoy intellectual, cultural, and recreational experiences that would be unavailable to many of them in a society with minimal government and laissez-faire capitalism.

Greer states that Roosevelt's desire to have the New Deal move beyond economic, material concerns arose from his spirituality. "He saw economic reforms as necessary for the succor of the spirit; they were therefore, in a deeper sense, moral propositions."[34] This somewhat idealistic, humanitarian aspect of Roosevelt's liberalism and that of the national Democratic Party developed and intensified during his presidency. This is evident in the clear ideological and policy differences between the relatively moderate regulatory proposals for business contained in Roosevelt's 1932 Commonwealth Club address and his 1944 message to Congress urging the implementation of an "Economic Bill of Rights" that would establish a comprehensive welfare state.

The liberalism that Roosevelt espoused and sought to establish within the Democratic Party also believed that the United States should take an active, leading role in international relations. Despite the widespread unpopularity of this issue among the voters in 1920, Roosevelt staunchly supported American membership in the League of Nations. He subscribed to Woodrow Wilson's belief that the United States must oppose imperialism and support every nation's right of self-determination. Like Wilson, Roosevelt believed that the United States should assume a position of leadership in building structures for international cooperation, namely, the

United Nations, and in achieving international agreements for peace, especially through arms control treaties.

This liberal belief that the United States has a moral responsibility for the survival and proliferation of democracy and human rights throughout the world was expressed in his Four Freedoms address of 1941. Roosevelt asserted that all people in the world must be able to enjoy four basic freedoms in order for universal peace and justice to be secured. These four freedoms are freedom of speech and expression; freedom of religion; freedom from want, which "means economic understandings which will secure to every nation a healthy peacetime life"; and freedom from fear, which "means a world-wide reduction of armaments" so "that no nation will be in a position to commit an act of physical aggression against any neighbor."[35] The protection of these freedoms would create a global "moral order" that depends on "the cooperation of free countries, working together in a friendly, civilized society" that assures "the supremacy of human rights everywhere."[36]

Consequently, the liberalism that Roosevelt succeeded in instilling within the Democratic Party strongly emphasized the protection and expansion of individual rights and liberties for both Americans and citizens of other nations. This belief expressed a high degree of tolerance for the expression of political dissent and controversial ideas. It also advocated an absolutist interpretation of the Bill of Rights as expressed by William O. Douglas and Hugo Black, both appointed to the Supreme Court by Roosevelt.

In foreign policy, this liberal belief in the United States' moral responsibility to protect and foster human rights and alleviate poverty throughout the world would be reflected in such later Democratic policies as Food for Peace, the Peace Corps, and the Carter administration's policy of denying foreign aid to governments that violated their citizens' human rights. These policies all reflected Roosevelt's belief, expressed in the Four Freedoms speech and other speeches, and the Atlantic Charter, that the survival and further enhancement of democracy in the United States were closely linked to the expansion of democracy in the world.

This liberalism that Roosevelt espoused and sought to instill in the Democratic Party, therefore, was not merely a politically calculated, self-serving reaction to the Great Depression and World War II. The landslide election of conservative Republican Warren G. Harding to the presidency in 1920 solidified Roosevelt's earlier conviction that the Democratic Party must become clearly and consistently liberal in its ideology and policy proposals by advocating greater federal intervention on economic issues that affected ordinary Americans—namely, the war boom. He believed that the Democratic Party would continue to be the minority party in national politics as long as its heavily compromised platforms offered nothing more to the voters than an ambiguous, diluted version of Republican conservatism.

Roosevelt was especially dismayed and angered by Al Smith's compliance with the 1928 Democratic platform. Its content, heavily influenced by Democratic National Committee chairman John Raskob, a wealthy corporate executive and former Republican, differed little from the Republican platform in its advocacy of high-tariff protectionism and opposition to greater federal intervention to solve such economic problems as the farm crisis. "It represented another intraparty triumph of extreme conservatism and, as such, another repudiation of Roosevelt's long effort to build the Democracy into a national party unified on liberal-progressive principles."[37]

Prior to the 1928 presidential campaign, Roosevelt had sensed that such conservative, big business domination of the Democratic National Committee (DNC) would occur because of Raskob's method of liquidating the debt incurred by the 1924 campaign. Raskob delegated this responsibility to Jesse Jones, the DNC's director of finance and a wealthy Houston banker. Jones simply collected large contributions from a small number of wealthy, influential patrons of the party. Roosevelt feared that such a method would make the Democratic Party obligated to and manipulated by conservative business interests, thereby hampering its development as a distinctly liberal alternative to the Republican Party. Roosevelt wanted to raise funds at the grassroots level by having all of the local party organizations solicit small donations among the masses of rank-and-file registered Democrats. He believed that such a populist-style fund drive would benefit the Democratic Party by revitalizing local party organizations, providing the masses of Democratic voters with a sense of participation and influence in their party, and making the Democratic Party financially independent of conservative business interests so that it could formulate ideas and policies that would benefit ordinary Americans.

In a letter to Myron D. Kings, dated June 15, 1925, Roosevelt expressed his exasperation with the DNC's conservative leadership and his fear that the party would become no different from the Republican Party in its subservience to big business. He wrote that "the fundamental Democratic idea that a political party is a piece of machinery by which the ideals of its principles can be put into actual practice in government should be carried into the financial side by refusing to permit large contributions and make almost every Democratic voter an equal partner through his subscription in our enterprize [*sic*]. If we believe in granting special favors to none, should we not be equally firm in refusing to accept special favors from none?"[38]

Roosevelt, therefore, believed that the proper role of the Democratic Party in the American two-party system entailed two functions.[39] First, it would represent liberalism and formulate and implement the liberal policy agenda, especially in economics. This would clearly distinguish the Democratic Party from the Republican Party and thus provide voters with a clear choice between the two parties. Roosevelt said to the Young Democrats in 1939, "The Democratic Party will not survive as an effective force in this nation if the voters have to choose between a Republican Tweedle Dum and a Democratic Tweedle Dummer."[40] Second, the Democratic Party, as the liberal party, would be an inclusive, pluralistic party that would attract into its ranks lower-income voters, especially minorities, who would benefit from the party's policies. In particular, small farmers, industrial workers, blacks, and urban ethnics would be attracted to party membership.[41]

Roosevelt, moreover, changed the Democratic Party so that it would provide more positions within the party and government to racial, religious, and ethnic minorities. Through the "Black Cabinet" and the prominence of Catholics and Jews in his administration, Roosevelt made the Democratic Party a greater source of access, status, and power in national politics for blacks and urban ethnics. Statistical analyses of voting behavior in presidential elections from 1932 to 1944 indicate that as the Democratic Party became more liberal and ethically diverse, Roosevelt's electoral support from non-Southern white Protestants, regardless of socioeconomic status, steadily declined.[42]

In refuting Burns's thesis about Roosevelt's failures as a party strategist, Russian political scientist Vladimir O. Pechatnov argues that Roosevelt successfully adapted the rhetoric, ideology, membership, and policy agenda of the Democratic Party to the economic and political circumstances of the depression. This type of party leadership by Roosevelt not only expanded the base of the Democratic Party but also enabled Roosevelt's party to co-opt and absorb the forces of economic protest and discontent, thereby saving American capitalism from revolution. The achievement of this strategic objective for his party made Roosevelt an incomparable success as a party leader, according to Pechatnov. "If by strategy we mean the fine art of using all proper means to achieve a basic goal, in FDR's case, channeling the huge energy of social protest into the legitimate political structures (his own party in particular) for the sake of preserving the existing sociopolitical system of capitalism, then Franklin D. Roosevelt is an outstanding political leader, having very few if any, peers in American history."[43]

The defeats and setbacks that Roosevelt's party leadership did suffer usually occurred when the pursuit of these two objectives (i.e., party expansion and liberalization) conflicted with each other. The pursuit of these two conflicting objectives explains why Roosevelt was sometimes willing to support, or at least not oppose, liberal Republicans, independents, and third parties. He usually did this not to destroy a particular Democratic organization but to pressure it to become a more liberal, reformist organization. This tactic was evident when Roosevelt directed DNC chairman James Farley and Bronx political boss Ed Flynn to help Socialist union leaders Sidney Hillman and David Dubinsky in establishing the American Labor Party in New York City in 1936.

Consequently, Roosevelt's loyalty to the Democratic Party was not blind or absolute.[44] His party loyalty was qualified according to how well the Democratic Party offered the voters a distinctly liberal alternative to the Republican Party.[45] He once remarked that he voted for Theodore Roosevelt in 1904 because his Republican cousin "was a better Democrat than the Democratic candidate."[46] Roosevelt told Josephus Daniels in 1938 that the 1940 Democratic presidential nominee had to be a liberal or else he would not support him, even if this meant party disunity and losing the election to the Republicans.[47]

In 1941, Roosevelt wrote the following passage in which he pledges to the American people his determination to continue being an advocate of liberal reform in both the Democratic Party and public policy. "I believe it to be my sworn duty, as President, to make steps necessary to insure the continuance of liberalism in our government. I believe, at the same time, that it is my duty as head of the Democratic Party to see to it that my party remains the truly liberal party in the political life of America. There have been many periods in American history, unfortunately, when one major party was no different from the other major Party—except only in name. In a system of party government such as ours, however, elections become meaningless when the two major parties have no differences other than their labels."[48]

ABBREVIATIONS IN NOTES

PL   Elliot Roosevelt (ed.), *F.D.R.: His Personal Letters*, 4 vols. (New York: Duell, Sloan & Pearce, 1947–1950). These are cited by volume number.

PPA   Samuel I. Rosenman (ed.), *The Public Papers and Addresses of Franklin D. Roosevelt*, 13 vols. (New York: Random House, 1938–1950). These are cited by volume number.

PPG   Franklin D. Roosevelt, *Public Papers of Governor Franklin D. Roosevelt*, 4 vols. (Albany, N.Y.: J. B. Lyon, 1930–1939). These are cited by volume number.

NOTES

1. James MacGregor Burns, *Roosevelt: The Lion and the Fox* (New York: Harcourt, Brace, 1956), p. 197.
2. Ibid., p. 207.
3. James MacGregor Burns, *Presidential Government* (New York: Avon Books, 1965), p. 207; and *Roosevelt: The Lion and the Fox*, p. 403.
4. Burns, *Presidential Government*, pp. 335–336.
5. James MacGregor Burns, *The Deadlock of Democracy: Four-Party Politics in America* (Englewood Cliffs, N.J.: Prentice-Hall, 1963), pp. 36–38.
6. Ibid., pp. 8–23.
7. Ibid., p. 260.
8. Ibid., pp. 323–340.
9. Ibid., p. 168.
10. E. E. Schattschneider, *Party Government* (New York: Holt, Rinehart and Winston, 1942), p. 7.
11. Everett C. Ladd, Jr., and Charles D. Hadley, *Transformations of the American Party System* (New York: Norton, 1975), p. 86.
12. Otis L. Graham, Jr., "The Democratic Party, 1932–1945," in *History of U.S. Political Parties*, ed. by Arthur M. Schlesinger, Jr. (New York: Chelsea House, 1973), vol. 3, pp. 1939–1964.
13. Ibid., p. 1963.
14. Burns, *Roosevelt: The Lion and the Fox*, pp. 191–202.
15. Ibid., pp. 210–220; and Alan Brinkley, *Voices of Protest* (New York: Vintage Books, 1982), pp. 107–241.
16. James Sundquist, *Dynamics of the Party System* (Washington, D.C.: Brookings Institution, 1973), p. 194; and Arthur M. Schlesinger, Jr., *The Crisis of the Old Order* (Boston: Houghton Mifflin, 1957), pp. 277–278, 389–393.
17. Thomas H. Greer, *What Roosevelt Thought* (East Lansing: Michigan State University Press, 1958), p. 208; and Albert V. Romasco, *The Politics of Recovery: Roosevelt's New Deal* (New York: Oxford University Press, 1983), p. 160.
18. Donald Brand, *Corporatism and the Rule of Law* (Ithaca, N.Y.: Cornell University Press, 1988), p. 264.
19. Ibid., p. 288.
20. Morton J. Frisch, *Franklin D. Roosevelt: The Contribution of the New Deal to American Political Thought and Practice* (Boston: S. T. Wayne, 1975), p. 79.

21. Ellis W. Hawley, *The New Deal and the Problem of Monopoly* (Princeton: Princeton University Press, 1966), p. 8; Eric F. Goldman, *Rendezvous with Destiny* (New York: Vintage Books, 1956), pp. 186–187; and Richard Hofstadter, *The Age of Reform from Bryan to F.D.R.* (New York: Alfred A. Knopf, 1974), pp. 222–251.

22. Richard Hofstadter, *The American Political Tradition* (New York: Vintage Books, 1973), p. 331.

23. Arthur S. Link and Richard L. McCormick, *Progressivism* (Arlington Heights, Ill.: Harlan Davidson, 1983), p. 23.

24. Kenneth S. Davis, *FDR: The Beckoning of Destiny, 1882–1928. A History* (New York: G. P. Putnam's Sons, 1972), pp. 239–242.

25. Frances Perkins, *The Roosevelt I Knew* (New York: Viking Press, 1946), pp. 9–12.

26. Frisch, *Franklin D. Roosevelt*, p. 79.

27. Ronald D. Rotunda, "The 'Liberal' Label: Roosevelt's Capture of a Symbol," *Public Policy* 17 (1968): 381–408.

28. PPA, vol. 1, pp. 14–15; PPG, vol. 3, pp. 172–180; Kenneth S. Davis, *FDR: The New York Years, 1928–1933* (New York: Random House, 1985), pp. 195–250; and Daniel S. Fusfeld, *The Economic Thought of Franklin D. Roosevelt and the Origins of the New Deal* (New York: AMS Press, 1970), pp. 123–165.

29. PL, vol. 3, p. 228.

30. Fusfeld, *Economic Thought*, p. 257; and Perkins, *The Roosevelt I Knew*, pp. 329–330.

31. Clinton Rossiter, "The Political Philosophy of Franklin D. Roosevelt," *Review of Politics* 2 (January 1949): 87–95.

32. PPA, vol. 7, p. xxix.

33. Ibid., vol. 3, p. 199.

34. Greer, *What Roosevelt Thought*, p. 10.

35. PPA, vol. 9, p. 672.

36. Ibid.

37. Davis, *FDR: The Beckoning of Destiny*, p. 825.

38. Frank Freidel, *Franklin D. Roosevelt: The Ordeal* (Boston: Little, Brown, 1954), p. 221.

39. PPA, vol. 7, pp. xxviii–xxx.

40. PPA, vol. 8, p. 437.

41. Frederick G. Dutton, *Changing Sources of Power: American Politics in he 1970's* (New York: McGraw-Hill, 1971), pp. 5–7; Samuel Lubell, *The Future of American Politics* (New York: Harper & Brothers, 1952), p. 49; and Sundquist, *Dynamics of the Party System*, pp. 202–203.

42. Graham, "The Democratic Party," p. 1947; Nancy J. Weiss, *Farewell to the Party of Lincoln* (Princeton: Princeton University Press, 1983), pp. 136–156; John Kirby, *New Deal Era and Blacks* (Urbana: University of Illinois Press, 1971), pp. 106–151; Ladd and Hadley, *Transformations*, pp. 46–67; and John

Allswang, *The New Deal and American Politics: A Study in Political Change* (New York: John Wiley & Sons, 1978), pp. 81–117.

43. Vladimir O. Pechatnov, "Franklin D. Roosevelt and the Democratic Party," in *Franklin D. Roosevelt: The Man, the Myth, and the Era, 1882–1945*, ed. by Herbert D. Rosenbaum and Elizabeth Bartelme (New York: Greenwood Press, 1987), pp. 56–57.

44. Frisch, *Franklin D. Roosevelt*, pp. 79–82; and PL, vol. 3, p. 827.

45. PPA, vol. 8, p. 437.

46. Ibid., vol. 7, p. 38.

47. PL, vol. 3, p. 827.

48. J.B.S. Hardman (ed.), *Rendezvous with Destiny: Addresses and Opinions of Franklin D. Roosevelt* (New York: Dryden Press, 1969), pp. 344–345.

8

FDR and the Prerogative Presidency

Mark J. Rozell

The presidential prerogative power entails the right of the chief executive, in extraordinary circumstances, to take any action deemed necessary to the nation's security and survival, even if such action is outside of the written law. President Franklin D. Roosevelt exercised this power on several occasions to meet threats to the nation, both domestic and foreign. Some scholars maintain that the American constitutional system makes no room for prerogative powers and that FDR therefore acted improperly and set dangerous precedents for future chief executives. I shall argue that FDR's actions were compatible with the American constitutional framers' conception of the executive, which recognized the need for the exercise of extraordinary powers in extraordinary circumstances.

THE THREAT FROM WITHIN

When Franklin D. Roosevelt assumed the duties of the presidency at noon on March 4, 1933, the nation was deep into its gravest economic crisis. The president wasted no time in acting. In his inaugural address FDR likened the domestic crisis to wartime conditions and left no doubt about his intentions.

It is to be hoped that the normal balance of executive and legislative authority may be wholly adequate to meet the unprecedented task before us. But it may be that an unprecedented demand and need for undelayed action may call for temporary departure from the normal balance of public procedure.

I am prepared under my constitutional duty to recommend the measures that a stricken nation in the midst of a stricken world may require. These measures or such other measures as Congress may build out of its experience and wisdom, I shall seek within my constitutional authority to bring to speedy adoption.

But in the event that the Congress shall fail to take these courses and in the event that the national emergency is still critical I shall not evade the clear course of duty that will then confront me. I shall ask the Congress for the one remaining instrument to meet the crisis—broad executive power to wage a war against the emergency as great as the power that would be given to me if we were in fact invaded by a foreign foe.[1]

FDR was true to his word and embarked on an extraordinary exercise of presidential powers during peacetime. During his famous first 100 days in office, FDR attacked the nation's banking and monetary crises nearly unfettered by any congressional restraints. Indeed, with broad-based public support for his emergency actions, Democratic majorities in Congress, and ineffectual Republican opposition, the president was accorded unprecedented discretion to act as he saw fit.

FDR's inaugural statement was extraordinary for its bold assertion that the president possessed broad emergency powers to act unilaterally in a domestic crisis in which an immediate response was necessary and the Congress moved either too slowly or not at all. Although this was a controversial view of his authority, FDR's belief that the president possessed such broad-based emergency powers appeared better suited to wartime conditions—a distinction acknowledged by FDR's own analogy that the domestic crisis required a wartime-like response.

To a nation gripped by economic crisis, the president's claim that the Great Depression directly posed a threat to the national security seemed inarguable. To many, the president's resolute leadership was nothing short of a godsend.

Congress was willing to defer to strong presidential leadership to confront the emergency. But total legislative deference to FDR did not last much beyond the early crisis phase of his presidency.

At times the president overreached his authority, only to be rebuked, as envisioned by the constitutional framers' conception of separation of powers. The most infamous case was the failed 1937 campaign to reconstruct the Supreme Court. FDR's ill-advised scheme was a response to his frustration with the Court's having declared crucial New Deal initiatives unconstitutional. This failure of leadership pointed out a fundamental aspect of the constitutional system: its flexibility both to allow for the exercise of prerogative powers and to constrain presidents who overreach their authority in nonemergency situations.

THE THREAT FROM WITHOUT

In 1933 the Congress and the public had conferred enormous, unprecedented authority on the president to confront a domestic crisis. But what about the looming crisis abroad that most Americans believed did not threaten them? In response to the widespread public desire to avoid "European entanglements," in the mid-1930s Congress passed neutrality laws that advocates believed would ensure peace for the United States. Although FDR put on a public face that assured a worried public that he was committed to avoiding U.S. involvement in war, privately he anguished over the threat to the free nations of the world should the United States remain neutral.

The spread of war in Europe convinced FDR that the United States had to be prepared to defend freedom. Nearly three months after the July 1937 Japanese invasion of China, the president traveled to Chicago, the heart of the isolationist Midwest, to deliver his "Quarantine the Aggressors" speech. It was FDR's first attempt to use the bully pulpit to rally the nation to defend freedom abroad. In response to widespread isolationist sentiment, FDR implored that "the people of the United States must, for the sake of their own future, give thought to the rest of the world." To convince isolationists of the futility of their position, FDR tried to convince them that it was turning our backs to the world that threatened the state of domestic peace. He presciently stated, "Let no one imagine that America will escape, that America may expect mercy, that this Western Hemisphere will not be attacked." The president asked Americans to "look ahead" because "the epidemic of world lawlessness is spreading." He added:

> And mark this well! When an epidemic of physical disease starts to spread, the community approves and joins in a quarantine of the patients in order to protect the health of the community against the spread of the disease.[2]

The president's speech failed to have the intended impact. Isolationist sentiment in the nation was too strong. Roosevelt publicly dropped his case and began to devise other, behind-the-scenes, strategies to achieve his objectives.

FDR's next major statement on the need for U.S. action to assist free nations was his January 4, 1939, annual message to Congress. The president favored the lifting of the U.S. arms embargo, and in his address he urged the adoption of measures "short of war, but stronger and more effective than mere words, of bringing home to aggressor governments the aggregate sentiments of our own people."[3]

In September 1939 the president called a special session of Congress to revise the Neutrality Act. In that session, he succeeded in getting Congress on November 3 to repeal the arms embargo provisions and to approve a "cash and carry" provision for the sale of war materials to the Allies.

But these efforts were not sufficient to protect the Allies. France fell and Great Britain was in a perilous state. British Prime Minister Winston Churchill implored Roosevelt to sell Britain a number of U.S. naval destroyers. As Robert Shogun pointed out in his fascinating account of the destroyers deal, Churchill's plea left FDR with the following choice: openly make the case before the public and Congress to legally aid the British, or circumvent Congress by entering into a secret deal.[4]

Roosevelt left nothing to chance and chose the latter course of action. He wrote to Frank Knox on July 22, 1940: "I fear Congress is in no mood at the present time to allow any form of sale."[5] The president wrote in a memorandum on August 2, 1940, that his Cabinet officers had agreed in a meeting with him that day that pursuing a legislative course to make the destroyers deal "would meet with defeat or interminable delay in reaching a vote."[6] Through the use of the executive agreement—which does not require congressional consent—FDR bypassed the isolationist Congress and thereby violated the neutrality laws. The secret deal sent fifty destroyers to Great Britain in exchange for the use of naval bases in the British West Indies. After making the deal, FDR announced his decision and the public overwhelmingly supported his action. In so doing, the president had made moot, in any practical sense, the issue of whether Congress should have any say in the matter. Over two months later, FDR brushed off legalistic denunciations of his action.

> There is virtually no criticism in this country except from legalists who think it should have been submitted to the Congress first. If I

had done that, the subject would still be in the tender care of the Committees of Congress![7]

FDR'S PREROGATIVE PRESIDENCY

Roosevelt exercised prerogative powers on a number of occasions. For example, despite a 1940 congressional prohibition on the deployment of U.S. troops outside of the Western Hemisphere, the president ordered the U.S. occupation of Iceland in July 1941. FDR unilaterally entered the United States in the Atlantic Charter. He negotiated an agreement with Denmark whereby the United States would defend Greenland.

The destroyers deal was FDR's most daring use of the prerogative power. To build the case for the deal, the president requested a legal memorandum on the subject from Attorney General Robert Jackson. The memorandum cited the president's commander-in-chief role and unique authority in foreign affairs as justification for entering into an executive agreement, rather than submitting the deal to the Senate in the form of a treaty. Jackson drew support for his view from the Supreme Court decision in *U.S.* v. *Curtiss-Wright Corporation*.[8] Writing for the Court, Justice George Sutherland offered his classic distinction between presidential powers in the domestic and international realms. He declared "the very delicate, plenary and exclusive power of the President as the sole organ of the Federal Government in the field of international relations." Furthermore, Congress "must often accord to the President a degree of discretion and freedom from statutory restriction which would not be admissible were domestic affairs involved."

Jackson's memorandum had given the president legal justification for entering into the executive agreement with Great Britain. To be sure, FDR had already made up his mind. Jackson's memorandum nonetheless provided the president with the appearance of having considered, and satisfied, the legal requirements of the deal.

The U.S. entrance into the war after the Japanese attack on Pearl Harbor emboldened the president to further exercise broad-based emergency powers both at home and abroad. FDR's boldest statement of the presidential prerogative power was his 1942 Labor Day address to Congress, in which he demanded the repeal of the Emergency Price Control Act. The president said that he would act alone if Congress did not do what he wanted.

In the event that the Congress should fail to act, and act adequately, I shall accept the responsibility, and I will act. . . .

> The President has powers, under the Constitution and under Congressional acts, to take measures necessary to avert a disaster which would interfere with the winning of the war. . . .
>
> The responsibilities of the President in wartime to protect the Nation are very grave. This total war, with our fighting fronts all over the world, makes the use of executive power far more essential than in any previous war. . . .
>
> The American people can be sure that I will use my powers with a full sense of my responsibility to the Constitution and to my country. The American people can also be sure that I shall not hesitate to use every power vested in me to accomplish the defeat of our enemies in any part of the world where our own safety demands such defeat.
>
> When the war is won, the powers under which I act automatically revert to the people—to whom they belong.[9]

In this message, FDR declared that his prerogative to act emanated not merely from his commander-in-chief role but, most important, from the people. The condition of national emergency, he reasoned, had justified his claim to exercise extraordinary powers to protect the ultimate sovereign— the people.

There is no shortage of opinion against the Rooseveltian notion of prerogative. William Howard Taft wrote in his memoirs that "there is no undefined residuum of power which [the president] can exercise because it seems to him to be in the public interest."[10] Regarding the destroyers deal, Shogun argued that FDR had acted illegally, unconstitutionally, and dishonestly, and had "set a pernicious precedent" for subsequent presidents to overreach their powers "in the name of national security."[11]

PRESIDENTIAL PREROGATIVE POWERS: THEORY AND PRACTICE

There is ample evidence that the chief executive possesses the right of prerogative. Roosevelt's actions were both necessary and constitutionally proper. Furthermore, his exercise of such authority, although extraordinary, was not unprecedented.

The rejection of the prerogative power frequently is based on the mistaken view that the American constitutional framers created a weak federal government with an executive power always subordinate to the legislative. But the framers instead had created a strong federal government with limited responsibilities. The framers envisioned a federal government that did little more than provide for the national security, preserve domestic tranquillity and coin money. But the Constitution enabled the government to carry out these vital functions vigorously and effectively.

As a part of their preparation for the Philadelphia Convention of 1787, the framers studied political theory and history. The ideas of the leading European philosophers of modern constitutionalism—John Locke and Baron de Montesquieu—weighed on the minds of the framers.

A careful reading of Locke and Montesquieu reveals that neither of these thinkers advocated weak government or a subordinate executive power at all times. Certainly, they emphasized restrained governmental powers and individual rights more than their predecessors, which has much to do with the appeal of these two thinkers to the American constitutional framers. Before examining the views of Locke and Montesquieu on executive power, let's briefly place those views in the proper context of modern political theory.

Political theorists today generally trace the origins of modern political thought to Niccolò Machiavelli. To simplify the distinction, the ancient philosophers focused on the need to create regimes that fostered citizen virtue and community. The modern thinkers, beginning with Machiavelli, concerned themselves with establishing regimes that controlled social and political strife and enabled people to cultivate their own interests without living constantly in fear of one another.

The regimes envisioned by the modernists required some form of executive power. In *The Prince*, Machiavelli advised a ruler on the cruel necessities of executive power during the founding of a regime. In order to gain control over a principality and the respect of its subjects, he believed, the ruler had to establish absolute authority through the exercise of often cruel measures. Only in such a way can order and authority be maintained, he reasoned.[12] Machiavelli, therefore, did not advocate overwhelming executive power for its own sake. His masterwork, *The Discourses*, goes to great length to show that there should be inherent limits on the executive power in the postfounding era. Machiavelli feared that an executive given overwhelming powers during the founding period might resist forfeiting such authority during normal times.[13] Hence, he proposed the eventual establishment of a "mixed-regime" composed of aristocratic, democratic, and monarchic elements, in which power checks power.[14]

Thomas Hobbes's *Leviathan* proposed that the sovereign power be granted extraordinary authority as the only means of overcoming civil strife. In Hobbes's regime, individuals sacrificed almost all of their liberties to the sovereign power in return for the relative comfort given them by the absolute dictator. The sovereign had absolute authority, but used it to promote peaceful coexistence in the community.[15]

Machiavelli and Hobbes thus established the necessity of executive power to a stable regime. The chief task of the modern constitutionalists—Locke and Montesquieu—was to create the conditions for such a stable regime while moderating the harsher prescriptions of Machiavelli and Hobbes. Whereas Machiavelli and Hobbes imagined circumstances under which citizens had to forfeit basic liberties to the sovereign power, Locke and Montesquieu sought to create regimes characterized by both strength and liberty. They believed that the way to ensure such a regime was through a system of institutionally separated governmental powers.

John Locke, in the *Second Treatise of Government*, offers a threefold distinction of governmental powers: the legislative, the executive, and the "federative."[16] Although on the surface Locke's emphasis on legislative supremacy seems unequivocal, he invests a considerable amount of power in the executive branch. For example, the "federative power"—the power to make war, peace, treaties, and alliances—is placed solely within the realm of the executive.[17] Locke's chapter "Of Prerogative" is the most revealing. In times of emergency, when the legislature is not in session, or where the laws are silent, the executive is given "the power of doing public good without a rule."[18] For Locke, the "supreme law" of the land is preservation of society. Only the executive can act with power and "despatch" in times of emergency. Whereas the legislative branch has supreme lawmaking powers during normal times, the executive branch is not denied the power to take extraordinary, even extralegal, actions in times of emergency. Therefore, Locke did not advocate either weak government or a subordinate executive power. Locke's "executive" is, in many ways, as powerful as Hobbes's "sovereign." The most important difference is that Hobbes takes the exception—civil strife and the need to overcome that through extraordinary executive power—and makes it the rule.[19] Locke's unique contribution to the American experience is showing us how to maintain a strong executive while moderating and checking this power at the same time.

Montesquieu also was concerned with the problem of reconciling freedom and coercion. Montesquieu more clearly formulated the proposition that power can be checked only by power than did his predecessors. The liberty of the citizenry, he wrote, can best be protected by preventing any one power from holding the authority to formulate and to execute the laws. He devised a governmental triad—legislative, executive, and judicial powers—as a means of preventing any one arm of the government from becoming tyrannical.[20]

... [C]onstant experience shows us that every man invested with power is apt to abuse it, and to carry his authority as far as it will go. . . . To prevent this abuse, it is necessary from the very nature of things that power should be a check of power.[21]

Although Montesquieu set forth a separation of powers system to limit governmental power as a means of enhancing individual liberty, he did not advocate weak government. Montesquieu's executive—the "monarch"—is empowered to act with a degree of discretion necessary in times of emergency, even if such actions are not specifically granted by the legislature. Montesquieu allows for a strong executive, independent of direct pressures from the "popular will," capable of acting with force and discretion.

The American constitutional framers created a republican form of government characterized by both liberty and power. They did not perceive any fundamental conflict between an energetic executive and ensuring the liberty of the people. Indeed, they understood energy in the executive as instrumental in protecting and preserving liberty.

The *Federalist Papers* evidence the framers' awareness of prerogative powers.[22] Our chief constitutional architect, James Madison, wrote in *Federalist* 41:

If a federal Constitution could chain the ambition or set bounds to the exertions of all other nations, then indeed might it prudently chain the discretion of its own government, and set bounds to the exertions for its own safety. . . .

The means of security can only be regulated by the means and danger of attack. They will, in fact, be ever determined by these rules, and by no others. It is in vain to oppose constitutional barriers to the impulse of self-preservation. It is worse than in vain; because it plants in the Constitution itself necessary usurpations of power, every precedent of which is a germ of unnecessary and multiplied repetitions.[23]

Alexander Hamilton defended a broad presidential discretion to protect the national interest. *Federalist* 70 offers the classic defense of the presidency uniquely possessing the qualities of "decision, activity, secrecy and despatch."[24] In *Federalist* 9 Hamilton extensively quotes Montesquieu to support the view that a large federal republic, as proposed at the constitutional convention, possesses the twin advantages of preserving liberty (like a small republic) and protecting the national security (like a monarchy).[25]

Federalist 23 supports the view that constitutional powers to provide for the common defense "ought to exist without limitation." Furthermore:

> The circumstances that endanger the safety of nations are infinite, and for this reason no constitutional shackles can wisely be imposed on the power to which care of it is committed. . . . [T]he *means* ought to be proportioned to the *end*; the persons, from whose agency the attainment of any *end* is expected, ought to possess the *means* by which it is to be attained.[26]

Even the ultradefender of individual liberty, Thomas Jefferson, adopted a broad view of the executive's power to take resolute action when compelled by necessity. In an 1810 letter defending some of his emergency actions as president, Jefferson wrote:

> A strict observance of the written laws is doubtless *one* of the high duties of a good citizen, but it is not the *highest*. The laws of necessity, of self-preservation, of saving our country when in danger, are of higher obligation. To lose our country by scrupulous adherence to written law, would be to lose the law itself, with life, liberty, property and all those who are enjoying them with us; thus absurdly sacrificing the end to the means.[27]

The constitutional framers and Jefferson recognized that the presidency possessed the institutional capacities uniquely suited to responding to emergency situations. As scholar Paul Peterson has written: "It is the executive power that most lends itself to energy. . . . To speak of energy in the legislative or judicial branches would be something akin to an oxymoron."[28] The judicial branch has recognized the executive's preeminence in national security and foreign policy-making on a number of occasions.[29] The constitutional provisions generally cited in defense of presidential emergency powers are the commander-in-chief clause, the take care clause, and the vesting clause. The vague language of Article II—in sharp contrast to that of Article I—bestows on the president considerable discretion to interpret his authority as he sees fit.

The concept of prerogative therefore entails the president's right to act for the public good without reference to any explicit constitutional or statutory provision. In exercising such authority, FDR had considerable precedent from which to draw. The adoption of the Constitution at the Philadelphia Convention was itself an extralegal action taken out of necessity. The delegates to the convention had merely been authorized to meet for the purpose of revising the Articles of Confederation. Through Madison's skillful maneuvering, the convention adopted the Virginia Plan for the creation of a large federal republic.

Among the most noted presidential exercises of prerogative were Jefferson's acquisition of the Louisiana Territory in 1803—a decision that Jefferson himself acknowledged had no explicit constitutional basis—and Lincoln's many extraconstitutional actions adopted out of necessity during the Civil War. According to scholar Richard M. Pious, Lincoln had created a "*constitutional dictatorship*: constitutional because the ultimate checks of elections and impeachment remained, but a 'dictatorship' because he disregarded the proximate checks and balances in the emergency."[30]

Among Lincoln's many extraconstitutional actions were the blockade of Southern ports without a congressional declaration of war; an increase in the size of the military without constitutional or statutory authorization; and the proclamations authorizing the commanding general of the armed forces to suspend the writ of habeas corpus. Lincoln's April 4, 1864, letter to A. G. Hodges best summarized the president's view of his powers in an emergency:

> [M]y oath to preserve the Constitution to the best of my ability, imposed upon me the duty of preserving, by every indispensable means, that government—that nation, of which that Constitution was the organic law. Was it possible to lose the nation and yet preserve the Constitution? By general law, life and limb must be protected, yet often a limb must be amputated to save a life; but a life is never wisely given to save a limb. I felt that measures otherwise unconstitutional might become lawful by becoming indispensable to the preservation of the Constitution through the preservation of the nation. Right or wrong, I assumed this ground, and now avow it. I could not feel that, to the best of my ability, I had even tried to preserve the Constitution, if, to save slavery or any minor matter, I should permit the wreck of government, country, and Constitution all together.[31]

In his classic study of the presidency, historian Clinton Rossiter called FDR a "constitutionalist" in the tradition "of Jackson, Theodore Roosevelt, Lincoln and Wilson." Rossiter likened FDR's actions to Lincoln's "constitutional dictatorship" and concluded that "Franklin Roosevelt is fixed firmly in the hierarchy of great presidents."[32] Few doubt that FDR deserved this exalted judgment. Like Lincoln, his prerogative presidency helped to save the nation and secure constitutional freedoms for future generations.

CONCLUSION

Contrary to the views of some critics of the prerogative presidency, the American constitutional system allows the chief executive to act unilaterally, in the national interest, in extraordinary circumstances—especially those in which the very survival of the system itself is threatened by events from within or without. In confronting calamity at home and abroad, FDR exhibited the very "energy and despatch" that the constitutional framers envisioned as necessary to the preservation of the republic. FDR's critics adopt a narrow, legalistic view of the president's powers that fails to take into account the broader purposes of Article II of the Constitution: to ensure the survival of the system itself as a prerequisite to guaranteeing all of the rights that the Constitution grants to the people.

None of this is to suggest that all presidents exercise such authority prudently or properly. The prerogative power can be—and has been—abused. That fact alone does not justify the view that such a power should not exist at all. The constitutional system of separation of powers provides for checks against executive abuse of the prerogative power. Congress and the courts possess sufficient countervailing powers to challenge the president's actions. In the case of the destroyers deal, for example, Congress could have challenged the president's decision. Not only did Congress choose not to do so, it quickly appropriated funds for the use of the naval bases.

For years legal scholars have celebrated the remarkable flexibility of our constitutional system and the ability of that system to meet numerous exigencies. The president's authority to exercise the prerogative power is a leading facet of that characteristic of the system. Prerogative powers allow for unified, resolute action during extraordinary circumstances so as to preserve and protect the basic rights and liberties ensured by the Constitution during normal times. Because of his skillful exercise of prerogative powers, FDR proved that democratic societies can both respond effectively to crises and preserve freedom.

NOTES

1. *The Public Papers and Addresses of Franklin D. Roosevelt*, Vol. 2, *The Year of Crisis, 1933* (New York: Random House, 1938), p. 15.

2. Basil Rauch, ed., *Franklin D. Roosevelt: Selected Speeches, Messages, Press Conferences, and Letters* (Norwalk, Conn.: Easton Press, 1989), pp. 187–188, 190–191.

3. Franklin D. Roosevelt, *Public Papers and Addresses, 1933–1941* (New York: Macmillan, 1939), p. 3.

4. Robert Shogun, *Hard Bargain; How FDR Twisted Churchill's Arm, Evaded the Law, and Changed the Role of the American Presidency* (New York: Scribner's, 1995), p. 178.

5. Elliot Roosevelt, ed., *The Roosevelt Letters*, Vol. 3, *1928–1945* (London: George G. Harrap, 1952), p. 325.

6. Ibid., p. 326.

7. Franklin D. Roosevelt, letter to King George VI, November 22, 1940. Cited in ibid., p. 340.

8. 299 U.S. 304 (1936).

9. Quoted in Edward S. Corwin, *The President: Office and Powers, 1789–1957* (New York: New York University Press, 1957), pp. 250–251.

10. William Howard Taft, *Our Chief Magistrate and His Powers* (New York: Columbia University Press, 1916), p. 138.

11. Shogun, *Hard Bargain*, p. 17.

12. Niccolò Machiavelli, *The Prince* (New York: Modern Library, 1950).

13. Niccolò Machiavelli, *The Discourses* (New York: Modern Library, 1950), book I, chs. 3, 9.

14. Ibid., book I, ch. 2; book III, ch. 1.

15. Thomas Hobbes, *Leviathan* (Cambridge: Cambridge University Press, 1991).

16. John Locke, *Second Treatise of Government* (Indianapolis: Bobbs-Merrill, 1952), ch. 12, secs. 143–148.

17. Ibid., secs. 146–148.

18. Ibid., ch. 14, sec. 166.

19. On this point see James W. Ceaser, "In Defense of Separation of Powers," in Robert A. Goldwin and Art Kaufman, eds., *Separation of Powers: Does It Still Work?* (Washington, D.C.: American Enterprise Institute, 1986), pp. 168–193.

20. Baron de Montesquieu, *The Spirit of the Laws* (New York: Hafner, 1966), book II.

21. Ibid.

22. Alexander Hamilton, James Madison, and John Jay, *The Federalist Papers* (New York: New American Library, 1961).

23. Ibid., p. 257.

24. Ibid., p. 424.

25. Ibid., p. 74–75.

26. Ibid., p. 153.

27. Thomas Jefferson, letter to John B. Colvin, September 20, 1810. Quoted in Dumas Malone, *Jefferson the President: First Term, 1801–1805* (Boston: Little, Brown, 1970), p. 320.

28. Paul Peterson, "The Constitution and the Separation of Powers," in Gary McDowell, ed., *Taking the Constitution Seriously: Essays on the Constitution and Constitutional Law* (Dubuque, Iowa: Kendall/Hunt, 1981), p. 194.

29. *First National Bank* v. *Banco Nacional de Cuba*, 406 U.S. 759 (1972); *Haig* v. *Agee*, 453 U.S. 291 (1981); *Oetjen* v. *Central Leather Co.*, 246 U.S. 297

(1918); *U.S.* v. *Curtiss-Wright Corp.*, 299 U.S. 304 (1936); *U.S.* v. *Truong Dinh Hung*, 629 F. 2d 908 (1980).

30. Richard M. Pious, *The American Presidency* (New York: Basic Books, 1979), p. 57.

31. "Letter to A. G. Hodges," in Carl Van Dorn, ed., *The Literary Works of Abraham Lincoln* (Norwalk, Conn.: Easton Press, 1980), p. 261. Morton J. Frisch argues that expediency cannot be the criterion for determining constitutionality. He interprets the Constitution as lacking a Lockean form of prerogative yet providing for presidential emergency powers. See his "Executive Power and Republican Government—1787," *Presidential Studies Quarterly* 17, no. 2 (Spring 1987): 281–291, as well as the several other scholarly articles in that issue that offer different interpretations of whether Lockean prerogative exists in the Constitution.

32. Clinton Rossiter, *The American Presidency* (Baltimore: Johns Hopkins University Press, 1987), pp. 135, 138.

9

The Prudential FDR

Ethan Fishman

What is the most accurate description of Franklin D. Roosevelt's presidential leadership style? What method did he use to guide the nation through the trials of the Great Depression and the tribulations of World War II? Scholars have had a difficult time dealing with these questions and agreeing on answers to them. The positions taken by Arthur Schlesinger, Jr., James MacGregor Burns, and Patrick Maney are typical of this scholarly divergence of opinion. Schlesinger maintains that Roosevelt was a pragmatist. Burns classifies him as a Machiavellian. Maney attributes Roosevelt's achievements to his positive outlook and an incredible amount of good luck.

Franklin D. Roosevelt was a proponent of classical Western prudence. In this chapter I will discuss the concept of classical prudence, provide a brief account of its historical development, and demonstrate how the concept can be used to explain why the Roosevelt presidency succeeded in some policy areas and failed in others. The conclusion will illuminate my differences with the interpretations of leading Roosevelt scholars.

CLASSICAL PRUDENCE

Classical prudence is based on certain assumptions about reality and human nature. It posits the existence of transcendent immaterial ideals accessible to human reason and assumes that reality is composed primarily of these ideals and, to a lesser extent, of transitory material phenomena accessible to our senses. According to this definition, for example, the reality of a square is found for the most part in its perfect universal definition but is imperfectly realized in material squares that eventually must break, rot, rust, or be erased.

Traditionally prudence has been understood as the process by which ideals manifest themselves through material elements to form reality. In this role, prudence functions to reconcile forever and today. Prudence also is the term used to describe the human faculty that permits us to comprehend and deal with the paradox that reality consists of apparently irreconcilable components. Prudence herein functions to combat the urge to simplify reality by portraying it as one-dimensional.

The view of reality underlying prudence may be called classical realism. Alternative interpretations of reality include idealism, materialism, and pragmatism. Idealism and materialism reduce reality either to transcendent ideals or to material phenomena alone. Pragmatism reverses the emphasis found in classical realism. It assumes that reality is composed primarily of material things, but not to the exclusion of universal ideals.

Consistent with its view of reality, the concept of classical Western prudence recognizes that human beings are a combination of soul and body, but emphasizes the primacy of the former. The supposition is that within each person there exists an ongoing conflict between the soul, striving to attain rational and moral perfection throughout eternity, and the body, settling for instant gratification. And although prudence champions the spirit, it harbors no illusions about the ability of the flesh to subvert the noblest of ideals.

Compared with proponents of classical prudence, idealists have a much more optimistic or romantic view of our capacity for justice. Materialists are pessimists or cynics in the sense that they abandon the struggle for justice to concentrate on exploiting our potential for evil. Pragmatists tend to bemoan our weaknesses but are more resigned to failure and more willing to tolerate cynicism than are proponents of classical prudence.

Because of its antireductionist orientation, classical prudence often is misidentified. Idealists tend to confuse the reference in classical prudence to material constraints with either cynicism or pragmatism. Yet cynics deny the reality of transcendent immaterial ideals altogether, and pragmatists are so concerned with tangible results that they are inclined to compromise the integrity of ideals when it becomes convenient to do so.

Cynics and pragmatists tend to confuse the emphasis in classical prudence on ideals with idealism. Yet idealists insist on meeting the most exacting rational and moral standards, regardless of the situation. In contrast, proponents of prudence consider universal ideals to be indispensable but insufficient. Ideals are thought to be indispensable because they imbue our mundane lives with meaning and direction by establishing an immutable order toward which we can strive. At the same time, proponents of classical prudence take extenuating circumstances very seriously because they regard ideals by themselves to be insufficient to meet the complex, diverse, and pressing demands of the here and how.

Classical prudence also has been mislabeled as "enlightened expediency."[1] Since "enlightened" modifies "expediency" in this term, the implication is that prudence constitutes a form of pragmatism, albeit of a principled kind. Yet expediency and pragmatism do not emphasize ideals enough to satisfy the criteria of classical prudence.

State university presidents whose curricula ignore job training for their students in favor of the arts and sciences are idealists. State university presidents who neither care about the arts and sciences nor require their students to learn about them are cynics. State university presidents who understand the traditional meaning of higher education in the West, but emphasize vocational courses in order to increase enrollments, are pragmatists. And state university presidents who require students to learn how to think critically about their nation, their culture, and the world, even while they are introduced to a trade, are proponents of classical prudence.

If the general purpose of prudence is to reconcile forever and today, its specific political function is to impart vision to the formulation of public policy. Most politicians in democracies pass laws designed solely to please temporary majorities of voters. Prudential democratic politicians legislate for the organic community of voters consisting, in Walter Lippmann's words, of "the entire living population, with their predecessors and successors."[2] Lippmann likened political prudence to the impulse that persuades young people to "die in battle for their country" and old people "to plant trees they will never sit under."[3]

Prudence also acts as an antidote to ideology and relativism in politics. Regardless of the situation, ideologues are prepared only to offer one dogmatic solution based on one doctrinaire mode of analysis to every political problem. Proponents of classical prudence reject such inflexibility. They stress abstract principles but realize that theories alone are unable to account for the shifting details of practical politics.

At the other extreme of the political spectrum lie relativists, who charge that all standards are culturally biased and untenable. Proponents of classical prudence argue, to the contrary, that the power of free will presupposes that we often will choose to make irrational and immoral decisions. The positing of and belief in infallible ideals toward which fallible humans can strive thus serve to minimize the dangers to the community posed by our inevitable mistakes. From this perspective, proponents of prudence emerge as genuine realists, according to the classical definition of the term, in their quest to balance the immaterial and material facets of the universe, the good and bad in human beings, and theory and practice in politics.

HISTORICAL DEVELOPMENT

The first and foremost philosopher of classical Western prudence was Aristotle. In Book VI of *Ethics*, he taught that there are two forms of science and two types of virtues or faculties that these forms of science employ. Theoretical science includes subjects such as physics and mathematics, involves knowledge for its own sake, and yields unadulterated transcendent ideals. Theoretical science employs intellectual virtues that are learned in theory and enables a thinker to contemplate reality. Practical science includes subjects such as politics and economics, involves knowledge for the sake of noble action, and yields ideals applied to material circumstances. Practical science employs moral virtues that are learned from life experiences and enables human beings to do the right thing to the right person at the right time.

Aristotle concluded that politics is the master practical science because he considered it to be essential for achieving justice in the community. He designated prudence as the chief moral virtue because of its ability to translate the vision of political justice into operationally just political institutions. When politics is practiced prudentially, he argued, human beings are treated as concrete persons, not abstractions, and their rights as individuals are balanced with their responsibilities as citizens.

In Book V of *Politics*, Aristotle illustrated how prudence can be utilized to oppose tyrannical regimes. Tyranny represented the antithesis of political justice to Aristotle because it elevates the self-interest of the tyrant over the public interest of the community. What can be done if revolution is neither feasible, because the tyrant controls all of the weapons, nor advisable, because citizens are not convinced that the new ruler would be more solicitous of their rights than the present one? In this event, Aristotle recommended, it might be possible for prudential reformers to exploit the tyrant's greed by warning that unless he restrains himself, a violent coup could deprive him of both his power and his head.

True to his prudential principles, it never occurred to Aristotle that such warnings would change a tyrant into a "half-good" or even "half-bad" guardian of the public interest. He did expect, however, that with proper motivation, a tyrant could be persuaded not to remain "wholly bad."[4]

In the thirteenth century St. Thomas Aquinas transformed Aristotelian prudence into one of the cardinal virtues of Christian theology. The value of prudence to Christianity, Aquinas maintained, is that it teaches Christians not to expect too little or too much from life. It simultaneously exhorts Christians to obey biblical commandments, warns about the pitfalls involved in this process, and counsels them on how to avoid cynicism in the face of temporary setbacks. The point, Aquinas wrote, is to aim high and accept less when one's efforts inevitably fall short of the mark.

Edmund Burke later invoked classical Western prudence to differentiate between the French and American revolutions. In their attempt to impose an abstract doctrine of freedom on a society historically unprepared for freedom, Burke wrote, the French pursued political change as if they were computing an algebraic equation. The effect, Burke warned in 1790, was to convert politics into a theoretical science and jeopardize the future of democracy in France by ushering in a period of repression unmatched by feudal monarchy.

Americans followed a more realistic strategy, according to Burke. Their goal was to adapt the philosophy of democratic government, as it had developed over the course of many centuries in England, to American soil. This integration of theory and practice, he predicted, would serve to lay a firm foundation for the continued evolution of freedom in the United States.

The neo-Thomist Jacques Maritain sought to apply classical prudence to twentieth century Western politics. During World War I, Maritain discussed the issue of how far decent people can go in their opposition to totalitarian dictatorships. Aristotle had recommended means to reform tyrannical regimes when the use of violence to bring about a tyrant's downfall is imprudent. Maritain took Aristotle one step further. He located in the philosophy of classical prudence moral justification for the temporary use of otherwise unjust methods to assassinate Hitler, defeat the Nazis, and end the Holocaust.

The most influential proponent of classical Western prudence in American history was Abraham Lincoln. Lincoln, Harry Jaffa writes, "undertook to guide political men, who need to know what is right here and now, but to guide them in the light of what is just everywhere and always."[5] He sought,

Jaffa observes, "to know what is good or right, to know how much of that good is attainable, and to act to secure that much good but not to abandon the attainable good by grasping for more."[6]

Lincoln's attitudes toward slavery and its spread to the American territories illustrate his political prudence. His opposition to slavery in principle was unequivocal. "I am naturally antislavery," he wrote in 1864. "If slavery is not wrong, nothing is wrong. I can not remember when I did not so think, and feel."[7] He nevertheless opposed interference with slavery in the South on the part of the national government. Attempting suddenly to abolish an institution that already had existed in that region for more than two centuries, he reasoned, would result in chaos and make matters worse for everybody, including the slaves themselves. Because Lincoln believed that technological changes soon would render slavery anachronistic, he counseled that it be allowed by the national government to die a natural death over time.

Concerning the territories, where slavery had not been firmly established, Lincoln reached a different conclusion. The principle, the absolute immorality of slavery, remained the same, but for the territories there were different conditions to consider. Lincoln thus made a stand against Stephen Douglas's plan to permit popular sovereignty to decide its fate there. In the American territories, he argued, neither citizens nor governments possess the authority to deny people their humanity.

Lincoln's prudential statesmanship was misunderstood while he was alive and continues to be misunderstood today. Idealists, who demanded the immediate abolition of slavery wherever it was found, considered him to be a cynic. Slave owners insisted that he was a radical abolitionist. Historian Richard Hofstadter concluded that Lincoln was a pragmatic "politician looking for votes."[8]

Americans have had an especially difficult time avoiding misconceptions about classical prudence because we generally do not share its paradoxical view of human nature. Aristotle, Aquinas, Burke, Lincoln, and Maritain taught that alone among living things, human beings possess a soul that gives us the power to choose between good and evil. Their prudential strategy of aiming for the moral high ground while grudgingly accepting less is meant to help us resist harmful choices in a world often overwhelmed by greed and power.

Americans have tended to hold a more optimistic view. Since the beginning of the seventeenth century our role models have been self-sufficient, rugged individualists. Our pantheon of heroes thus includes James Fenimore Cooper's frontiersman, Thomas Jefferson's small freehold farmer,

Henry David Thoreau's civilly disobedient naturalist, Frederic Remington's cowboy, Horatio Alger's entrepreneurial capitalist, and the famed "Lone Eagle," Charles Lindbergh. Even Lincoln is remembered by Americans more for his "log cabin to the White House" success story than for his prudential politics.

Much of American thinking about government, from Jefferson to Ronald Reagan to Newt Gingrich, has revolved around the axiom that "governments which govern least govern best." When Jefferson wrote in the Declaration of Independence that all people are endowed with the God-given right to explore their own routes to happiness, unburdened by government intervention, he was unable to imagine that someday many would choose to pursue happiness through drugs and crime. The point is that historically Americans have not felt the need to think seriously about prudence as a resource to cope with life's temptations because we have not tended to take these temptations very seriously in the first place.

The term "prudence" has not disappeared from our vocabulary. It just has conveyed a different meaning in the United States than it did in the formation stages of Western history. Previously prudence referred to an imaginative process by which determined people actively sought to accomplish the difficult task of imbuing their lives and politics with dignity and respect. Today it tends to suggest timidity, caution, and a certain cunning in avoiding challenges to the status quo.

ROOSEVELT'S PRUDENCE

Franklin Roosevelt should be added to the short list of Americans who have adhered to the concept of classical Western prudence. His successes as a political leader can be explained largely by his ability to conform to its precepts.

Those who follow classical prudence emphasize moral ideals over material circumstances. The moral ideal to which Roosevelt adhered was the Golden Rule. He once wrote: "I doubt if there is in the world a single problem, whether social, political, or economic, which would not find ready solution if men and nations would rule their lives according to the plain teaching of the Sermon on the Mount."[9]

From his parents and his teachers at Groton and Harvard, Roosevelt learned that the most powerful classes have personal and social responsibilities to their neighbors, especially to the least fortunate. From his experience with polio he developed an acute sensitivity to the suffering of others. From Theodore Roosevelt he learned to view the presidency as a "bully pulpit," a place of moral leadership from which to spread humanitarianism to the nation and the world.

As president, Roosevelt sought to put his Golden Rule ideal into practice. To those who opposed an increase in taxes to pay for government-financed unemployment relief in the midst of the Great Depression, he replied: "It is clear to me that it is the duty of those who have benefited by our industrial and economic order to come to the front in such a grave emergency and assist in relieving those who, under the same industrial and economic order, are the losers and sufferers. I believe their contribution should be in proportion to the benefits they receive and the prosperity they enjoy."[10]

To those in the American Liberty League who published a series of "commandments" dedicated to the preservation of unrestricted property rights, he asked: "What about other commandments? What about loving your neighbors? . . . There is no mention made . . . about the concern of the community, in other words the government, to try to make it possible for people who are willing to work, to find work to do. For people who want to keep themselves from starvation, keep a roof over their heads, lead decent lives, have proper educational standards, those are the concerns of Government; besides these points, and another thing which isn't mentioned is the protection of the life and liberty of the individual against elements in the community which seek to enrich or advance themselves at the expense of their fellow citizens."[11]

To those who objected to his pre–Pearl Harbor "lend-lease" strategy of contributing arms to the beleaguered Allied cause, Roosevelt invoked the image of neighbors helping neighbors: "Suppose my neighbor's home catches fire. . . . if he can take my garden hose and connect it up with his hydrant, I may help him to put out his fire. Now, what do I do? I don't say to him before that operation, 'Neighbor, my garden hose cost me $15; you have got to pay me $15 for it.'"[12]

Referring to the difficult task proponents of classical prudence face when they attempt to balance ideals and material circumstances, Roosevelt once described himself as a "juggler."[13] The domestic circumstances he inherited were marked by the worst economic crisis in our history. In 1932, 12 million Americans, nearly one out of every four workers, were jobless. Almost 200 banks were closing every month, depriving depositors of their cash, savings, and futures.[14] Violence erupted on the farms, where rapidly decreasing crop prices and rapidly increasing rates of foreclosure sowed the seeds of rebellion.[15] Confidence in the nation clearly was at low ebb. Cries arose throughout the land for a dictator to put an end to the chaos.

Chief among Roosevelt's obstacles to alleviating these hardships and restoring public trust was the laissez-faire tradition. Against the prevailing view that political power is inherently evil, Roosevelt proposed that it is necessary to actively pursue the public interest. Indeed, Roosevelt's vision that government can help to create a social environment conducive to living by the Golden Rule and his skill at convincing Americans to accept this vision represent both the measure of his prudence and his major contribution to American political thought.

Invariably the message he conveyed through carefully orchestrated press conferences and "fireside chats" was that laissez-faire in the twentieth century had come to mean "that government is best which is most indifferent" to human hardship.[16] According to Roosevelt, a powerful national government elected to protect all Americans was necessary as a counterbalance to the mammoth multinational corporations being organized to defend the self-interest of the privileged few. Given the complex interrelationships of citizens and nations in the modern world, he argued, it was no longer realistic to expect that private initiative, individual philanthropy, and local governments alone could achieve justice.

National political power of this magnitude would have been unthinkable earlier in American history, when social problems rarely crossed state and national boundaries. But times had changed, Roosevelt maintained, and unprecedented conditions called for unprecedented approaches.

Roosevelt found the agricultural crisis in the United States to be especially troubling. He feared that if farmers were to revolt, the rest of the nation would soon follow. His response was to establish the Agricultural Adjustment Administration to remunerate farmers for regulating their plantings on the basis of coordinated national formulas, buy nonperishable crops that subsequently were put into storage, and provide mortgage relief. In 1933 many farmers objected to this agenda because they were unable to imagine that greater profits could result from less work and production. Yet by 1936 it had become clear that Roosevelt's gamble was beginning to pay off. Agricultural income had increased by 50 percent, at least for the largest farmers, and the incipient farm rebellion was averted.[17]

Although the Great Depression disrupted the lives of so many Americans in every walk of life, for prudential reasons Roosevelt focused his attention on agriculture. An idealist would have attempted to help all Americans indiscriminately. A cynic would have ignored the suffering. And a pragmatist would have provided the most help to those groups that could pay him back with the most votes.

Only a short while later, Roosevelt did extend aid to other Americans. He established, for example, the Civilian Conservation Corps to provide jobs for young men between the ages of eighteen and twenty-five. He passed the Social Security Act, which inaugurated unemployment compensation and insurance for retired people, widows, and orphans. He initiated the Federal Deposit Insurance Corporation, which protected bank savings deposits. He created the Securities and Exchange Commission, which punished fraud in the sale of securities. And he abolished child labor. Toward the end of World War II, moreover, he produced the G.I. Bill of Rights, which guaranteed such veterans' benefits as business and home loans, hospital services, and college tuition. Each of Roosevelt's reforms reflected enduring Judeo-Christian values.

The international circumstances Roosevelt inherited presented a set of equally formidable challenges. Through foreign policy he sought to achieve Woodrow Wilson's ideal of helping to create a world in which independent democratic governments, representing themselves in a viable international peace organization, could flourish. The problems he encountered were that neither the Axis powers nor the Russians were friends of democracy, and the British wanted to maintain their extensive colonial empire.

As a proponent of classical prudence, moreover, Roosevelt was determined not to commit Wilson's error of getting too far ahead of the American public on international issues. Nor did he favor the pursuit of a cynical foreign policy that would manipulate the international scene to favor American interests or a pragmatic one that would be convenient for the United States.

Roosevelt's first critical foreign policy test came during the period between the Nazi invasion of Poland and the Japanese attack on Pearl Harbor, when Americans had not yet accepted the inevitability of their entrance into the war. In order to fortify the Allies while he educated American public opinion about the nature of the Axis threat, Roosevelt invented lend-lease. The plan, he said, was for the United States to become the "great arsenal of democracy" by producing ships, planes, and guns to insure an Allied victory in Europe.[18]

After Pearl Harbor, Roosevelt had to confront the problem of competing battlefronts. Many Americans assumed that since we had been attacked by the Japanese, we ought to concentrate our efforts in the Pacific. But Roosevelt knew better. He realized that Germany, with its control over most of Europe, interest in Latin America, and superior technological capability, presented a greater threat to the United States.

Roosevelt's position on American war aims remained consistent from before Pearl Harbor to his death on April 13, 1945. In January 1941, he described for Congress his vision of a postwar world "founded upon four essential freedoms": freedom of speech and expression, freedom of religion, freedom from want, and freedom from fear.[19] In August 1941 he secured Churchill's reluctant acceptance of an Atlantic Charter dedicated to world peace through national self-determination and equal access to trade and raw materials.

In March 1944 Roosevelt told reporters that we were "fighting to make a world in which tyranny and aggression cannot exist; a world based upon freedom, equality, and justice; a world in which all persons regardless of race, color, or creed may live in peace, honor, and dignity."[20] In August–September 1944 he hosted a meeting of Allied representatives to plan for the formation of a permanent international peace organization. And at Yalta in February 1945 he arranged for a conference to establish the United Nations.

The ability Roosevelt demonstrated during the Great Depression and World War II to transform what was morally preferable into what was politically feasible qualifies him as a successful proponent of classical Western prudence. The goal to which he consciously subscribed and at which he generally succeeded was to combine Woodrow Wilson's integrity and moral idealism with Theodore Roosevelt's ebullience, political shrewdness, and communication skills.

"There were indeed many times," Doris Kearns Goodwin writes, "when it seemed that he could see it all—the relationship of the home front to the war front; of the factories to the soldiers; of speeches to morale; of the government to the people; of war aims to the shape of the peace to come."[21] Archibald MacLeish observed; "Let no man miss the point of Mr. Roosevelt's hold upon the minds of the citizens of this republic. . . . It is only to the free, inventive gestures of the human soul that men wholly and believingly respond."[22] These are precisely the qualities—the penetrating vision and open-mindedness in the face of domestic and foreign catastrophes—that define classical prudence and describe Franklin D. Roosevelt's presidential leadership style.

ROOSEVELT'S IMPRUDENCE

There are a number of mistakes common to the practice of classical Western prudence. It is possible to identify the most realizable ideal pertinent to a situation yet choose means that fail to carry it out. Roosevelt miscalculated the proper relationship between means and ends when he attempted to pack the Supreme Court in 1937. It is possible to lose touch temporarily with universal ideals. Roosevelt made this mistake when he signed the Japanese Exclusion Act of 1942. It also is possible to wind up emphasizing material circumstances over universal ideals. Roosevelt reversed the priorities of classical prudence with his approaches to the adversities faced by European Jews and African Americans.

During Roosevelt's first term the Supreme Court had found seven out of nine pieces of New Deal legislation to be unconstitutional. Frustrated by the Court's laissez-faire majority, Roosevelt sought at the beginning of his second term to appoint an additional justice committed to the New Deal for every federal court judge aged seventy or over. The plan would have allowed him to add a maximum of six new members to the Supreme Court and forty-four new lower federal court judges.

Reaction to Roosevelt's initiative was almost unanimously adverse. The Senate Judiciary Committee described it as "a needless, futile and utterly dangerous abandonment of constitutional principle."[23] Even ardent supporters accused him of misplaced idealism. While they agreed with his democratic and humanitarian goal to aid the "one third of a nation ill-housed, ill-clad, ill-nourished,"[24] they found his contempt for the separation of powers indefensible.

The Japanese Exclusion Act of 1942 has been called "the worst single wholesale violation of civil rights of American citizens in our history."[25] Roosevelt's performance in this sorry episode was nothing less than cynical. In February 1942 he signed an order permitting the Army to move 112,000 Japanese Americans from the West Coast to ten inland relocation centers, where they remained for the duration of the war. Two-thirds of the evacuees were U.S. citizens.

In fact, Roosevelt was pressured on every side by military authorities, state government officials, the media, congressmen, senators, and members of his Cabinet to issue the order. It also is true that the Supreme Court later validated the order in three separate decisions: *Hirabayashi* v. *U.S.* (1943), *Korematsu* v. *U.S.* (1944), and *Ex parte Endo* (1944). Nevertheless, Roosevelt must take responsibility for this serious miscarriage of justice. The relocation of an ethnic group based on unconfirmed charges of sabotage was a racist act in direct contradiction to his stated ideals.

Roosevelt's attitude toward European Jews and African Americans was pragmatic at best. He did just enough to help them, but not enough to do much good. During the 1930s, when the Nazis were allowing Jews to leave Germany, Roosevelt opened the door to 105,000 refugees.[26] Although this number exceeded that admitted by any other country, it represented only a small percentage of those who desperately wanted to immigrate. Roosevelt claimed that he couldn't relax immigration quotas any more because he couldn't afford to lose the support of anti-Semitic congressmen for his New Deal reforms.

After 1940, when the Nazis were implementing their "final solution" by rounding up European Jews into death camps, Roosevelt denied requests by American Jewish representatives to bomb either the rail lines used to transport Jews to the gas chambers or the death camps themselves. His excuse was that such bombing missions would divert military attention from ending the war at the earliest possible date.

Roosevelt took a similar approach to the problems encountered by African Americans. With the exception of Lincoln, he probably did more for civil rights than any president before him—outlawing, for example, racial discrimination in the federal government and defense industries. Yet he did not support Senator Robert Wagner's antilynching bill and refused to desegregate the armed services. He rationalized the hypocrisy between fighting racism abroad and essentially ignoring it at home by reiterating the excuse he used with regard to the European Jews—a more active approach would jeopardize other New Deal legislation and interfere with the war effort.

Each of these mistakes involved a miscalculation of the classic prudential equation. In the Court-packing fiasco he identified a valid democratic ideal but used incommensurate means to achieve it. With the Japanese Exclusion Act he operated without a valid democratic ideal. His treatment of the European Jews and African Americans wasn't idealistic enough to qualify for classic prudential status.

CONCLUSION

Despite these and other serious errors, the record indicates that Roosevelt consciously practiced politics according to the measure of classical Western prudence and, more often than not, was successful at it. Why, then, has the prudential nature of his presidential leadership style been generally ignored?

The problem is that Americans historically have not shared the views of reality and human nature upon which the concept of classical Western prudence is based. Proponents of classical prudence believe that human beings possess the ability to act both morally and immorally, rationally and irrationally. They emphasize the reality of transcendent immaterial ideals in order to provide us with direction and stability so that we can avoid making immoral and irrational decisions as much as possible.

One consequence of our tendency to deny this paradoxical interpretation of human nature in favor of a more sanguine view is that American scholars generally have missed the opportunity to apply classic prudential standards to their analyses. Leading Roosevelt scholars Arthur Schlesinger, Jr., James MacGregor Burns, and Patrick Maney are among many who have missed this opportunity.

Schlesinger classifies Roosevelt as "the eternal pragmatist."[27] Roosevelt "had no philosophy save experiment," he observes.[28] He portrays the New Deal as "trial and error pragmatism."[29] The strengths of the New Deal, he writes, were "that it had no doctrine, that it was improvised and opportunistic, that it was guided only by circumstance."[30]

On the other hand, Schlesinger claims that Roosevelt's "greatest resources . . . lay in his ability to stir idealism in people's souls."[31] He also agrees with Harry Hopkins's consideration that Roosevelt was "a great spiritual figure . . . an idealist."[32] And he argues that "at bottom" Roosevelt "had a guiding vision with substantive content of its own."[33]

Schlesinger seems to confuse pragmatism with classical Western prudence. The two terms share an aversion to dogmatism, but their similarity ends there. While pragmatism does not deny ideals, it is dedicated to tangible results and lacks a substantive "guiding vision." Since classical prudence emphasizes transcendence over the here and now, it is less apt than pragmatism to compromise principles for the sake of practical politics. By definition, therefore, one cannot be an idealist and a pragmatist at the same time.

Perhaps Schlesinger means that Roosevelt was idealistic on some occasions and pragmatic on others. But this is not what he writes. Perhaps he means that Roosevelt was prudential but was not familiar with the classical definition of prudence. Although classical Western prudence contains elements of idealism and pragmatism, its distinguishing feature is the ability to integrate these alternative views of reality into a whole that is greater than the sum of its parts.

James MacGregor Burns develops the theme that Roosevelt suffered from a "derangement of ends and means."[34] He criticizes Roosevelt for possessing what he identifies as a Machiavellian split personality: one personality devoted to transcendent moral goals, the other to the acquisition of political power. By likening Roosevelt to Machiavelli, however, Burns contradicts himself. Consider the infamous quotation from *The Prince* with which Burns introduces his book *Roosevelt: The Lion and the Fox*:

A prince must imitate the fox and the lion, for the lion cannot protect himself from traps, and the fox cannot defend himself from wolves. One must therefore be a fox to recognize traps, and a lion to frighten wolves. Those that wish to be only lions do not understand this. Therefore, a prudent ruler ought not to keep faith when by so doing it would be against his interest, and when the reasons which made him bind himself no longer exist. If men were all good, this precept would not be a good one; but as they are bad, and would not observe their faith with you, so you are not bound to keep faith with them.[35]

Although he uses the term "prudent," Machiavelli is describing the leadership style of an amoral tyrant, not a proponent of classical Western prudence. Machiavelli counseled leaders to follow whatever strategy, moral or immoral, was necessary to maintain power and further their own interests—even if their interests were contrary to the commonweal. Since Burns considers Roosevelt to be at heart "a moral man"[36] and Machiavelli's leader is a wholehearted cynic, his analogy is flawed. To use Machiavelli's own metaphor, lions and foxes struggle in their ways to survive, but neither possesses a soul or pursues moral ideals.

Burns refers to Roosevelt's wartime relationship with Stalin to illustrate his charge that Roosevelt failed generally to integrate ends and means. He suggests that if Roosevelt had treated Stalin more forthrightly in terms of rapidly opening up a second front and sharing with him the secrets of the atomic bomb, the Cold War might have been averted. "For a brief shining moment during World War II," he writes, "democratic and Communist nations were united in a euphoria of hope and idealism about how people might live in brotherhood, with common goals, sacrifices, and triumphs. But behind the facade of unity statesmen were pursuing *Realpolitik* and national interest. The resulting cynicism was the breeding ground of postwar disillusion and disunity."[37]

Now Stalin came as close to being a Machiavellian tyrant as one can imagine. By 1970, the year Burns's book first appeared, even the Russian people had come to terms with the scope of Stalin's evil. Why Burns would be more trusting of Stalin than of Nikita Khrushchev is not clear. Perhaps Burns believes that transcendent, immaterial ideals and material circumstances are inherently irreconcilable. Perhaps he is correct. Yet it is important to realize that some of the founding fathers of Western culture once thought that prudence could be used to unite these disparate elements into a functional political whole.

Roosevelt's "main trouble was intellectual," Burns concludes.[38] Roosevelt's atheoretical approach, he charges, clouded his judgment about the proper relationship between democratic ends and means and led him unwittingly down the road to Machiavellianism. His "mind was an eminently operative one," Burns writes. "He disdained elaborate, fine-spun theories. . . . He hated abstractions. His mind yearned for the detail, the particular, the specific. . . . He had a passion for the concrete."[39]

Burns here misses the distinction made originally by Aristotle between theoretical and practical science. He attributes Roosevelt's "derangement of ends and means" to what Oliver Wendell Holmes called his "second class intellect."[40] Aristotle, however, taught that there are two different types of intelligence, only one of which is useful in government. Aristotle considered hatred of abstractions to be essential to dealing not with figures and equations, but with human beings in organic political communities.

A critique of a different sort is offered by Patrick Maney. He surveys Roosevelt's accomplishments and concludes that Roosevelt's greatest attributes were his "extraordinary sunny disposition and abiding sense that all was right with the world."[41] Through these attributes, Maney argues, Roosevelt was able to buoy the flagging hopes of Americans during the darkest days of the Great Depression and World War II. Maney recognizes that a positive attitude is indispensable for overcoming tragedy and clearly is grateful for Roosevelt's contribution. Yet one gets the distinct impression that he considers Roosevelt's optimism to be a relatively unimportant leadership quality, and somehow odd and unnatural in view of the severe hardships that were involved.

How could a person with only relatively moderate leadership skills have guided the nation through such major crises? Maney decides that luck must have been on FDR's side. He refers to the attack on Pearl Harbor to illustrate his point. Prior to the attack, Maney observes, Roosevelt was frustrated by the question of American entrance into the war. On the one hand, he recognized that it was only a matter of time before we would start fighting. On the other, he realized that the mood of the country was not sufficiently pro-war to guarantee a concentrated effort. "As it were," Maney concludes, "Pearl Harbor rallied and united the American people to an extent that even Roosevelt could never have equaled. Even in tragedy, it seemed, his luck had held."[42]

Schlesinger admires Roosevelt. Despite his many negative judgments, Burns is able to see in him "the lineaments of greatness."[43] Maney is more critical, preferring to damn him with faint praise with regard to his temperament and fate. He concludes that Roosevelt's accomplishments were "specific to a particular time and place in history."[44] Among American chief executives, he determines, "Franklin Roosevelt was not a man for all seasons."[45]

For proponents of classical prudence, however, as times change, the governing universal ideal changes as well. During the Great Depression, for example, Roosevelt proposed certain reforms to relieve the hardships of the American people. Sixty years later these innovations have achieved entitlement status. Were he alive today, Roosevelt surely would reconsider their relevance. The same man who was troubled in 1932 by destitute people selling apples on street corners would be similarly troubled by such contemporary phenomena as welfare dependency and the savings and loan scandal.

Proponents of classical prudence are not superhuman. They just seek to do the very best they can under the circumstances. "I have no expectation of making a hit every time I come to bat," Roosevelt confessed. "What I seek is the highest possible batting average not only for myself but for the team."[46] Roosevelt also liked to compare himself to a football quarterback.[47] The universal ideal constituted his pregame plan. He would initiate a policy or call a play in the huddle based on that plan, he said, and then feel free to change the policy or call an audible at the line of scrimmage based on the specific defensive formation he encountered.

For moral idealists, nevertheless, a .300 batting average or an occasional incomplete pass in politics is unacceptable. It is not enough that Roosevelt demonstrated his concern for the interests of all Americans. Not enough that he sought to replace an obsolete laissez-faire public philosophy in the United States with a vital new middle way encompassing both capitalism and socialism, individualism and collectivism. Not enough that he helped to defeat a sinister totalitarian movement bent on world domination. Not enough that he opposed colonialism and set into motion the organization of the United Nations. Not enough that the presidential leadership he exercised was based on a classic Western prudential vision unequaled by any other public figure in the twentieth century.

NOTES

1. Francis Canavan, "Edmund Burke's Conception of the Role of Reason in Politics," *Journal of Politics* 21 (1959): 79.

2. Walter Lippmann, *The Public Philosophy* (New York: New American Library, 1955), 32.

3. Ibid., 35.

4. Aristotle, *The Politics*, trans. by Ernest Barker (New York: Oxford University Press, 1962), 250.

5. Harry Jaffa, *Crisis of the House Divided* (Chicago: University of Chicago Press, 1982), 1.

6. Ibid., 371.

7. Richard Current, ed., *The Political Thought of Abraham Lincoln* (Indianapolis: Bobbs-Merrill, 1967), 197.

8. Richard Hofstadter, *The American Political Tradition* (New York: Vintage Books, 1961), 116.

9. Roosevelt quoted in Arthur Schlesinger, Jr., *The Coming of the New Deal* (Boston: Houghton Mifflin, 1958), 587.

10. Roosevelt quoted in Patrick Maney, *The Roosevelt Presence* (New York: Twayne, 1992), 34.

11. Roosevelt quoted in James MacGregor Burns, *Roosevelt: The Lion and the Fox* (New York: Harcourt, Brace and World, 1956), 206–207.

12. Roosevelt quoted in Frank Freidel, *Franklin D. Roosevelt: A Rendezvous with Destiny* (Boston: Little, Brown, 1990), 360.

13. Doris Kearns Goodwin, *No Ordinary Time* (New York: Simon and Schuster, 1994), 137.

14. John Blum, Edmund Morgan, et al., *The National Experience* (New York: Harcourt Brace Jovanovich, 1977), 618.

15. Ibid., 636.

16. Roosevelt quoted in Freidel, *Rendezvous with Destiny*, 207.

17. Blum, Morgan, et al., *The National Experience*, 637.

18. Roosevelt quoted in Goodwin, *No Ordinary Time*, 194.

19. Roosevelt quoted in Freidel, *Rendezvous with Destiny*, 361.

20. Roosevelt quoted in James MacGregor Burns, *Roosevelt: The Soldier of Freedom* (New York: Harcourt Brace Jovanovich, 1970), 468.

21. Goodwin, *No Ordinary Time*, 10.

22. MacLeish quoted in Arthur Schlesinger, Jr., *The Politics of Upheaval* (Boston: Houghton Mifflin, 1960), 192.

23. Maney, *The Roosevelt Presence*, 97.

24. Roosevelt quoted in Blum, Morgan, et al., *The National Experience*, 648.

25. Goodwin, *No Ordinary Time*, 321.

26. Ibid., 101.

27. Schlesinger, *The Coming of the New Deal*, 257.

28. Schlesinger, *The Politics of Upheaval*, 654.

29. Ibid., 155.

30. Ibid., 654.

31. Schlesinger, *The Coming of the New Deal*, 544.

32. Hopkins quoted in ibid., 585.

33. Schlesinger, *The Politics of Upheaval*, 652.

34. Burns, *The Soldier of Freedom*, 609.

35. Burns, *The Lion and the Fox*, i.

36. Ibid., 475.

37. Burns, *The Soldier of Freedom*, 374.
38. Burns, *The Lion and the Fox*, 334.
39. Ibid.
40. Ibid., 157.
41. Maney, *The Roosevelt Presence*, 1.
42. Ibid., 139.
43. Burns, *The Soldier of Freedom*, 611.
44. Maney, *The Roosevelt Presence*, xiv.
45. Ibid., 203.
46. Roosevelt quoted in Freidel, *Rendezvous with Destiny*, 120.
47. Burns, *The Soldier of Freedom*, 295.

10

The Veto Record of FDR

Samuel B. Hoff

Presidents possess a plethora of tools to wield in the legislative arena. One formal power is the veto, which is normally utilized when a president faces a minority of partisans in Congress or when the legislature is dominating the issue agenda.[1] However, the employment of the qualified negative by Franklin Roosevelt contradicted both of these trends. The intent of this chapter is to investigate the manner by which FDR's use of the veto coincided with the advent of the modern presidency, to examine precedent-setting actions of the Roosevelt administration relating to different types of vetoes, and to assess the extent to which the veto's employment during the New Deal affected not only Franklin Roosevelt's presidency but subsequent chief executives as well. Previous studies have ignored the importance of this constitutional power for FDR's activist legislative program and his historical standing as one of the nation's most successful political leaders.

VETO USE BEFORE FDR

Veto frequency changed considerably after the Civil War. Up to the beginning of Abraham Lincoln's administration there were thirty-four regular vetoes of bills, an average of slightly fewer than one per Congress, and only eighteen pocket vetoes, or one per two Congresses. From 1860 to

1932, presidents vetoed 606 bills by regular means, an average of 16 per Congress, and 476 bills by pocket means, about 13 per Congress. Shaw noted the extensive employment of the veto by Grover Cleveland and its ramifications:

> Before Cleveland became President, only Andrew Johnson and Grant had cast more than a dozen vetoes. But after Cleveland showed the way by casting 584 vetoes, his successors up to 1933 used the veto more frequently than Presidents who served before Cleveland. From 1900 to 1933 . . . Presidents vetoed about nine bills per year.[2]

The reasons for greater reliance on the veto following the Civil War are varied. One explanation identifies the developing practice of attaching policy measures, called riders, to appropriation bills.[3] Another factor was the bitter postwar fight over Reconstruction between President Andrew Johnson, who succeeded Lincoln, and a dominant Republican Congress. Between 1870 and 1888, a large number of vetoes were applied to private bills seeking payment of Civil War claims as well as to legislation addressing the gold standard and immigration policy. From 1889 to 1909, vetoes were issued in order to protect the money supply and to maintain personal rights.[4] Higgins cites several areas covered by vetoes, such as immigration and tariff policy, and appropriation bills. He concludes that "[b]y far the greater number of vetoes during the period, 1889–1929, seem to have been justified."[5]

Perhaps the most basic change in veto use at the beginning of the twentieth century was the issuance of the qualified negative for other than constitutional reasons. Mason asserts that after the Civil War, "[q]uestions as to the administration of the government then became important, and the veto accordingly became a weapon of expediency."[6] Lewis claims that the change from unconstitutionality to expediency as the primary ground for releasing vetoes augmented their use.[7]

FDR AND THE MODERN PRESIDENCY

In order to understand why and how the veto was used by Franklin Roosevelt, it is necessary to explore Binkley's belief that "President Roosevelt seems to have been the first President of the United States to establish and utilize systematically and continuously an elaborate organization designed to gauge public sentiments and mold public opinion."[8] Leuchtenburg contends that FDR "recreated the modern presidency."[9]

Kessel asserts that "[t]he most frequently cited 'beginning point' of the modern presidency is the administration of Franklin Roosevelt."[10] Barger postulates that "[t]he modern White House staff was born with Roosevelt's 1939 reorganization of the Executive Branch."[11] Rossiter contends that FDR "created the modern Presidency."[12] Rose finds that

> [t]he modern presidency was created by Franklin D. Roosevelt's response to the depression of the 1930's. Although Roosevelt was not the first occupant of the Oval Office of the White House to believe in an active Presidency, he was the first to become an active leader in peacetime.[13]

Davis delineates factors that affected executive–legislative relations and contributed to the modern presidency in the FDR era: an increase in federal regulations, the emergence of the United States as a world power, the concentration of authority in the executive branch during World War I, establishment of the presidential budget initiative in 1921, and Supreme Court decisions that strengthened presidential power.[14] According to Shaw,

> [t]here have been major changes in the relationship between the modern Presidents and Congress as compared with the corresponding relationship prior to the New Deal. A vital aspect of this change has been that post-1933, with notable exceptions, Presidents tended to be much less conspicuously involved in the legislative process. . . . Since 1933, by contrast, initiatives from the White House have been viewed as crucial inputs into the congressional process.[15]

Greenstein holds that "[d]uring Franklin Roosevelt's administration, in response to presidential leadership and such social and political conditions as the Great Depression, World War II, and the availability of network radio, the presidency began to change in at least four major ways." These changes included more power to make unilateral decisions, increased agenda-setting of federal policy, the augmenting of staff and advisory personnel, and heightened visibility of the executive branch vis-à-vis other actors in the political system.[16] Edwards and Wayne observe that "[w]hile nineteenth-century presidents formulated some legislative proposals and even drafted bills in the White House, it was not until the twentieth century that the practice of presidential programming developed on a regular basis."[17] This procedure was institutionalized during FDR's White House years.

VETO EMPLOYMENT BY FDR

General Use

A plethora of writers have evaluated Roosevelt's exercise of the veto. Neustadt conjectures that FDR conceived of the veto as "among the presidency's greatest attributes, an independent and responsible act of participation in the legislative process, and a means of enforcing congressional and agency respect for presidential preferences or programs."[18] Burns explains FDR's unbridled employment of the veto by pointing to his penchant for being a presidential activist who used all tools available to him.[19] Carlton Jackson compares the veto patterns of FDR and Andrew Jackson:

> An analysis of Roosevelt's vetoes shows that he was most like Andrew Jackson, since both Presidents were tremendously influential with Congress while retaining the support of the general populace. Like . . . Jackson, he was a pragmatic President, not committing himself to inflexible programs, and not making apologies for apparent inconsistencies.[20]

Metz mentions that FDR "regarded the veto as one of the most important powers of the President. As his programs shifted and his preference changed, he applied the veto to public and private legislation in order to realize his purposes both within the bureaucracy and with Congress."[21]

Bass believes that Roosevelt's veto use "forces one to conclude that the only outstanding characteristic of the negative's employment was in its quantity, not its quality."[22] He elaborates:

> The President was an executive who used other means to gain his ends, who knew the threat of the negative to be more powerful in many respects than its use and who accomplished a few exceptional things through his interpretation of the veto power. . . . Consequently, he used the veto power not as a weapon of first resort but as a reminder, when other measures failed, that an ultimate weapon rested in his hands. It was a tool to guide, more than to punish, and he brought to culmination what was intended to be over one hundred and fifty years before.[23]

Several scholars relate Roosevelt's request to "bring me a bill I can veto."[24] Mullen holds that the request served "as a reminder that legislation that did not conform to his program would not be allowed to become law."[25] Wayne states that "Roosevelt realized the potential of the veto both as a positive and negative instrument of presidential power. . . . By using the veto so frequently, he was able to employ it effectively to prevent riders, amendments, and laws he considered unwise, impolitic, or both."[26] Koenig contends that FDR wanted to periodically "remind legislators that they had the President to reckon with."[27] Davis finds that Franklin Roosevelt "refined leadership techniques which had been employed less effectively by his predecessors," including the veto as well as presidential messages and patronage.[28]

Public and Private Bill Vetoes

In analyses of FDR's vetoes, there are discrepancies between authors on the total number. For instance, Metz shows that FDR vetoed 214 public bills and 418 private bills, for a total of 632.[29] Bass concludes that Roosevelt turned back 242 public bills and 393 private bills, for a sum of 635 by both regular and pocket means.[30] Spitzer claims that FDR vetoed 138 public bills and 497 private bills, totaling 635.[31] McKay counts 134 public bill vetoes and 632 overall.[32] Wayne, Fisher, and Mervin each find that FDR vetoed 635 bills.[33]

In terms of issues covered by legislation disallowed by FDR, Robinson identifies "agricultural relief, adjusted service compensation, interstate commerce, alien deportation, judicial review of administrative tribunals, flood control, protection of fisheries, homestead administration, Indian relief, tax and tariff policy, national defense, Philippine independence, Memorial Day observances, cemetery approaches, short-hand reporting, homing pigeons, District of Columbia designations, parking meters, credit for beer wholesalers, control of funerals" among others.[34]

Several authors note historical precedents achieved by Roosevelt in his regular vetoes. FDR was the first chief executive to personally read a veto message to a joint session of Congress. The legislation that precipitated his veto was a 1935 bill to provide payment of veterans' service certificates that were due to mature in 1945. The veto followed an unsuccessful attempt by the president in the preceding year to kill an appropriation bill that furnished pension benefits to Spanish-American War veterans. According to Campbell and Jamieson, "[o]n May 22, 1935, with the country listening on a national radio hookup, the president forcefully defined his veto."[35] Spitzer describes the act as "pure theater, designed to sway congressional, as well as popular sentiment."[36] After his arguing that the federal government could not afford to spend $2 billion on 4 percent of the population during such time of economic hardship, FDR's veto was upheld in the Senate, having been overridden by the House of Representatives.[37]

Also setting a precedent, in 1944, the president rejected a revenue bill, the first time a chief executive had vetoed such a measure. Bass asserts that Roosevelt ignored the advice of the Democratic Party leaders in Congress and "denounced the tax bill as providing 'relief not for the needy but for the greedy.' "[38]

Few quantitative studies of veto use have been undertaken. Neustadt, who illustrates how the Bureau of the Budget "came into control of agency communications to the President on signature or veto of enrolled bills," finds that in 1939 the bureau handled agency reports on 2,448 pending public bills and 438 drafts of proposed legislation.[39] Metz relies on descriptive statistics in his analysis of public bill vetoes by presidents over the 1889–1968 time frame. He reveals that 57 percent of FDR's decisions to veto public bills were unanimously supported by agency personnel, whereas 41 percent had divided recommendations. The Bureau of the Budget backed the president's decision to veto a public bill in 95 percent of instances.[40]

Lee examines veto frequency and overriding actions from 1828 through 1968. He claims that Roosevelt killed one out of every twelve bills presented to him. Lee uncovers four sets of relationships between president and Congress and places FDR in the conflict-type pattern, illustrated by the high number of vetoes and overriding actions.[41]

Copeland sought to replicate Lee's findings while adding a few new variables and identifying the year rather than the Congress as the unit of analysis. He probes reasons for the use of the veto over two time periods, 1789–1860 and 1861–1980. In the post-1860 period he concludes that when control variables representing the presidencies of Grover Cleveland and Franklin Roosevelt are added to the equation, "[b]oth of the additional variables are strong determinants of the use of the veto, and interestingly, considerably lessen the impact of being democrat on the use of the veto." These control variables are likewise statistically significant in Copeland's all-years veto frequency equation.[42]

Watson investigates the reasons provided by presidents for vetoing legislation over the 1933–1981 time frame. He limits cases to important public bills negated by regular means. Of the thirty-eight Roosevelt veto messages included in the study, he finds that twenty-nine, or about 76 percent, cited unwise policy as justification; six claimed the bill was fiscally unsound; two argued that the public bill was unconstitutional; and one veto message stated that the legislation was administratively unworkable.[43]

Hoff examined annual veto frequency of presidents over the last century. By focusing on Roosevelt, it was found that he disapproved 105 public bills by regular means over his twelve-year presidency.[44] This total corresponds closely to Bass's figure of 107 vetoes of public bills by regular means.[45] FDR vetoed no public bills in 1933, three in 1934, eight in 1935, ten in 1936, nine in 1937, five in 1938, fourteen in 1939, thirty-three in 1940, six in 1941, nine in 1942, four in 1943, and four in 1944. He vetoed 8.75 public bills annually by regular means, placing second in usage over the span from 1889 to 1992. FDR's nine public bills negated in 1937 is tied for second for most initial-year-of-term vetoes, whereas his six public bills vetoed by regular means in 1941 is tied for fourth in first-year vetoes by chief executives from Benjamin Harrison through George Bush.

The greater number of total vetoes in Roosevelt's second (sixty-one) and third (twenty-three) terms in contrast to his first four years may be attributed not only to the decline of the Democratic Party majority after 1937 but to issues and actions as well. Davidson suggests that FDR's phenomenal early legislative achievements "did not endure a smooth course with Congress after 1937. The second Roosevelt administration confronted such explosive issues as anti-lynching, tax reform, farm policies, and the president's disastrous Court-packing scheme."[46] Barone postulates that "[t]he deadlock between an activist president and recalcitrant legislators had begun when Congress rejected Roosevelt's court-packing proposal in 1937; it continued as Congress cut appropriations for Harry Hopkins's WPA, passed the Hatch Act, and refused to give any serious consideration to Roosevelt's Third New Deal proposals."[47]

Regarding congressional responses, 12 of 105 (11 percent) public bill vetoes during FDR's tenure were overridden by the first chamber. This finding is 10 percent lower than the average number of initial overturns suffered by all presidents over the last century. Of the ninety-two sustaining actions, the first chamber actually voted on only five occasions. At the second chamber stage, Congress successfully voted to override Roosevelt's public bill vetoes in nine of twelve instances. The average proportion of second chamber decisions resulting in override is higher for FDR (75 percent) than for other chief executives who faced such legislative challenges over the last century (68 percent), although the mean successful override percentage garnered by the second chamber during FDR's presidency (80 percent) is less than that suffered by other presidents over the 1889 to 1989 time span (84 percent).[48]

Private bills generally encompass two categories: those dealing with claims against the United Sates and those excepting individuals from certain immigration and naturalization requirements.[49] In his study of FDR's private bill vetoes, Metz shows that 81 percent received unanimous support from pertinent agency personnel, while 19 percent of these vetoes were accompanied by divided recommendations. Congress sought to override just two private bills negated by regular means, and failed in both.[50] Bass compares the veto records of Roosevelt and Grover Cleveland. He indicates that 62 percent of FDR's total vetoes were applied to private bills; 59 percent of Cleveland's vetoes were issued on private bills. In both cases, veterans' claims comprised the majority of subjects covered by such legislation.[51]

Pocket Vetoes

Although there are differences in the frequency of pocket vetoes administered by Roosevelt cited by various authors, the divergence is less than that for bills vetoed by regular means. Vose and Metz tabulate 260 pocket vetoes,[52] while Fisher and Spitzer count 263 bills pocket-vetoed by FDR.[53] FDR rates first in issuance of pocket vetoes among all presidents since 1789. As for the topics of his pocket vetoes, "Roosevelt applied the pocket veto to 153 private items and thirty-one public items of local concern. These two categories account for 71% of all pocket items."[54]

Roosevelt affected the development of the pocket veto in two major ways. One manner in which this was accomplished was the June 26, 1934, White House announcement that the president would provide a written rationale for pocket vetoes as well as for regular ones:

> In the past, it has always been customary in most cases involving vetoes for the President to withhold his signature, thereby, in effect, allowing the bill to die without becoming law. The President has desired, however, to take a more affirmative position than this, feeling that in the case of most legislation, reasons for definite disapproval should be given. Therefore, he has written on the copy of each bill the words "Disapproved and Signature Withheld" and has appended in every case a brief statement giving the reason or reasons for disapproval.[55]

Vose declares that Roosevelt actually attached written messages to 258 of his 260 pocket vetoes. He finds that only 4 of 447 pocket vetoes by presidents from 1934 to 1963 were not accompanied by written messages. He concludes that "[a]s Presidential routine the silent pocket veto is a thing of a past."[56] Bass holds that written memoranda justifying pocket vetoes had "fallen into desuetude since Cleveland's brief attempt in his first administration," but that "every president succeeding Roosevelt continued the practice."[57] Fisher and Spitzer claim that written messages for pocket vetoes were provided by presidents from James Madison through Andrew

Johnson, ceased with Ulysses Grant, and were reinstated by FDR.[58] Spitzer states that "[s]ince 1963, virtually all pocket vetoes have been accompanied by messages."[59]

Roosevelt also contributed to the development of the pocket veto through a June 11, 1940, regular veto of a public bill, H.R. 3233, aimed at repealing most past pocket veto measures. In *La Abra Silver Mining Co.* v. *U.S.* (9175 U.S. 423), the Supreme Court in 1899 "rejected the contention that the president could not sign bills when Congress was not in session despite the court's recognition that the president was participating in a legislative act."[60] In the 1929 Pocket Veto Case, the Supreme Court unanimously ruled that adjournment between sessions of a Congress prevented the president from returning a bill, declaring that over one-fourth of all pocket vetoes up to 1929 (119 out of 400) had occurred between sessions rather than at the conclusion of a two-year Congress.[61] In his message informing Congress that he was disallowing H.R. 3233, Roosevelt included the following defense:

> I am constrained to pursue this course in view of the fact that an approval of the bill may have far reaching implications in that it is based on an interpretation of the constitutional "pocket veto" power of the President which is much narrower than that which has been placed upon its continuous usage for over a century, and which has met the express sanction of the Supreme Court. The acceptance of such new construction of the "pocket veto" power would make a serious inroad on the pertinent constitutional provision. In fact, it would render the authority of the President to "pocket veto" bills almost nugatory.[62]

FDR's veto message likewise claimed that of the over 600 pocket vetoes since 1789, "almost half occurred following a sine die adjournment of a session as distinguished from a sine die adjournment of a Congress."[63]

The question of whether the president could pocket-veto bills during an intersession adjournment arose in 1943. When Congress adjourned from July 8 until September 14 of that year pursuant to a concurrent resolution, FDR requested Attorney General Francis Biddle to advise him on the legality of pocket-vetoing legislation that he had received less than ten days before the legislative break.[64] In his reply to the president's July 13 memorandum, the attorney general concluded that "[i]n my opinion the adjournment of the present congress is the Adjournment contemplated by Clause 2, Section 7, Article I of the Constitution; and, therefore, you may prevent enactment of any bill which is presented to you by refusing to sign it."

Biddle furnished evidence showing that Presidents Johnson, Cleveland, and Benjamin Harrison had not signed bills during such within-session adjournments, and that the bills "were never promulgated as Law." He likewise forwarded the opinions of Attorney Generals William Miller and John Sargent, who advised Presidents Benjamin Harrison and Calvin Coolidge, respectively, that they had the authority to disapprove bills during brief legislative adjournments.[65]

FDR's Position on the Line-Item Veto

From 1937 until 1942, various Roosevelt administration documents reveal the president's view of the proposed line-item veto power. An August 19, 1937, letter from Senator Arthur Vandenberg, a Michigan Republican, informed FDR that he had presented an item veto constitutional amendment and that he shared the president's criticism of legislative riders on tax and appropriation bills.[66] In a letter to the president on September 20, 1937, Solicitor General Stanley Reed stated that "[t]his does not seem the opportune time, however, to actively support such an amendment." His attached draft reply to Vandenberg's letter contained the following sentence: "Not withstanding the apparently satisfactory experience which the States have had with the item veto, I am not convinced that anything more is needed, at this time, than that the Congress should more carefully avoid the use of riders or special interest items, whether in tax, appropriation, or general bills."[67] However, in his response to Vandenberg's correspondence on September 24, 1937, FDR revised the latter reply:

> I understand that thirty-nine States have had satisfactory experience with the item veto in general appropriation acts. During my four years as Governor of New York, I came to the conclusion that the right to veto items in general appropriation acts met with general favor on the part of the Legislature and the public. It seems to me, therefore, that it is appropriate at least to discuss the subject.[68]

Senator Vandenberg's September 29, 1937, letter to the president appears to have caused some concern in the White House. After thanking the president for his September 24 letter, the senator requested permission to make their correspondence public in order to "stir up some general interest in this proposition." Vandenberg further wrote that "[c]ertainly *our* agreement on the general principle would lift the proposition out of partisan politics—and that is where it belongs."[69] However, an October 28, 1937, letter from Senator Alben Barkley indicated that FDR solicited the Kentucky Democrat's opinion on the issue. Barkley responded by asserting that although he opposed attaching riders to appropriation bills, "I doubt whether such an amendment would arouse a great amount of interest among the people without a good deal of additional work being done on it, and I think such an arousement on the subject would be calculated to stop Congress from including such riders in bills dealing with other subjects."[70] FDR relayed Barkley's points to Vandenberg in a December 21, 1937, letter.[71]

Roosevelt provided a public statement on the item veto a few weeks later. In his annual budget message, sent to Congress on January 3, 1938, the president said:

> An important feature of the fiscal procedure in the majority of our States is the authority given to the executive to withhold approval of individual items in an appropriation bill, and, while approving the remainder of the bill, to return such rejected items for further consideration of the legislature. This grant of power has been considered a consistent corollary of the power of the legislature to withhold approval of items in the budget of the executive; and the system meets with general approval in many States which have adopted it. A respectable difference of opinion exists as to whether a similar item veto power could be given to the President by legislation or whether a constitutional amendment would be necessary. I strongly recommend that the present Congress adopt whichever course it may deem to be the correct one.[72]

The item veto power was raised again in late 1940. In a December 19 memorandum for Attorney General Robert Jackson, the president contended that he favored the item veto, regardless of the method by which Congress empowered the chief executive with such authority. But FDR also warned that he "would not want this to become a party issue because while I think the proposal has very definite merits, the world crisis makes it advisable not to have a long drawn out fight on it at this time."[73]

Finally, another series of communications between Roosevelt and Senators Barkley and Vandenberg on the item veto transpired during the first few months of 1942. In a February 28 letter, Vandenberg thanked the president for his comments at a press conference held the preceding day where FDR condemned the inclusion of legislative riders upon "must bills." The senator concluded, "I respectfully suggest that we have reached a point where the 'ITEM VETO'—which we have discussed before—is indispensable." Vandenberg reminded FDR that "[m]y proposal is still pending."[74] In a March

4, 1942, memorandum for Barkley, the president asked to speak to the Democratic leader about Vandenberg's latest letter.[75] Roosevelt's March 9, 1942, letter to Senator Vandenberg mentions that he favored having Congress "pass legislation with the item in it" over a constitutional amendment.[76]

FDR's LEGISLATIVE LEGACY

In assessing FDR's achievements it is vital to include discussion of his contribution to the veto power. Regarding the veto, Jackson postulates that "[t]he Presidents following Roosevelt have generally conformed to the various veto patterns set by their predecessors" and that vetoes issued after FDR's tenure "have rarely become the subject of great interest and controversy."[77] Exceptions to the latter premise include President Harry Truman's veto of the Taft–Hartley Act and President Ronald Reagan's refusal to sign the Highway Reauthorization Act, each of which resulted in heated debate and eventual override of the veto.

Wayne conjectures that an outcome of the fact that Roosevelt issued more vetoes than any chief executive before or since is that he "expanded the legislative expectations and demands on the presidential office."[78] Keefe and Ogul identify the increase in international involvement, rising expectation and demands for government action, and the growing scope and intensity of political conflict as leading to persistent veto use by presidents in this century, particularly after FDR's administration.[79]

Hargrove and Nelson point out that the post-1953 period was dominated by Republican presidents and democratic Congresses. They suggest that "the tendency of conservative Republican presidents such as these to veto bills is more pronounced"; chief executives serving under an opposition Congress vetoed seven more bills on average per year than leaders whose party controlled the legislature from 1955 to 1981.[80] Ringelstein's study reveals that the categories of vetoes from 1953 through 1984 were remarkably similar from president to president; he attributes part of the explanation to "the enlarged scope of government in recent years."[81] Presidents issued 779 regular vetoes from 1933 through 1988, for an average of 28 per Congress, and 556 pocket vetoes, or about 20 per two-year legislative session.

Others delineate the impact that Roosevelt had on presidential–congressional relations. According to Allswang, the ascent of the presidency to a position of influence and power "has not diminished; rather, the contrary has resulted."[82] Referring to later chief executives, Leuchtenburg laments

that FDR's legislative successes "made it much less likely that their achievements would equal or surpass his,"[83] and surmises that "few would deny
that Franklin Delano Roosevelt continues to provide the standard by which
every successor has been and may well continue to be measured."[84] Rossiter
remarks that "Roosevelt's influence on the Presidency was tremendous."[85]
Berman observes that "FDR's legacies were numerous: the New Deal, the
institutional expansion of the presidency, increased expectations for government itself."[86] Whicker and Moore mention that Roosevelt's "personal
and political style were so strong that he was able to mobilize public
opinions as an effective form of congressional leverage."[87] Seligman and
Covington suggest that FDR created a condition of perpetual conflict
between presidents and their party members in Congress,[88] but Neustadt
refutes that charge.[89]

Perhaps it is most appropriate to conclude that President Roosevelt
possessed a positive orientation toward Congress together with a proclivity
to use the veto if the decision on its employment by staff and agency
personnel was close.[90] It is apparent that FDR's readiness to say "no deal"
to legislative proposals that he opposed gave impetus to his outstanding
accomplishments during the New Deal era and significantly shaped the
governing strategies of ensuing chief executives.

NOTES

1. See Katherine A. Towle, "The President's Veto Since 1889," *American
Political Science Review* 31 (1937): 51–56; Joseph E. Kalenbach, *The American
Chief Executive* (New York: Harper & Row, 1966); Frederick E. Taylor, "An
Analysis of Factors Purported to Influence the Use of, and Congressional Re-
sponses to the Use of, the Presidential Veto" (Ph.D. diss., Georgetown University,
1971); Jong R. Lee, "Presidential Vetoes from Washington to Nixon," *Journal of
Politics* 37 (1975): 522–546; Gary W. Copeland, "When Congress and the Presi-
dent Collide: Why Presidents Veto Legislation," *Journal of Politics* 45 (1983):
696–710; David W. Rhode and Dennis M. Simon, "Presidential Vetoes and
Congressional Response: A Study of Institutional Conflict," *American Journal of
Political Science* 29 (1985): 393–427.

2. Malcolm Shaw, "The Traditional and Modern Presidencies," in Malcolm
Shaw, ed., *The Modern Presidency* (New York: Harper & Row, 1987), 257.

3. Charles J. Zinn, *The Veto Power of the President* (Washington, D.C.: U.S.
Government Printing Office, 1951).

4. Carlton Jackson, *Presidential Vetoes, 1792–1945* (Athens: University of
Georgia Press, 1967).

5. John L. B. Higgins, "Presidential Vetoes, 1889–1929" (Ph.D. diss., Georgetown University, 1952), 240.

6. Edward C. Mason, *The Veto Power, 1789–1889* (New York: Russell and Russell, 1890), 130.

7. Henry M. Lewis, "The Veto Power of the President" (Ph.D. diss., American University, 1927).

8. Wilfred E. Binkley, *President and Congress* (New York: Random House, 1962), 304.

9. William E. Leuchtenburg, *Franklin D. Roosevelt and the New Deal, 1932–1940* (New York: Harper & Row, 1963), 327.

10. John H. Kessel, *The Domestic Presidency: Decision-Making in the White House* (North Scituate, Mass.: Duxbury Press, 1975), 17.

11. Harold M. Barger, *The Impossible Presidency* (Glenview, Ill.: Scott, Foresman, 1984), 204.

12. Clinton J. Rossiter, *The American Presidency* (Baltimore: Johns Hopkins University Press, 1987), 128.

13. Richard Rose, *The Postmodern President* (Chatham, N.J.: Chatham House, 1988), 2.

14. James W. Davis, *The American Presidency: A New Perspective* (New York: Harper & Row, 1987).

15. Shaw, "The Traditional and Modern Presidencies," 255–256.

16. Fred I. Greenstein, "Toward a Modern Presidency," in Fred I. Greenstein, ed., *Leadership and the Modern Presidency* (Cambridge, Mass.: Harvard University Press, 1988), 3.

17. George C. Edwards and Stephen J. Wayne, *Presidential Leadership: Politics and Policy Making* (New York: St. Martin's Press, 1990), 283.

18. Richard E. Neustadt, "Presidency and Legislation: The Growth of Central Clearance," *American Political Science Review* 48 (1954): 656.

19. James MacGregor Burns, *Roosevelt: The Lion and the Fox* (New York: Harcourt, Brace and World, 1956).

20. Jackson, *Presidential Vetoes*, 223.

21. John Carl Metz, "The President's Pocket Veto Power, 1889–1968: An Instrument of Executive Leadership" (Ph.D. diss., University of Pittsburgh, 1971), 259.

22. David J. Bass, "The Veto Power of the President: Its Theory and Practice" (Ph.D. diss., University of Chicago, 1972), 218.

23. Ibid., 218, 233.

24. See William F. Mullen, *Presidential Power and Politics* (New York: St. Martin's Press, 1976); Stephen H. Wayne, *The Legislative Presidency* (New York: Harper & Row, 1978); Louis W. Koenig, *The Chief Executive* (San Diego: Harcourt Brace Jovanovich, 1968); Robert J. Spitzer, *The Presidential Veto: Touchstone of the American Presidency* (Albany: State University of New York Press, 1988); William E. Leuchtenburg, "Franklin D. Roosevelt: The First Modern President," in Fred I. Greenstein, ed., *Leadership and the Modern Presidency;*

Robert E. DiClerico, *The American President* (Englewood Cliffs, N.J.: Prentice-Hall, 1990).

25. Mullen, *Presidential Power*, 55.

26. Wayne, *The Legislative Presidency*, 18.

27. Koenig, *The Chief Executive*, 162.

28. Davis, *The American Presidency*, 24.

29. Metz, "The President's Pocket Veto Power."

30. Bass, "The Veto Power of the President."

31. Spitzer, *The Presidential Veto*.

32. David McKay, "Presidential Strategy and the Veto Power: A Reappraisal," *Political Science Quarterly* 104 (1989): 447–461.

33. See Wayne, *The Legislative Presidency*; Louis Fisher, *The Politics of Shared Power: Congress and the Executive* (New York: Harper & Row, 1987); David Mervin, "The President and Congress," in Malcolm Shaw, ed., *The Modern Presidency*, 83–118.

34. George C. Robinson, "The Veto Record of Franklin D. Roosevelt," *American Political Science Review* 36 (1942): 76.

35. Karlyn Kohrs Campbell and Kathleen Hall Jamieson, *Deeds Done in Words* (Chicago: University of Chicago Press, 1990), 91.

36. Spitzer, *The Presidential Veto*, 67.

37. Bass, "The Veto Power of the President."

38. Ibid., 222.

39. Neustadt, "Presidency and Legislation," 654.

40. Metz, "The President's Pocket Veto Power."

41. Lee, "Presidential Vetoes from Washington to Nixon."

42. Copeland, "When Congress and the President Collide," 707.

43. Richard A. Watson, "Reasons Presidents Veto Legislation," paper presented at the 1987 Annual Meeting of the American Political Science Association, Chicago, September 3–6.

44. Samuel B. Hoff, "Saying No: Catalysts of Presidential Vetoes, 1889–1989," *American Politics Quarterly* 19.3 (July 1991): 310–323.

45. Bass, "The Veto Power of the President."

46. Roger H. Davidson, "The Presidency and Congress," in Michael Nelson, ed., *The Presidency and the Political System* (Washington, D.C.: Congressional Quarterly Press, 1984), 384.

47. Michael Barone, *Our Country: The Shaping of America from Roosevelt to Reagan* (New York: Free Press, 1990), 145.

48. Samuel B. Hoff, "Presidential Support and Veto Overrides, 1889–1989," *Midsouth Political Science Journal* 13 (Summer 1992): 173–189.

49. "Private Bills in Congress," *Harvard Law Review* 79 (June 1966): 1684–1706.

50. Metz, "The President's Pocket Veto Power."

51. Bass, "The Veto Power of the President."

52. See Clement E. Vose, "The Memorandum Pocket Veto," *Journal of Politics* 26 (May 1964): 397–405; Metz, "The President's Pocket Veto Power."

53. See Louis Fisher, *Constitutional Conflicts Between Congress and the President* (Princeton: Princeton University Press, 1985); Spitzer, *The Presidential Veto*.

54. Metz, "The President's Pocket Veto Power," 269.

55. *Public Papers and Addresses of Franklin D. Roosevelt 1934* (New York: Random House, 1938), 306.

56. Vose, "The Memorandum Pocket Veto," 398.

57. Bass, "The Veto Power of the President," 221.

58. See Fisher, *Constitutional Conflicts Between Congress and the President*; Spitzer, *The Presidential Veto*.

59. Spitzer, *The Presidential Veto*, 116.

60. Ibid., 109.

61. Pocket Veto Case, 297 U.S. 694 (1929).

62. President's Veto Message on H.R. 3233, June 11, 1940, White House Official File 47: Veto Messages, FDR Library, Hyde Park, NY.

63. Ibid.

64. Memorandum from President Roosevelt to Attorney General Francis Biddle, July 13, 1943, White House Official File 47: Veto Messages, FDR Library.

65. Letter from Attorney General Francis Biddle to President Roosevelt, July 16, 1943, White House Official File 47: Veto Messages, FDR Library.

66. Letter from Senator Arthur Vandenberg to President Roosevelt, August 19, 1937, White House Official File 47: Veto Messages, FDR Library.

67. Letter from Solicitor General Stanley Reed to President Roosevelt, with draft of suggested reply, September 20, 1937, White House Official File 47: Veto Messages, FDR Library.

68. Letter from President Roosevelt to Senator Arthur Vandenberg, September 24, 1937, White House Official File 47: Veto Messages, FDR Library.

69. Letter from Senator Arthur Vandenberg to President Roosevelt, September 29, 1937, White House Official File 47: Veto Messages, FDR Library.

70. Letter from Senator Alben Barkley to President Roosevelt, October 28, 1937, White House Official File 47: Veto Messages, FDR Library.

71. Letter from President Roosevelt to Senator Arthur Vandenberg, December 21, 1937, White House Official File 47: Veto Messages, FDR Library.

72. *Public Papers and Addresses of Franklin D. Roosevelt 1938* (New York: Macmillan, 1941), 22–23.

73. Memorandum from President Roosevelt to Attorney General Robert Jackson, December 19, 1949, White House Official File 47: Veto Messages, FDR Library.

74. Letter from Senator Arthur Vandenberg to President Roosevelt, February 28, 1942, White House Official File 47: Veto Messages, FDR Library.

75. Memorandum from President Roosevelt to Senator Alben Barkley, March 4, 1942, White House Official File 47: Veto Messages, FDR Library.

76. Letter from President Roosevelt to Senator Arthur Vandenberg, March 9, 1942, White House Official File 47: Veto Messages, FDR Library.

77. Jackson, *Presidential Vetoes*, 224.

78. Wayne, *The Legislative Presidency*, 18.

79. William Keefe and Morris Ogul, *The American Legislative Process: Congress and the States* (Englewood Cliffs, N.J.: Prentice-Hall, 1981).

80. Erwin C. Hargrove and Michael Nelson, *Presidents, Politics, and Policy* (New York: Alfred A. Knopf, 1984), 209.

81. Albert C. Ringelstein, "Presidential Vetoes: Motivations and Classifications," *Congress and the Presidency* 12 (1985): 187.

82. John M. Allswang, *The New Deal and American Politics* (New York: John Wiley and Sons, 1978), 130.

83. William E. Leuchtenburg, *In the Shadow of FDR* (Ithaca, N.Y.: Cornell University Press, 1983), 240.

84. Leuchtenburg, "Franklin D. Roosevelt: The First Modern President," 40.

85. Clinton Rossiter, *The American Presidency* (Baltimore: Johns Hopkins University Press, 1987), 205.

86. Larry Berman, *The New American Presidency* (New York: John Wiley and Sons, 1987), 205.

87. Marcia Lyn Whicker and Raymond A. Moore, *When Presidents Are Great* (Englewood Cliffs, N.J.: Prentice-Hall, 1988), 55.

88. Lester G. Seligman and Cary R. Covington, *The Coalitional Presidency* (Chicago: Dorsey Press, 1989).

89. Richard E. Neustadt, *Presidential Power and the Modern Presidents: The Politics of Leadership from Roosevelt to Reagan* (New York: Free Press, 1990).

90. Neustadt, "Presidency and Legislation."

11

FDR and the "Use Theory": Robert Worth Bingham at the Court of St. James's, 1933–1937

William E. Ellis

Robert Worth Bingham (1871–1937) demonstrated several tendencies during his lifetime. Though a reconstructed Southerner in many ways, he never completely transcended his Southern upbringing. For example, while ambassador to the Court of St. James's, he reacted effusively to Margaret Mitchell's *Gone with the Wind*, believing that the book more than vindicated the Bingham family's history in his native North Carolina.[1]

Moreover, he demonstrated many of the ideals of Wilsonian progressivism during his professional life as a lawyer and political leader. After moving to Louisville in 1896, he married into a prominent local family and soon became one of the leading young lawyers there. Though a registered Democrat, he sometimes supported Republicans he thought progressive, cooperating with them in Louisville and Kentucky politics in the first two decades of the twentieth century. While serving as interim mayor in 1907, he infuriated the local Democratic machine with his attempts to reform the body politic.[2]

After the death of his first wife, Bingham's life drifted for a time until his marriage to the widow of Henry Flagler, Mary Lily Kenan Flagler. She died in 1917 under circumstances that spawned a cottage industry of books in the 1980s, all of which accused her husband of varying degrees of complicity in her death because of a codicil to her will leaving him $5 million.[3]

Bingham took $1 million of his bequest and purchased the *Louisville Times* and the *Courier-Journal* in 1918. Over the next two decades he made the papers his fiefdom, using them for crusades against what he considered to be the enemies of Wilsonian progressivism and internationalism. Moreover, he led crusades for cooperative marketing in the 1920s and took an active interest in state and national affairs.[4]

Not long after the Great Crash, Bingham began searching for a progressive Democratic standard-bearer for 1932. He became one of the staunchest supporters of Franklin D. Roosevelt. "I have no doubt in my mind that you are the best hope not merely for the Democratic Party, which is a minor consideration, but for our country, which is the major consideration," Bingham told Roosevelt in September 1931. More important, he contributed substantially to the Democratic Party's coffers and used his papers to push for FDR's election.[5]

Soon after Roosevelt's election, Bingham visited Roosevelt at Warm Springs, Georgia, and there may have been talk then of a substantive reward. "You worked long and faithfully," FDR wrote in a letter, "and I am more than grateful to you." Although talk about other posts circulated, Bingham had already set his sights on an ambassadorship, "something on the outside," which, he maintained, would allow his newspapers a semblance of independence.[6]

Bingham's interest in appointment to the Court of St. James's came from his genealogical attachment to England, his long association with numerous English and Scottish friends, and his firm belief that the future welfare of the world depended on closer Anglo–American ties. "In my judgment, civilization, as we have known it, is at its greatest crisis," he explained to an English friend. "If it is to be saved at all, it can only be saved through the joint effort of the British and ourselves." Although he was challenged as an "Anglophile" and an "apologetic American" for previous statements about Britain and the United States, the Senate confirmed Robert Worth Bingham as "Ambassador Extraordinary and Plenipotentiary of the United States to Great Britain" after a brief delay. *Newsweek* asked the inevitable question directed to all new ministers to Great Britain: "Will you wear knee pants?" Bingham emphatically declared: "I will not."[7]

Recurring health problems plagued Bingham during his stay in London. He was unable to leave the United States until mid-May 1933 and became ill on board the S.S. *Washington*. Upon stepping off the ship at Plymouth, Bingham took the diplomatic offensive and expressed the view that the grave problems of the world could be solved only "by genuine understanding and cooperation between Great Britain and ourselves."[8]

Throughout his tenure as ambassador, Bingham jealously guarded what he considered to be his prerogatives. As chief representative of the U.S. government in Great Britain, he objected to the continual flow of special delegations from Washington to conferences in London and other European capitals in the 1930s, believing that these detracted from his own diplomatic usefulness and that of the embassy. Moreover, he disliked FDR's penchant of assigning two people to work on the same task, so well illustrated by the fiasco that became the London Economic Conference. Keeping the Department of State and the White House informed about other members of the American diplomatic corps took much of Bingham's time and energy. Sometimes these intrigues proved detrimental to American foreign policy, but more often they only demonstrated the whims of individual personalities and the inefficiency of the American diplomatic system. Moreover, in his earliest days in office Roosevelt did little to set the tone of American diplomacy, preferring to allow contending forces within the administration to test the water of public opinion.[9]

Owing to the depths of the depression, foreign policy took second place to domestic concerns in the early New Deal. During the campaign of 1932, FDR scolded Hoover for blaming the depression on international factors and thereby trying to lift responsibility from his own shoulders. However, Roosevelt soon modified his foreign policy directives to gain the support of more conservative Democrats. In return for the backing of William Randolph Hearst, Roosevelt dropped his support for membership in the League of Nations. The Democratic candidate moved toward isolationism, or economic nationalism, during the campaign, contradicting his Wilsonian internationalist inclination.[10]

British political scientist Harold Laski's estimation of Bingham's appointment to the Court of St. James's summed up the ideas of not a few Americans about the English and also provided a scathing social commentary on his own nation's leaders. Bingham's appointment "will enable our aristocracy to feel that the best Americans are really like themselves," the Englishman explained. "They share the same tastes, they have the same ambitions, they dream the same dreams."[11] Anglophobic representatives of the press such as William Randolph Hearst had a wide audience in the early to mid-1930s, capitalizing on such statements as vindications of their own mind-set.

Bingham sought closer ties with the British and a more prominent role for American foreign policy in European and world affairs. He thought of his function as educational in nature, his primary responsibility being to explain America to the British. In the process he defended Roosevelt and the New Deal at every opportunity. Significantly, he often appeared to be ahead of the times. Most of his speeches called for closer Anglo–American relations, often in contrast to official American policy.[12]

For his speeches Bingham received heated criticism from both British and American sources. While officials in the State Department disliked the candor of these remarks, Roosevelt never repudiated Bingham. In a press conference on 31 May 1933, for example, the president displayed his usual confident control over the proceedings when asked if he agreed with a statement made by Ambassador Bingham about Norman H. Davis, concerning war debt problems. FDR replied, "off the record," that the ambassador had given a "wrong impression on the American viewpoint" on disarmament. However, he neither publicly nor privately reprimanded Bingham. In another instance Roosevelt refused to take the bait in a reporter's query about Bingham's urging closer Anglo–American relations, saying that he had not seen the statement, when "in fact he had."[13]

If Bingham appeared to be an alarmist on international matters, Roosevelt understood those reactions. Bingham's responses mirrored ones that Roosevelt would have made if not constrained by political exigencies. FDR used Bingham, as he did others, to test either the domestic or international political waters. Some proof of this thesis is based on the fact that Roosevelt apparently never seriously considered replacing his controversial ambassador to Great Britain even after a much publicized and highly criticized anti-Nazi speech by Bingham in 1937.[14]

On the job it did not take Bingham long to show his colors. His first speech, at the annual meeting of the Pilgrims' Society, came only ten days after he assumed the post in London and just before the opening of the London Economic Conference. Though still suffering from a debilitating infection, Bingham delivered a forceful speech, one that not only set the tone for his later speeches but also clearly established the course of his ambassadorship.[15]

"I would have you know that I believe the hope for a stricken world rests entirely upon understanding, co-operation and confidence among the English-speaking peoples of the world," the ambassador announced, "and to the task of maintaining and promoting this attitude of mind, I come here resolved to dedicate all that I can, all that I have of mind and spirit." Moreover, he issued a solemn warning that though "our civilization is trembling in the balance . . . there is no time for any other thought except 'what shall we do to be saved?' " He concluded that the "hope of the world lies in whole-hearted, concerted action between Great Britain, the great self-governing British Commonwealth, and the United States."[16]

If this speech set the tone for Bingham's ambassadorship, the reactions in Britain and in the United States were also an indication of things to come. On the American side, Hearst, "always the isolationist" if inconsistent about other matters, allowed his *Chicago Herald-Examiner* to take the offensive with an article entitled "Who Put the Ass in Amb-ass-ador?," claiming that Bingham had already spoken out of turn on several occasions during his brief tenure. "He is a danger to the peace and good understanding which all Americans desire with the people of England," the editorialist exclaimed. "This country has already had enough of Bingham. We imagine that England has, too." Senator Joseph Robinson repeated an earlier attack on Bingham from the floor of the Congress, while the more even-handed *New York Times* cited Bingham's pronouncement about the need for tariff reduction as a legitimate concern.[17]

On the other side of the Atlantic, reactions also were mixed and heated. The London *Daily Telegraph* found the ambassador's pleas for Anglo–American cooperation to have "the authentic ring of sincerity." The *Evening News* proclaimed Bingham to be "the best, the clearest and the most decisive speaker that Washington has sent us as Ambassador for many a year past." However, several papers like Lord Beaverbrook's *Evening Standard* and the *Daily Mail*, republished the Hearst article and contributed their own critical appraisals of the ambassador. Bingham would later claim that the "Hearst gang in our country and the Beaverbrook gang over here . . . hooked up with each other" in a conspiracy to discredit him. The most eminent Briton, King George V, however, apparently thought well of the ambassador, at least from first impressions.[18]

During the ill-fated London Economic Conference, special envoy Raymond Moley and Bingham, who served the president as a conduit of information, clashed from the start. Although Bingham did not take direct part in the conference, he kept in close touch with Secretary of State Cordell Hull, who often talked with him about the negotiations. The ambassador did everything he could to oppose Moley. Bingham interpreted Moley's hyperactivity as upsetting the embassy's routine and especially disliked Moley's constant use of the code room. Moreover, Bingham visualized a cabal, controlled by Bernard Baruch and consisting of William E. Bullitt, Moley, Herbert Feis, and others, intent on undermining Hull and taking over negotiations.[19]

After FDR removed all doubt about American intentions by issuing his "Bombshell Message" on 2 July 1933, Bingham put a gloss on the whole affair. He reported to the president that Hull "did a really magnificent job here and emerged as the great figure of the Conference . . . I know of no finer incident in American diplomatic history than his achievement here."[20]

In the spring and summer of 1934, diplomatic maneuvering for reconsideration of earlier naval treaties developed into a test of wills between the major naval powers of the world. FDR instructed Bingham to "feel out the British on their attitude towards cooperation with us, in the event a war should break out in Europe or elsewhere." Specifically, the president ordered Bingham to relay to the British the American apprehension about giving Japan parity in any new naval agreement.[21]

After the beginning of negotiations in London, Bingham recommended that the United States should allow the British to run the course of their present state of mind about armaments and security. "On the whole, they need us and will need us much worse than we shall need them, and they will come to us in time," he concluded, "if we leave them entirely alone, and make it clear that we have nothing to talk to them about."[22]

Though often criticized as being an Anglophile, Bingham took a far more critical view of the British than his detractors perceived. He did not believe that America should bend to the British proposals at the 1935 London Naval Conference. Although the anti-American *Evening Standard* claimed that the ambassador had "acquired a remarkably good imitation of an English accent," Bingham himself poked fun at the variety of English accents and criticized the "underlying supercilious attitude" of the English upper class. Moreover, he echoed the feelings of many of his countrymen by deploring the lack of British sensitivity about the debt question. To Bingham the attitude of the British government needed a complete overhaul. Judging from his correspondence and notations in his diaries, he continually reminded British officials and friends that the majority of Americans felt betrayed by the British course on war debts and the question of stabilization. Nevertheless, Bingham voiced his pleas for Anglo–American cooperation. To Lord Queensborough, a pro-American friend, he said that "you may be sure that as you love my . . . country next to your own, I love your country next to my own."[23]

Bingham became embroiled in controversy in October 1934 after a speech before the Edinburgh Philosophical Institution. He explained that neither Americans nor the English adequately understood the culture, politics, and needs on the other side of the Atlantic, and both should immediately begin to make amends for such misunderstandings. Of course, he stressed the importance of cooperation, emphasizing that the welfare of both nations "is inextricably bound together." He told his British audience that the depression had created worse conditions in the United States than in Great Britain because of the banking crisis of the early 1930s in the former. More important, he urged stabilization of the dollar and the pound as necessary for improvements in the economies of both countries.[24]

After the initial reaction of Bingham's critics, Hull and Roosevelt hinted at the same stance in public addresses. Bingham believed that he had been vindicated for the statement at Edinburgh. Apparently given his head by the administration, he plunged back into the fray by making a similar speech before the Plymouth Branch of the English-Speaking Union.[25]

In 1935 the world moved closer to war. The Roosevelt–Bingham correspondence of mid-1935 offers two examples of the dilemma American policy-makers faced during this era, a time in which the general mood of Americans inclined toward isolationism. In late March, Bingham declared "the European atmosphere is surcharged" with fear of Nazi aggression. "I am more than doubtful whether we could keep out of a great European conflagration," the ambassador said. The president voiced a more cautious concern: "A very wise old bird tells me that a number of important world forces, including the British, would much like to involve us in some way—any way—in the world's critical problems." Of course, the question in the coming months would be how much leadership, moral or otherwise, the United States could muster without a consensus of public opinion.[26]

Anglo–American relations in 1935 remained strained because of the unsettled debt and pound–dollar stabilization questions. Bingham continually probed British opinion, not only within Whitehall but among the English people as well. His suggestion of linking the value of the dollar and the pound "at the proper time" drew immediate repudiation from the U.S. Department of the Treasury. However, Roosevelt said nothing about Bingham's statement. The ambassador reacted by redoubling his efforts to bring about better Anglo–American relations. When the BBC began broadcasting a series, "The American Half-hour," hosted by Alistair Cooke, Bingham kept close tabs on the programs' content; he officially complained about one segment that did not "tend to promote a spirit of friendly understanding." Within days, Sir John Reith, director of the BBC, apologized and promised to make amends during the airing of the next program.[27]

Mussolini's pressure on Ethiopia in 1935 created a tense situation. Bingham reacted to the crisis by not accepting any speaking engagements, claiming that the "situation here is too serious and too tense, and I should be a hypocrite if I made any suggestion which could possibly be construed as indicating a possibility that our country would take any hand in their troubles here." In late July he returned to the United States for consultation with Roosevelt and Hull on the London Naval Conference, the Italo–Ethiopian crisis, British–American relations, and other matters. While home, Bingham lobbied for the administration's neutrality legislation. When the First Neutrality Act passed Congress on 31 August 1935, Bingham predicted that "history may mark this as Mr. Roosevelt's greatest achievement." Not long afterward Italy invaded Ethiopia.[28]

The bad blood between Bingham and Norman Davis intensified when FDR appointed the latter to head an American delegation to the London Naval Conference. Moreover, the ambassador refused to serve as a special delegate at the conference. Throughout his tenure in London, Bingham argued that sending special delegations to Europe, especially headed by dignitaries like Davis, presented a false message of imminent American participation among Western nations. In the long run, when America did not assert itself, European heads of state became even more cynical about the intentions of the United States. On at least one occasion in early 1935, Roosevelt told Colonel Edward House that he agreed with Bingham "about having no special missions abroad this summer," accepting the reasoning that it might be better to function only through regular diplomatic missions for a while.[29]

The Davis–Bingham relationship deteriorated as Davis stayed in London. Bingham interpreted Davis's actions there as a political game that had nothing whatsoever to do with good diplomacy. He suggested that Davis be recalled before any more damage could be done. Aft first the president appeared to agree with Bingham, but then reversed his tack. Bingham asserted that he did not receive adequate explanation for this decision from the White House.[30]

Apparently, Davis exceeded instructions from the beginning of his negotiations with the British. Roosevelt finally dashed off an urgent note, asking Hull to "keep me in daily touch with what Davis is doing—I hear several dispatches have come from him showing that Davis is talking debts and economics. That is not his job!" Later in November 1935, in nearly identical letters, Hull and Roosevelt apologized to Bingham for the behavior of Davis and for their decision to send him to London. Both extolled Bingham as occupying the "premier position of all the notable Americans" serving in diplomatic posts. Bingham could hardly contain his elation at being vindicated in his judgment of Davis. In early 1936 the conference sank into impotence after the Japanese walked out, and apparently another chance had been lost to keep the peace in the world. But events as well as the efforts of Bingham and others began easing Anglo–American tensions of the early 1930s, and both nations moved ever so slowly toward cooperation.[31]

Poor health plagued Bingham while he was in London. Never entirely free from pain and weakness, he submitted to complete medical examinations in England in December 1935, and at the Brady Institute in Baltimore in March of 1936. When neither examination revealed any cause for Bingham's recurring health problems, he blamed his suffering on the ravages of advancing age. The ambassador began to develop "a bit of a stomach" that was particularly noticeable to his son Barry; it seemed unusual because of his spare diet and a fastidious concern about his health and appearance.[32]

Other factors also made Bingham's life uncomfortable. Throughout his time in Britain, his critics often cited his allegedly pro-British stance. For example, one anonymous correspondent, who signed the letter "An American for America Only" railed: "Honored Sir; Be Damn careful with secretive agreements and diplomatic pitfalls with the wily hipricritical [sic] English, lest you emulate the disgraceful pro-English record of Walter Hines Page." He also continued to receive periodic broadsides because he appeared to be anti-Irish. And there was always William E. Bullitt, who, Bingham argued, worked against him within the State Department. After weathering these verbal storms for over three years, Bingham seriously considered retiring from his post in 1936. Discussions with Hull, Colonel House, and Roosevelt brought an agreement that Bingham should remain on the job until January 1938.[33]

In a critique of the early years of New Deal diplomacy, Howard Jablon has argued that the single-minded, domineering leadership of Secretary of State Cordell Hull blunted any hope for more creative policy from 1933 to 1937. Hull was obsessed with free trade and reciprocal trade agreements to the exclusion of more substantive foreign policy. In several ways Bingham played a part in this "devotion to the reciprocal trade program." First, the secretary of state and Colonel House headed a powerful interest group within the administration, and the ambassador followed their lead. Second, Southern congressmen and Southerners historically had accepted the ideal of world peace through better trade relations. Perhaps most important of all, the American people and the administration in Washington indicated no consensus on any policy save that on domestic issues in the early New Deal years. Bingham's early suggestion that the United States should "stay on our side and let them come to us" suited the times. No one agreed more than President Franklin D. Roosevelt.[34]

If the United States lacked a coherent foreign policy in 1936, Bingham went about his task from another perspective. His efforts to bring about closer relations between the United States and Great Britain finally began to bear fruit as British attitudes began to shift. While the British government hesitated to talk about a reciprocal trade agreement early in 1936 because of the uncertainty of the reelection of FDR, the English people moved ever so slowly toward a consensus that allowed them to produce a coherent defense and rearmament policy.[35]

War clouds grew more intense over Europe and the world in 1936. Bingham relayed to Roosevelt his feeling that Germany would go to war "if they feel they can get away with it, and it may happen through some untoward event which we cannot immediately foresee." To an English friend he declared, "There is grave reason to suspect that Hitler and Mussolini are beginning to work together on the basis of dividing up the world between them." He also found a strong pro-German sentiment among a minority in Britain and people "more anxious and apprehensive than I have ever seen them before."[36]

In 1936, as Germany grew stronger, Bingham intensified his pleas to Hull and Roosevelt for closer ties with the United Kingdom. Throughout that year he kept up a steady barrage of cooperationist speeches and press releases. Before the Association of British Chambers of Commerce he praised the benefits of Wilsonian internationalism and Hull's proposal for reduced tariffs. "The surest method of preventing war," he argued, "lies in the restoration of normal international trade, bringing with it the promise to the peoples of the world of a better standard of living and the hope of a fuller life." More specifically, he declared his belief that the United States and Great Britain were at last ready to arm against aggression.[37]

On 4 July 1936, in a short speech to the American Society in London, broadcast to the United States on CBS, Bingham expounded on the same themes he had been preaching for over three years. The English-speaking and "other free peoples in the world" must cooperate to confront the forces of "tyranny." "In a world armed and arming, we must and will be fully prepared, gun for gun, ship for ship, plane for plane, man for man, to protect our homes and our country," Bingham challenged. Dramatically, he ended his address: "I say again that ours is the supreme heritage among men, to be cherished, to be loved, to serve, to live and, if need be, to die for!"[38]

Bingham "should be recalled," one Irish-American lawyer in Philadelphia demanded of FDR. Another critic told Hull that the American ambassador's remarks would lose votes in the upcoming presidential race. Bingham did not relent. Not long after the revolt of Francisco Franco and the beginning of the Spanish Civil War, Bingham spoke before an English-Speaking Union garden party at Capestone in Cheshire. Although he appeared to back off slightly from his previous call for Anglo–American cooperation in the early part of his speech, he continued to stress the common culture, language, and ethnic background of the two countries. The United States did not desire an alliance with any nation; however, Bingham said, "There are many ties which draw the English-speaking nations together. . . . We are the great free peoples of this earth."[39]

Bingham served Roosevelt at every turn. The 1936 presidential election presented him with another such opportunity. Early that spring, Louis Howe, the president's oldest staff member, imposed on Bingham's support for FDR by asking for and receiving a contribution of $10,000 for an "educational campaign." Howe's plans presumably included organizing a publishing company to print pro-administration material. After Bingham asked for a clarification from Roosevelt, James A. Farley discovered that Howe had been using the money for personal expenses. FDR stopped this practice and the accelerating "embarrassment" that Howe had brought to him. Within weeks Howe died.[40]

Several months before the Democratic National Convention, Kentucky governor "Happy" Chandler suggested that Bingham head Kentucky's delegation to the Philadelphia meeting. The ambassador declined, maintaining that such a move would make him too much of a "partisan." However, he fully intended to play some role in the upcoming election. As much as he wanted to get back to the States, he suggested that the turbulent political climate in Europe prevented him and other American diplomats from leaving their posts for long. The president insisted that Bingham come back home briefly to work on press relations, specifically "to lay a lot of ground work in the Associated Press organization looking toward complete fairness by them." Bingham acceded to FDR's wishes that he should "be on hand to watch every move by the Associated Press control, and to do anything else which you may think desirable," a duty that included working with the radio networks.[41]

After the nomination of Roosevelt and the lull in campaigning before the post–Labor Day push, Bingham returned to his post in London. Tensions in Europe continued to concern him, and although he would have liked nothing better than participating directly in the election back home, he remained in Britain. FDR reported to Bingham in mid-September that "THINGS HERE ARE GOING ALL RIGHT." To make sure that all went smoothly, the ambassador assigned Ulric Bell, the *Courier-Journal* Washington bureau chief, and Herbert Agar to write special articles and editorials in support of Roosevelt. Bell kept in close contact with the White House and "Fairfax," the code name for FDR in the Bingham–Bell correspondence. Bingham charged Bell with the special task of keeping "a close watch on the AP." As usual, Bingham made substantial contributions to the Democratic Party's campaign chests.[42]

The *Literary Digest* public opinion poll to the contrary, a "Landon-slide" did not materialize in the fall of 1936. With nationwide voter participation at its highest since 1916, Roosevelt won with over 60 percent of the votes, taking every state except Maine and Vermont.

Ulric Bell's lead article in the *Courier* the day after the election claimed that the election endorsed liberalism and the New Deal. He scolded Al Smith, Father Charles Coughlin, Congressman William Lemke, Dr. Francis Townsend, and "all the other motley Republicans" for their folly in opposing the president. Bingham could not contain his elation in a telegram to FDR: "I have no doubt yours is the supreme achievement since the union of states was formed."[43]

Bingham immediately made the obligatory resignation from his post; as expected, Roosevelt asked him to stay on as the chief American diplomat to His Majesty's Government. A few days after the election Bingham explained the reaction of the British to the president. While the average English person "warmly" appreciated FDR's victory, Bingham declared that the "British press service is so bad and so insufficient" that it reported Governor Alf Landon stood a good chance of winning. Unfortunately, the British government did not believe Bingham's statements to the contrary, and correspondingly temporized its policies toward the United States for several months prior to the election.[44]

Nevertheless, in the latter months of 1936 Bingham noticed a discernible shift in relations between the United States and Great Britain. A combination of factors led to this trend. First, the overwhelming reelection of Roosevelt finally convinced the British government that the president had a majority behind him. Second, war appeared more ominously on the horizon than ever in late 1936, and Bingham's letters and dispatches often relayed that feeling to Washington. Third, the British experienced difficulty rebuilding their defenses, having particular trouble in their aircraft construction program. Combined with the aggressiveness of Germany, Italy, and Japan, this led to a developing British consensus that the United States could again be their best ally in case of war in Europe.[45]

In his meetings with British leaders, particularly with Foreign Secretary Anthony Eden, Bingham stressed the necessity for Anglo–American trade agreements as a beginning for closer general ties between the two nations. The Imperial Study Group, made up of fifty-five members of Parliament, offered some hope when it urged that the British government seek monetary and trade agreements with America. One prominent member of the group reported to Bingham in early October that after an extensive tour of European capitals, his entourage concluded that "quite clearly our path must lie alongside the United States, and as far away from Europe as possible." Although Roosevelt agreed with Bingham that such moves were welcome, he refused to recognize "unofficial foreign missions of any kind," such as the Imperial Policy Group, fearing adverse reaction in the press.[46]

Bingham was perceptive enough to discern that although there was "a wide-spread, persistent, increasing feeling that it is to their interest to cultivate better relations with the United States," the British government lacked the will to move in late 1936. In the British effort to improve relations with America, several members of the House of Commons informed Bingham that they were forming an organization to promote better understanding with the United States. As part of this obvious change, Commons gave a dinner in honor of Bingham in mid-December. In his remarks the ambassador suggested that when the English visited the United States, they would be well served to explore areas other than the East in order to find a true understanding of his country. Two days later the London *Spectator* praised such meetings as valuable and editorialized that Britain should never have suspended "token payments" of its war debt. This admission represented fulfillment of Bingham's prediction that the United States should bide its time and allow the British "to come to us."[47]

Even as the aggressiveness of Germany, Italy, and Japan increased, events in Britain took on an appearance of more style than substance in late 1936 and early 1937. A constitutional crisis developed when Edward VIII, who had followed his father, George V, to the throne but had not yet been crowned, ran afoul of the court and tradition by romancing an American divorcée, Wallis Warfield Simpson. As one who greatly admired Britain and feared for its safety, Bingham rejoiced that the "crisis" had "successfully and triumphantly" concluded with the accession of George VI to the throne. "The Duke of Windsor [Edward VIII] was surrounded by a pro-German cabal and many people here suspected that Mrs. Simpson was actually in German pay," the ambassador told Roosevelt.[48]

Bingham's diplomatic duties continued unimpeded into early 1937. Through early spring he fought a valiant rearguard action in his attempt to keep from having to wear the detested knee breeches at the upcoming coronation. The court made one concession when they stated that the American ambassador could wear breeches made of the same material as his coat rather than of silk. Bingham's mild protestations to Roosevelt brought a humorous response from the Oval Office: "My ruling is: that Ambassadors should wear trousers unless the Sovereign of the State to which he is accredited makes a personal demand for knee breeches. I am fortified in this ruling by the pictures I have seen of Comrade Litvinoff in the aforesaid short pants. If Soviet Russia can stand it I guess we can too."[49]

As the British constitutional crisis resolved itself, other events in 1937 reinforced Bingham's forebodings of war. Early that year, Roosevelt signed into a law a new neutrality resolution in response to the continuing Spanish Civil War. Bingham's advice to retain a "wide measure of discretion" had by that time become the view of many Americans, who feared complete neutrality would be both impossible and unwise. Although Adolf Hitler only engaged in verbal saber-rattling for the remainder of the year, the Japanese moved one step closer to all-out war in Asia by storming across the Marco Polo Bridge into China in early July.[50]

While the United States and Great Britain could not agree on any form of action to impede the Japanese in 1937, they moved closer toward cooperation. The trend that Bingham sensed in 1936 continued into the new year. Undoubtedly, the reelection of Roosevelt helped. In early January 1937, Bingham reported an obvious British "drive" under way to gain American support, reinforcing "my thesis that events must eventually force the British to come to us." Hull's determination to gain an Anglo–American trade agreement apparently now had the blessing of several leaders in the British cabinet, particularly Foreign Secretary Anthony Eden. Neville Chamberlain agreed after he replaced Stanley Baldwin as prime minister at midyear. One member of Parliament assured Bingham that "effective economic co-operation between Great Britain and the United States is the only ultimate hope of saving what is left of civilization." Whether of government official or private citizen, in public or in private, the British disposition toward the United States had obviously changed by mid-1937.[51]

Regardless of the rumors about Bingham's recall, the president continued his support. Bingham reciprocated and never relented in his support of FDR through thick and thin. Even during the ill-fated attempt to pack the Supreme Court, Bingham put a gloss on the effort: "I think you won the war, and that this will mean unlimited benefit to our country." Roosevelt thanked Bingham for his support during the crisis but admitted to "laying low" for the time being.[52]

The Spanish Civil War increasingly confounded both British and American diplomats in mid-1937. Bingham relayed Eden's belief that "a Franco victory would not jeopardize British interests in the Iberian peninsula," but that an American embargo would "complicate his task" in working toward a peaceful solution there. He accepted Eden's conclusion that anything other than "strict neutrality" by the United States in that conflict "would be

regarded by Europe as a gratuitous interference in continental affairs."
British policy followed strict neutrality to the point of allowing warring
"parties in Spain" full "belligerent rights at sea." Their rearmament and
public relations efforts to win American approval to the contrary, Hull told
FDR that "the British tories are still tories and in spite of Eden's denial,
want peace at any price." Bingham sensed that the continuation of the
Spanish crisis generally deepened suspicions among the major nations of
Europe.[53]

Bingham maintained a spirited censure of Germany and her allies. At
the annual Pilgrims' Dinner in mid-May, he praised Anglo–American
efforts for world peace and scored the militarization of the Axis powers.
"They rearmed and for what—for aggression," the ambassador charged.
"No nation needs bombing airplanes, big tanks and heavy artillery unless it
tends to plunder its neighbors."[54]

However, these remarks paled in comparison with those made a few
weeks later at the American Society's annual Fourth of July festivities at
the embassy in London. After a crowd of over 300 heard Columbia University President Nicholas Murray Butler give an appropriately patriotic
speech, Bingham's brief remarks left no doubt about his views of Germany,
Italy, and Japan. "Let us admit for the moment that the dictatorships are
better prepared for war," he explained, "but if the dictatorships are better
prepared to begin war, certainly the democracies are better able to finish it."
Now the British and Americans were rearming, he said. Although Bingham
refused to be totally pessimistic about world peace, he faced up to the threat
to democracy. In the strongest possible terms he proposed: "If we must deal
with people who cannot and will not listen to reason, if we must deal with
despotism and people who regard war as a cult, and blood and honour as
something to teach little children, and who only listen to the argument of
force, then we must fall back on that. But my hope is that there must be in
these despotisms at least some remnant of reasoning power and of sanity."[55]

Disparaging reaction came within hours. Ambassador William E. Dodd
in Berlin sent Hull word about strong Nazi press reaction. A Berlin newspaper scolded Bingham for an "inbred Anglo-Saxon habit of playing the
schoolmaster." One paper charged that Bingham's speech "incited the
so-called democracies in almost unbelievable fashion." Another asked:
"Should an American ambassador accredited in a European capital make
agitative speeches against other European peoples?"[56]

The speech also caught the eye of critics in the United States. The
Chicago Daily Tribune, an old Bingham foe, replied with a front-page
cartoon with Uncle Sam remonstrating, "I don't remember ever authorizing

him to enter into a military alliance with Great Britain" as a prim Bingham spoke to a circle of English friends in the background. Personal correspondence to the ambassador kept up the attack. One American critic addressed Bingham as "R. Worthless Bingham, You Bumbling British So-&-So," while another assumed that "President Roosevelt will hand you a good stiff kick in the pants."[57]

Not only did Nazi newspapers and Bingham's American critics score the Fourth of July speech, but the Department of State scrutinized the ambassador's remarks. Undersecretary of State Sumner Welles submitted a circular letter to FDR, asking that thereafter ambassadors submit all speeches to the department before they were delivered. The president replied by requesting more information as well as a copy of Bingham's speech. The latter proved impossible. Bingham either had no copy of his speech, it having been spontaneous and made off the cuff, or he destroyed any notes or script. Only newspaper accounts are extant today. Attempts by Welles to find a copy elsewhere or obtain one from the London embassy failed. Bingham chose to ignore Welles. More important, FDR supported Bingham. A couple of weeks later the president made no criticism of Bingham's outburst against totalitarianism, declaring: "You are doing a grand job." In a few weeks the incident was nearly forgotten, but Bingham refrained from making such public statements for a while.[58]

Bingham's correspondence after the Fourth of July remarks revealed an increasing mood of pessimism. He explained his diplomatically intemperate talk by telling friends that he had lost patience. "I thought it was high time that those of us who believe in liberty, justice and democratic institutions should have a word to say to these bloody dictators who repeatedly broadcast their contempt for democracy, which they describe as being rotten, inefficient, and decadent," Bingham told one colleague. He denied having called for a military alliance between the United States and Great Britain, although he believed "in a decent and reasonable mutual and beneficial cooperation among the English-speaking peoples." Unfortunately, the "only language the Japanese and the Germans understand is guns, and neither Britain nor the United States is prepared to go to war." Moreover, he believed "the Germans intend to attack as soon as they think they are ready."[59]

Bingham's outburst at the Fourth of July festivities coincided with deteriorating health. Indeed, physical pain may well have contributed to his blunt remarks. He complained of a lack of energy and unexplained pain throughout his body. Nothing seemed to ease his discomfort and, being unable to carry out his diplomatic tasks, he applied for leave from his post in late August. After reaching New York, Bingham immediately traveled to Baltimore, where his old friend Dr. Hugh Young examined him at Johns Hopkins. However, no cause could be found for his deteriorating health. After a brief stay in the hospital, Bingham talked with Secretary Hull in Washington for an hour about world affairs and then traveled to Hyde Park for a brief conference with FDR. At both locations he denied press allegations that either leader had sought his resignation.[60]

During Bingham's stay at Johns Hopkins Hospital, Roosevelt delivered his Quarantine Speech on 5 October. In a telegram to the president Bingham declared: Your Chicago speech undoubtedly encouraging and helpful to all decent people throughout the world and may well lay foundation for their salvation from the murderous brigands infesting the world. Isolationists like Hearst cried foul, but an increasing number of Americans agreed with the White House and Bingham. However, this "uncertain feeler," as it was described by diplomatic historian H. G. Nicholas, failed to bring immediate change.[61]

After he resumed his duties in London, Bingham's health deteriorated and he set sail for home on 20 November 1937. After checking into Johns Hopkins, Bingham officially resigned on 8 December. He thanked FDR for the opportunity of serving as ambassador to Great Britain. He predicted that the physicians would be able to find the cause of his "peculiar recurrent periodic form of fever." Although Barry Bingham reported to Roosevelt that his father was "making slow progress," by 11 December the press reported that FDR had already chosen a replacement, Joseph P. Kennedy, who vigorously sought the ambassadorship.[62]

Meanwhile, Hugh Young convinced Bingham and his family that exploratory surgery was needed for an inflamed abdomen. On 14 December, Young and his team of surgeons discovered that Bingham suffered from abdominal Hodgkin's disease. Young immediately understood there would be no hope of saving his old friend's life. After briefly regaining consciousness, Bingham lapsed into a coma. He died on the third day after the operation, at the age of sixty-six.[63]

Roosevelt issued the following, somewhat perfunctory, statement: "I feel the loss of Ambassador Bingham keenly. He was not only an old personal friend, but as one of the foremost citizens of Kentucky and of the nation, he exercised an active and consistent influence in the cause of decent government and of high ideals. As Ambassador of the United States to Great Britain he truly represented the best interests of his country. All of us have suffered a heavy loss." In the end he had taken no official action on Bingham's resignation and wrote a note of tribute to Barry with the explanation that his father "died on December eighteenth—still American Ambassador to Great Britain."[64]

Bingham proved to be a perceptive diplomat as U.S. representative at the Court of St. James's and not the Anglophile his critics charged. He was not just a conduit of information and observer as diplomat, but worked incessantly for better Anglo–American relations at a crucial time in the histories of both countries. He hated fascism in all its forms. His warnings about the dangers of fascism and German militarism, and the necessity of a united front by the Western democracies against totalitarianism, proved prescient.

If Bingham was used by Roosevelt as a diplomat stalking-horse, he was a willing one because he implicitly trusted the leadership of FDR. He found no alternative to unquestioning support of New Deal foreign policy, at the same time pushing FDR toward closer ties with Britain. Moreover, he never doubted that Roosevelt saved the United States from the ravages of the Great Depression. The ambassadorship represented not only the highlight of Bingham's career but also symbolized to him the acceptance of himself and his region into the American mainstream.

NOTES

1. RWB to Margaret Mitchell, 16 February 1937, RWB Papers, Manuscript Division, Library of Congress [hereafter cited as RWB-LC].

2. William E. Ellis, "Robert Worth Bingham and Louisville Progressivism, 1905–1910," *Filson Club History Quarterly* 54 (April 1980): 169–195.

3. The cause of the publication of these books was the breakup of the Bingham family in the mid-1980s. The family sold off its considerable media holdings after the siblings of Barry Bingham, Sr., could not agree on publication policies of their papers. These books include David Leon Chandler and Mary Voelz Chandler, *The Binghams of Louisville: The Dark History Behind One of America's Great Fortunes* (New York: Crown, 1987); Marie Brenner, *House of Dreams: The Bingham Family of Louisville* (New York: Random House, 1988); Sallie Bingham, *Passion and Prejudice: A Family Memoir* (New York: Alfred A. Knopf, 1989); and Susan E. Tifft and Alex A. Jones, *The Patriarch: The Rise and Fall of the Bingham Dynasty* (New York: Summit Books, 1991).

4. William E. Ellis, "Robert Worth Bingham and the Crisis of Cooperative Marketing in the Twenties," *Agricultural History* 56 (January 1982): 99–116; and "The Bingham Family: From the Old South to the New South and Beyond," *Filson Club History Quarterly* 61 (January 1987): 5–33.

5. RWB to FDR, 22 September 1931, Private Correspondence, 1928–32, FDR Papers, Franklin D. Roosevelt Library, Hyde Park, N.Y.

6. FDR to RWB, 3 December 1932, Private Correspondence, 1928–32, FDR Papers; RWB to Shepard Bryan, 24 October 1932, Southern Historical Collection, University of North Carolina, Chapel Hill.

7. RWB to Reverend R. W. Paul, [n.d.] 1932, RWB-LC; Key Pittman to Cordell Hull, 16 March 1933, RWB-LC; *Louisville Herald-Post*, 18, 27, and 29 September 1927; *Chicago Daily Tribune*, 14 March 1933; *Newsweek*, 27 May 1933.

8. *New York Times*, 11 May 1933; Dr. Edward H. Linneham to "Dear Doctor," 16 May 1933, Dr. William F. Rienhoff, Jr. to Bingham, 9 June 1933, RWB-LC; *London Daily Express*, 18 May 1933.

9. Oral history interview with Barry Bingham, Sr., 3 December 1980, Eastern Kentucky University Archives, Richmond, Ky.; Hull to Embassy, Paris, 24 March 1933, 123 Bingham, Robert W./32, Department of State Papers, National Archives, Washington, D.C.; *New York Times*, 20 May 1933.

10. Robert D. Schulzinger, *American Diplomacy in the Twentieth Century* (New York: Oxford University Press, 1984), 150–153; Robert Dallek, *Franklin D. Roosevelt and American Foreign Policy, 1932–1945* (New York: Oxford University Press, 1979), 23–34; Wayne S. Cole, *Roosevelt and the Isolationists* (Lincoln: University of Nebraska Press, 1983), 23, 108, 123–124.

11. Reprint from the *London Daily Herald* in the *Chicago Daily Tribune*, 8 May 1933.

12. *New York Times*, 31 May 1933.

13. Edgar B. Nixon, *Franklin D. Roosevelt and Foreign Affairs*, Vol. I, *January 1933–February 1934* (Cambridge, Mass.: Belknap Press of Harvard University, 1969), 193; *Foreign Relations of the United States, 1933*, Vol. I (Washington, D.C.: Department of State, 1950), 166–168; James MacGregor Burns, *Roosevelt: The Lion and the Fox* (New York: Harcourt, Brace, and World, 1956), 189.

14. Burns, *The Lion and the Fox*, 189; Arthur S. Link, *American Epic: A History of the United States, Vol. II, 1921–1941* (New York: Knopf, 1963), 470–471.

15. *Raleigh News and Observer*, 31 May 1933.

16. Ray Atherton to Hull, telegram, 23 March 1933, 123 Bingham, Robert W./6, Department of State Papers; Pilgrims' Dinner Speech, 30 May 1933, Speech File, RWB-LC; *The Times*, 31 May 1933.

17. *Chicago Herald-Examiner*, 4 June 1933; Emmanuel Levi to RWB, 5 June 1933, RWB-LC; Rodney P. Carlisle, *Hearst and the New Deal* (New York: Garland, 1979), 9, 19; RWB to FDR, 26 May and 11 June 1933, OF 491, FDR Papers; *New York Times*, 1, 7, and 22 June 1933; W. A. Swanberg, *Citizen Hearst* (New York: Charles Scribner's Sons, 1961), 473; Cole, *Roosevelt and the Isolationists*, 23, 108, 123–124.

18. *London Daily Mail*, 5 June 1933; *London Daily Telegraph*, 31 May 1933; Bingham Diaries, Vol. I, 21 June 1933, Bingham to Ulric Bell, 27 October 1934,

Bingham to Grover Page, 23 June 1933, RWB-LC; Nixon, *FDR and Foreign Affairs*, I, 238.

19. Ted Morgan, *FDR: A Biography* (New York: Simon and Schuster, 1985), 393; Bingham Diaries, I, 1 and 5 March 12, 19, 22, and 30 June, 6 July 1933, RWB-LC.

20. Bingham Diaries, I, 13, 14, 23, and 24 June, 2, 6, 12, 26, and 28 July 1933, RWB to Lincoln MacVeagh, 11 September 1933, RWB-LC.

21. Bingham Diaries, I, 20 February and 1 March 1934, II, 16 July and 7 November 1934, RWB-LC; RWB to FDR, 8 May 1934, PSF, GB:1934–36, FDR Papers.

22. *Foreign Relations of the United States, 1934*, Vol. I (Washington, D.C.: Department of State, 1934), 264; Bingham Diaries, "Memorandum of Conversations Between Prime Minister MacDonald and Norman H. Davis, 2 March 1934, inserted in Vol. I, also I, 22 June 1934, II, 16 July 1934, 18–19 June 1934, 19 November 1934, and 13 December 1934, RWB-LC; Hull to RWB, 30 June 1934, OF 491, FDR Papers.

23. *New York Times*, 24, 25, 29, 30, and 31 October 1934; London *Evening Standard*, 9 November 1934; RWB to Lord Queensborough, 14 April 1934, RWB to William E. Dodd, 29 October 1934 and 16 April 1935, RWB to Mary M. French, 7 May 1935, copy of *Fortune* magazine article from Ulric Bell, 25 June 1934, RWB-LC; Bingham Diaries, I, 12 April 1934, II, 10 April 1935, IV, 27 October and 4 December 1936, RWB-LC; Anne Trotter, *Britain and East Asia, 1933–1937* (London: Cambridge University Press, 1975), 170–172.

24. *Courier-Journal*, 25 and 30 October 1934; *New York Times*, 26 October 1935; "Address to Edinburgh Philosophical Institution," 23 October 1934, RWB-LC.

25. Hull to George Holden Trinkam, 16 January 1935, 123 Bingham, Robert W./87, Department of State Papers; RWB to Lawrence K. Callahan, 26 October 1934, RWB-LC; *Manchester Daily Express*, 24 October 1934; Bingham Diaries, II, 23 October 1934, 162–163, RWB-LC.

26. RWB to FDR, 26 March 1935, PPF 716, FDR Papers; FDR to RWB, 11 July 1935, PSF, GB:RWB, FDR Papers.

27. *Courier-Journal*, 26 March 1935; RWB to Cordell Hull, 28 June 1935, Sir John Reith to RWB, 28 February and 26 April 1935, RWB to Reith, 17 April 1935, Reith to Ray Atherton, 27 March 1935, RWB-LC.

28. *Courier-Journal*, 7 August 1935; RWB to Barry Bingham, 8 April and 16 October 1935, RWB to Ulric Bell, 3 July 1935, RWB-LC; Dallek, *FDR and American Foreign Policy*, 111; *New York Times*, 25 July, 1, 7, 8, 12, and 30 August, and 11 September 1935.

29. Elliot Roosevelt, ed., *FDR: His Personal Letters*, Vol. I, (New York: Duell, Sloan & Pearce, 1950), 473–474; Nixon, *FDR and Foreign Affairs*, III, 45–47, 88–90; RWB to FDR, 9 May 1935, PSF, GB:RWB, FDR Papers; Bingham

Diaries, II, 21 February 1935, RWB-LC; *Foreign Relations of the United States, 1935*, Vol. I (Washington, D.C.: Department of State, 1953), 772–773.

30. Dallek, *FDR and American Foreign Policy*, 90; Davis to RWB, 12 and 27 January 1935, RWB to Barry Bingham, n.d., Family Correspondence, 1935, RWB-LC.

31. Bingham Diaries, III, 28 October and 17 November 1935, and 23 page insert, IV, 25 January 1936, RWB-LC; Roosevelt, *FDR Letters*, Vol. I, 525–527; Hull to RWB, 19 and 23 November 1936, PPF 716, "Memo for Secretary of State," n.d., PSF Confidential, Department of State Papers.

32. Interview with Barry Bingham, Sr., 4 April 1987; Bingham Diaries, III, 17 December 1935 and IV, 19 March 1936, RWB-LC.

33. House to FDR, 17 November 1936, PPF 222, FDR to House, 9 December 1936, OF 491, FDR Papers; "An American for America Only" to RWB, 11 October 1935, Barry Bingham to RWB, 18 November 1936, Charles Edward Russell et al., to Cordell Hull, 8 June 1936, 123 Bingham, Robert W./123, Department of State Papers; RWB to Barry Bingham, 4 December, 1936, RWB-LC.

34. Howard Jablon, *Crossroads of Decision: The State Department and Foreign Policy, 1933–1937* (Lexington: University Press of Kentucky, 1983), 131–138; Bingham Diaries, II, 29 March 1935, RWB-LC.

35. *Foreign Relations of the United States, 1936*, Vol. I (Washington, D.C.: Department of State, 1953), 296–298, 304–305; Richard N. Kottman, *Reciprocity and the North Atlantic Triangle, 1932–38* (Ithaca, N.Y.: Cornell University Press, 1968), 133, 143, 272–279.

36. RWB to FDR, 4 September 1936 and 21 July 1937, FDR to RWB, telegram, 14 September 1936, PSF, GB:RWB, FDR Papers; RWB to Lady Grogan, 28 July 1936 and 1 October 1937, RWB-LC.

37. Speech to the Association of British Chambers of Commerce, 30 April 1936, 123 Bingham, Robert W./119, Department of State Papers.

38. *New York Times*, 26 June 1936; Bingham Diaries, IV, 10–17 June 1936, 330–331, "Remarks of the American Ambassador at the American Society Dinner in London on July 4, 1936," RWB-LC.

39. Arnold A. Offner, *American Appeasement: United States Foreign Policy and Germany, 1933–1937* (Cambridge, Mass: Belknap Press of Harvard University, 1969), 154; *New York Times*, 15 July 1936; Michael J. Ryan to FDR, 5 July 1936, OF 491, FDR Papers; Celei Lyman to Cordell Hull, 9 July 1936, 123 Bingham, Robert W./126, *Ottawa Journal*, editorial, 123 Bingham, Robert W./127, Speech, English-Speaking Union garden party, 7 August 1936, 123 Bingham, Robert W./130, Department of State Papers.

40. Morgan, *FDR: A Biography*, 442; RWB to Howe, 16 March 1936, RWB to FDR, 19 March 1936, PSF, GB:RWB, FDR Papers; Bingham Diaries, IV, 18 March 1936, insert, RWB-LC.

41. Barry Bingham to RWB, 9 April 1936, RWB to Barry Bingham, 22 April 1936, RWB-LC; FDR to RWB, 4 May 1936, RWB to FDR, 5 May 1936, PSF, GB:RWB, FDR Papers; FDR to Jesse I. Straus, 4 May 1936, Roosevelt, *FDR Letters, 1928–1945*, Vol. I, 585–586.

42. Bell to RWB, 6 September and 6 October 1936, Bingham Diaries, IV, 5 August and 16 September 1936, RWB-LC; FDR to RWB, 14 September 1936, telegram, 123 Bingham, Robert W./132, Department of State Papers; Dallek, *FDR and American Foreign Policy*, 125.

43. *Courier-Journal*, 2, 4, and 5 November 1936; RWB to FDR [November 1936], RWB-LC; RWB to FDR, 13 November 1936, PSF, GB:RWB, FDR Papers.

44. RWB to FDR, 13 November 1936, PSF, GB:RWB, FDR Papers; RWB to Major James S. Iredell, 11 November 1936, RWB to Barry Bingham, 14 December 1936, RWB-LC; FDR to George VI, 19 December 1936, 123 Bingham, Robert W./125, Department of State Papers.

45. *Courier-Journal*, 26 November 1937; *Foreign Relations of the United States, 1936*, Vol. I, 684, 702–703; Nixon, *FDR and Foreign Affairs*, Vol. III, 412–413; Bingham Diaries, IV, 2 December 1936, Sir Evelyn Wrench to RWB, 5 November 1936, RWB to Wrench, 6 November 1936, Roy Howard to RWB, 1 September 1936, RWB to Howard, 9 September 1936, RWB-LC.

46. Bingham Diaries, IV, 19 September and 26 October 1936, RWB to Cordell Hull, 7 April [1936], RWB-LC; Hull to FDR, 1 August 1936, PSF, GB:1933–36, FDR Papers; RWB to Kenneth de Courcy, 6 October 1936, de Courcy to RWB, n.d. [1936], OF 491, FDR to RWB, 27 October 1936, OF 491, FDR Papers; Nixon, *FDR and Foreign Affairs*, Vol. III, 449–452.

47. *London Spectator*, 18 December 1936; *The Times*, 16 December 1936; J. Taylor Peddie to RWB, 17 January 1936, OF 491, FDR Papers; Nixon, *FDR and Foreign Affairs*, Vol. III, 461–462, 484–486, 547–549.

48. Morgan, *FDR: A Biography*, 486; RWB to Shepard Bryan, 15 December 1936, RWB-LC; RWB to FDR, 5 January 1937, PSF, Diplomatic, GB:1937–38, FDR Papers.

49. *New York Times*, 4 May 1937; RWB to Sir John Wilson Taylor, 18 May 1937, RWB to the Spanish ambassador, 22 April 1937, FDR to RWB, 18 June 1937, RWB to FDR, 5 July 1937, RWB-LC.

50. Nixon, *FDR and Foreign Affairs*, Vol. III, 568–569; Offner, *American Appeasement*, 157, 177–179.

51. *The Times*, 29 April and 20 May 1937; Offner, *American Appeasement*, 178, 195–196; Peter Lowe, *Great Britain and the Origins of the Pacific War: A Study in British Policy in East Asia, 1937–1941* (Oxford: Clarendon Press, 1977), 18, 22; RWB to FDR, 5 January 1937, PSF, GB:RWB, RWB to Cordell Hull, 6 July 1937, PSF, Diplomatic, GB:1937–38, FDR Papers; *Foreign Relations of the United States, 1937*, Vol. II (Washington, D.C.: Department of State, 1954), 22–23, 81; RWB to Hull, 30 April 1937, Hull to RWB, 25 September 1937, RWB

to Ulric Bell, 6 April 1937, RWB to William Murray, 11 March 1937, RWB to Lady Reading, 14 October 1937, Robert Boothby to RWB, 11 November 1937, RWB-LC.

52. FDR to RWB, 23 July 1937, RWB to FDR, 11 March and 1 August 1937, RWB-LC; Roosevelt, *FDR Letters, 1928–1945*, Vol. I, 702; RWB to FDR, 12 August 1937, PSF, GB:RWB, FDR Papers.

53. Cordell Hull, *The Memoirs of Cordell Hull*, Vol. I (New York: Macmillan, 1948), 510–512; Dallek, *FDR and American Foreign Policy*, 143; *Foreign Relations of the United States 1937*, Vol. I, 317–318, 342–343; RWB to Hull, 14 July 1937, PSF, Diplomatic, GB:1937–38, FDR Papers; Memorandum for the Secretary of State from FDR, 7 July 1937, PSF, Confidential, State Department:1937–38, FDR Papers.

54. *New York Times*, 20 May 1937.

55. *The Times*, 6 July 1937; *New York Times*, 6 and 7 July 1937; *Louisville Times*, 6 July 1937. No copy of the speech has been found by the author in either the Robert Worth Bingham file of the Department of State Papers, the Roosevelt Library, or the Bingham Papers at the Library of Congress. The accounts of his speech come entirely from newspaper sources.

56. *Louisville Times*, 6 and 7 July 1937; William E. Dodd to Hull, 7 July 1937, 123 Bingham, Robert W./151, Department of State Papers.

57. *Chicago Daily Tribune*, 8 July 1937; "An American Tourist" to RWB, 12 July 1937, William Seymour to RWB, 123 July 1937, John V. Hynes to RWB, 22 July 1937, A. Jukes-Ham to "R. Worthless Bingham," 17 August 1937, M. S. Watts to RWB, 22 August 1937, RWB-LC; Lady Lister Kaye to Hull, 11 August 1937, 123 Bingham, Robert W./155, Department of State Papers.

58. Welles to FDR, 7 July 1937, FDR, Confidential Memorandum, 8 July 1937, PPF 716, FDR Papers; Pierrepont Moffat to Welles, 23 July 1937, 123 Bingham, Robert W./152, Department of State Papers; FDR to RWB, 23 July 1937, RWB-LC.

59. RWB to Jan Masaryk, 6 July 1937, RWB to Jess Pope, 20 August 1937, RWB to F. W. Paul, 2 August 1937, RWB to William E. Chilton, 12 November 1937, RWB to Ralph E. Moreton, 23 July 1937, RWB to Dr. William Rienhoff, Jr., 19 August 1937, RWB to Raymond Buell, 15 July 1937, RWB-LC.

60. *Courier-Journal*, 31 August 1937; *Louisville Times*, 30 August 1937; *The Times*, 15 July, 23 August, 1, 2, and 18 September, 13 October 1937; *New York Times*, 1, 2, and 17 September, 21 October 1937.

61. James Roosevelt to RWB, telegram, 11 October 1937, RWB-LC; RWB to FDR, telegram, 6 October 1937, OF 491, FDR Papers; H. G. Nicholas, *The United States and Britain* (Chicago: University of Chicago Press, 1975), 87.

62. *New York Times*, 9 and 10 December 1937; David E. Koskoff, *Joseph P. Kennedy: A Life and Times* (Englewood Cliffs, N.J.: Prentice-Hall, 1974), 114–115, 512; Cole, *Roosevelt and the Isolationists*, 276; Barry Bingham to FDR, 11

December 1937, PPF 716, FDR Papers; RWB to FDR, 8 December 1937, RWB-LC.

63. *New York Times*, 15, 16, and 19 December 1937; *The Times*, 15 December 1937.

64. *The Times*, 20 December 1937; FDR to Barry Bingham, 22 December 1937, PSF, GB:RWB, FDR Papers.

12

Defining Eleanor, Defining Power: World War II, Racism, and a Preoccupied White House

Allida M. Black

Eleanor Roosevelt disagreed with FDR over the purpose of World War II. While her husband looked to the immediate necessity of defeating European and Asian fascism, she focused on the long-range effects wartime policies would have on the nation's political and social development. Refusing to abandon the New Deal to "Dr. Win the War," she insisted that winning the war was only half the battle. To secure lasting victory, to rendezvous with destiny, America must also win the peace.

More than any other politician in the wartime Roosevelt White House, Eleanor Roosevelt understood the fragile underpinnings of the American home front. The bombing of Pearl Harbor, the ferocious language of Aryan propaganda, and the dramatic appeal of Office of War Information propaganda could unite the nation only for so long before the social fissures deferred by New Deal platitudes would threaten Americans' resolve. Thus, as FDR prepared for war by wooing manufacturers and a reluctant Congress to the benefits of defense production, his wife prepared for war by arguing that wartime policy must balance military preparedness with democratic social and economic policies.

To Eleanor Roosevelt, the New Deal was not a dream to be deferred but an approach with which to fight fascism, expand democracy, and spur economic growth. Repeatedly she argued that the only way to mobilize the nation to fight foreign aggression was to make sure the nation understood how this threat not only jeopardized America's basic interests but also violated democratic ideals. Habitually she asked the public how it could curse Hitler and embrace Jim Crow.

Historians have frequently interpreted Eleanor Roosevelt's commitment to liberal reform during wartime as the result of "conscience" or as a continuation of her role as ombudswoman for the disenfranchised and the downtrodden. While there can be no doubt that Eleanor Roosevelt did prod the nation to accept its democratic and humanitarian responsibilities, there also can be no doubt that such a moral stereotyping of her positions not only discounts the power she tried to wield within the administration but also makes her appear uninterested in pragmatic political realities.

Nothing could be further from the truth. Eleanor Roosevelt was, in the words of Arthur Schlesinger, Jr., a tried and true "political warhorse." She possessed a keen understanding of the steps necessary to implement new policy. She just became increasingly impatient with the excuses offered by officials cowed by propaganda and the domestic crises of wartime. Indeed, as the war progressed and the administration delayed social and economic reform, Eleanor Roosevelt left the White House in 1945 more convinced than ever that for America to flourish, it must address the domestic issues it neglected during wartime.[1]

This chapter will focus on Eleanor Roosevelt's actions on two domestic racial crises the administration confronted during World War II—segregation and internment—and argue that in each instance, Eleanor Roosevelt pressured FDR to change his policy. In attacking Jim Crow, she succeeded somewhat, despite initial setbacks. In the other, internment, she lost the battle and, in the process, lost respect for herself, only to emerge from the war determined never to make the same concession again. Both experiences made her more determined to attack racial injustice and galvanized her outspoken Cold War assault on American complacency.

Eleanor Roosevelt entered the war the unquestioned white champion of African-American civil rights. Her strong influence on the establishment of New Deal programs such as the National Youth Administration (NYA), the Federal Writers' Project, the Federal Theatre Project, the Federal Art Project, Arthurdale and the Homestead Subsistence Division, and numerous WPA projects ensured that African-American interests would at least be given token recognition by the administration. Her consistent intercession on behalf of the NAACP, the National Urban League, Howard University, Bethune Cookman College, the Southern Conference for Human Welfare,

Marian Anderson, the Fair Employment Practices Commission (FEPC), and the National Committee to Abolish the Poll Tax drew such attention that all became major issues in the conservative attack on the New Deal.[2]

Aryanism increased Eleanor Roosevelt's disgust with American racism. By 1939, she decided to attack the hypocritical way in which the nation dealt with racial injustice. She wanted her fellow citizens to understand how their guilt in "writing and speaking about democracy and the American way without consideration of the imperfections within our system with regard to its treatment . . . of the Negro" encouraged racism. Americans, she told Ralph Bunche in an interview for Gunnar Myrdal's *American Dilemma*, wanted to talk "only about the good features of American life and to hide our problems like skeletons in the closet." Such withdrawal only fueled violent responses; Americans must therefore recognize "the real intensity of feeling" and "the amount of intimidation and terrorization" racism promotes and act against such "ridiculous" behavior.[3]

By the early 1940s Eleanor Roosevelt firmly believed civil rights were the real litmus test for American democracy. Thus, she declared over and over again throughout the war, there could be no democracy in the United States that did not include democracy for blacks. In *The Moral Basis of Democracy* she asserted that people of all races have inviolate rights to "some property." Continually she insisted that education, housing, and employment were basic human rights that society had both a moral and a political obligation to provide for its citizens. The government must not only provide protection against discrimination but also develop policies that create a level economic playing field. In making clear exactly what she meant, Eleanor Roosevelt explained: "This means achieving an economic level below which no one is permitted to fall, and keeping a fairly stable balance between that level and the standard of living."[4]

When white America refused to see how segregation mocked American values, Eleanor Roosevelt addressed this issue sternly and directly: "We have never been willing to face this problem, to line it up with the basic, underlying beliefs in Democracy." Racial prejudice enslaved blacks; consequently, "no one can claim that . . . the Negroes of this country are free." She continued this theme in a 1942 article in the *New Republic*, declaring that both the private and the public sector must acknowledge that "one of the main destroyers of freedom is our attitude toward the colored race." "What Kipling called 'The White Man's Burden,' " she proclaimed in the *American Magazine*, is "one of the things we can not have any longer." Furthermore, she told those listening to the radio broadcast of the 1945

National Democratic Forum, "democracy may grow or fade as we face [this] problem."[5]

Eleanor Roosevelt realized that rhetoric alone did little to ease the pain African Americans encountered on a daily basis, and she tried very hard to understand the depths of African-American anger. "If I were a Negro today, I think I would have moments of great bitterness," she confessed to readers of *Negro Digest*. "It would be hard for me to sustain my faith in democracy and to build up a sense of goodwill toward men of other races." This empathic response underpinned her appreciation of African-American rage. Nevertheless, she cautioned African Americans against letting their anger go unchecked. The war was not the time to explode in hot-tempered righteous indignation, just as it was not the time to yield in quick defeat. Eleanor Roosevelt did not deny the validity of anger; rather, she saw it as a powerful tool that should empower reform. It should not be dissipated in defeat because "there now remains much work to be done to see that freedom becomes a fact and not just a promise for [the Negro] people."[6]

However, just as African Americans should be wary of promises, Eleanor Roosevelt cautioned all Americans to be suspicious of those social reformers who preach tolerance. She believed that "we must . . . take the word 'tolerance' out of our vocabulary and substitute for it the precept live and let live, cooperate in work and play and like our neighbors." "The problem is not to learn tolerance of your neighbors," she lectured to those who promoted complacency and defended the social status quo, "but to see that all alike have hope and opportunity and that the community as a whole moves forward." She minced no words responding to those critics who argued that her policies would destroy the moral fiber of the nation. They had it backward. Make no mistake about it, Eleanor Roosevelt retorted. Refusing to address racial justice in a conscientious manner would kill the nation. As she told a nationwide radio audience in late 1944, America must not neglect justice where race is concerned, because to do so would be denying its heritage, tainting its future, and succumbing to the law of the jungle.[7]

When Eleanor Roosevelt dared during the war to equate American racism with fascism and argued that to ignore the evils of segregation would be capitulating to Aryanism, hostility toward her reached an all-time high. Newspapers from Chicago to Louisiana to New York covered the dispute and citizens pleaded with J. Edgar Hoover to silence her. Typical of such outrage is the argument presented by one irate American who accused her of "deliberately aiding and abetting the enemy abroad by fermenting racial troubles at home." Trying to turn the allegations of fascist behavior back onto the first lady, the author labeled the *Negro Digest* a publication dedicated to promoting Communist-inspired racial propaganda and proclaimed Mrs. Roosevelt guilty by association. The vast majority of the *"loyal* American population . . . are not afraid to express . . . their honest opinion that the wife of our nation's President and Commander-in-Chief heads the list [of enemies]." Although she professed "to speak as a private citizen," if any other private citizen expressed her opinions, "all loyal Americans would name her a traitor." Moreover, Eleanor Roosevelt's statements on behalf of black Americans "are calculated to arouse distrust and suspicion between the white and negro race here in the United States." Outraged that "white citizens of the United States have sacrificed their careers" to advance the stature of blacks, he predicted that if Mrs. Roosevelt were not silenced, veterans would come home "only to return to find the Roosevelts and the negroes in complete charge of our so-called 'democracy' they fought to save." Moreover, she not only damaged American morale but encouraged the Axis powers to think the nation weak. "Can you wonder that the Germans and Reds are laughing up their sleeves at us?" he concluded.[8]

Even those Americans professing to support economic equality for blacks objected to Eleanor Roosevelt's positions. For example, Frank McAllister, a socialist who sat on the Southern Conference for Human Welfare board with her, was so jealous of Mrs. Roosevelt's influence within the conference that he spread rumors that she was having an affair with Paul Robeson (and therefore was nothing more than a closet Communist) as part of his efforts to undermine her stature.[9]

Nothing could prepare the administration, however, for the venomous attacks Eleanor Roosevelt received throughout 1943 after she continued to argue that black defense workers should be allowed to occupy federally constructed housing units in Detroit. She argued unsuccessfully within the administration that the critical housing shortage could be used as a cover for slum clearance, that the housing constructed should last longer than the war, and that proper planning could produce integrated neighborhoods. Opposed by Charles Palmer, who coordinated the federal housing program, Eleanor Roosevelt watched as Congress stripped slum clearance from its housing appropriations bill. Then she encouraged Clark Foreman's plan to divert some housing funds to the Sojourner Truth Project in Detroit. Outraged that their neighborhood could be integrated against their will, Polish neighbors of Sojourner Truth appealed to their congressman to stop the plan. Representative Rudolph Tenerowicz labeled the African-American tenants "Communist pawns" and then had a rider attached to the appropriations bill declaring that "no money would be released unless that 'nigger lover'

[Foreman] was fired and the project returned to white occupancy." The Federal Works Agency capitulated, forced Foreman out, and stopped recruiting African-American tenants.[10]

Eleanor Roosevelt then appealed to the president on behalf of the civil rights leaders who requested her intercession. Arguing that the African-American tenants had support from a variety of leading white politicians, such as Mayor Edward Jeffries, Walter Reuther, and other United Auto Workers officials, she convinced the president to reverse the whites-only policy. By the end of February 1942, FDR yielded and two dozen African-American families, accompanied by 300 African-American supporters, prepared to move into the project, only to be met by cross burnings and a crowd of 700 armed white resisters. The families turned back, the police arrested 104 rioters, and, after a series of compromises failed, the city delayed occupancy for over a year.

In April 1943, the city of Detroit, supported by the White House and 800 state police, moved the African-American families into their new homes. Within two months, tensions boiled over as fights broke out between African Americans and whites seeking refuge from the summer heat at Belle Isle, the amusement park located on an island in the Detroit River. As rumors flooded the housing districts adjacent to Sojourner Truth, sporadic outbreaks of violence coalesced into a sustained, brutal riot on June 21. Twenty-five African Americans and nine whites died. The week before, Eleanor Roosevelt had returned to Washington from Chicago, where she met with a predominantly African-American crowd distraught over the race riot that had closed the Addsco shipyard in Mobile, Alabama, three weeks earlier. She used her speech as a plea for racial cooperation. When White House aides told her of the Detroit uprising, she mourned the deaths but was not surprised. She later wrote to Trude Pratt (Lash), "Detroit never should have happened, but when Congress behaves as it does why should others be calmer?"[11]

The country was stunned, and many held Eleanor Roosevelt responsible. One Detroit resident told the FBI the first lady had "done more to agitate the whites and over-encourage the negroes . . . than any other single group outside of the Communists in the United States." Another wrote to FDR that his wife and the mayor encouraged the outbreak by "their coddling of the negroes." The Southern press abandoned all decorum. "It is blood on your hands, Mrs. Roosevelt," the *Jackson Daily News* pronounced the day after the riot. "You have been personally proclaiming and practicing social equality at the White House. . . . What followed is now history." By August, the White House, concerned that her positions were too damaging to the president, began its own counteroffensive. As Henry Wallace and Gardner Jackson later recalled, "Mrs. R . . . was ordered to go [to New Zealand]" because "the Negro situation was too hot." Although she had long wanted to visit the troops, she understood why the administration suddenly honored her request. "I suppose when one is being forced to realize that an unwelcome change is coming, one must blame it on someone or something."[12]

Although her tour of the South Pacific got Eleanor Roosevelt out of the country, it did nothing to deter her commitment to racial justice at home. Haunted by her visits with soldiers on bases, in hospitals, and in battle zones, she obsessed over how to honor their sacrifices. More and more she referred to the prayer she had carried with her. "Dear Lord, Lest I continue my complacent way, help me to remember, somewhere out there a man died for me today. As long as there be war, I must ask and answer am I worth dying for?" She confessed to a friend that her visit with the troops filled her with "a sense of obligation which I can never discharge."[13]

Thus, she accepted the CIO's invitation to host the opening of their canteen in Washington in February 1944. When the wire services carried photographs of a smiling Eleanor Roosevelt serving refreshments to a crowd of African-American soldiers and white hostesses, the furor over her racial policies resurfaced. Typical of this reaction is the caption the *Greensboro Watchman* placed under the photo—"This is Mrs. Roosevelt at the CIO canteen party in Washington as she served negroes along with whites, and joined in singing love songs as negro men danced with white girls." Letters poured into the White House objecting to her participation, and newspapers from Tampa to Houston to Memphis editorialized against her conduct.[14]

Furthermore, throughout the 1944 campaign, Republicans capitalized on this fear and spread allegations that Eleanor Roosevelt "advocated intermarriage of the negro with the whites." To one columnist, her "innocent, wholehearted, humane enthusiasms" were "only a disguise" for "some scheme containing the most binding elements of Communism and Hitlerism." And the *Alabama Sun* devoted an entire issue to "Eleanor Demands Equality for Negroes in Address" and featured numerous photographs under the caption "Eleanor and Some More Niggers."[15]

With such criticism escalating as the war drew to a close, Eleanor Roosevelt's warnings about the future increased. Worried that an uncertain postwar economy would exacerbate white racism and that a refusal to recognize the contributions of African-American veterans would encourage African-American distrust of whites, she urged America to recognize that racial injustice was the biggest threat to American democracy. The United States must "stop generalizing about people" and recognize stereotypes as racist propaganda. "If we really believe in Democracy," Eleanor Roosevelt said to African-American and white audiences throughout 1945, "we must face the fact that equality of opportunity is basic" and that grievances expressed by African-Americans were "legitimate." We have expected [the Negroes] to be good citizens and . . . we haven't given them an opportunity to take part in our government." Refusing to concede to her opponents, she asserted that if the nation continued to honor Jim Crow, America would have defeated fascism abroad only to defend racism at home.[16]

Eleanor Roosevelt said the same things in private that she did in public. Whether interceding with the president for Walter White, Mary McLeod Bethune, A. Philip Randolph, or W.E.B. Du Bois; raising money for Howard University or Bethune Cookman College; investigating discrimination that African-American women encountered while stationed at the Women's Auxiliary Army Corps base in Des Moines, Iowa; pressing the FEPC to investigate complaints; or supporting antisegregation campaigns and antilynching legislation, she pressed to keep civil rights issues at the top of the domestic political agenda.[17]

Nor did Eleanor Roosevelt limit her energy to confronting national problems. Frequently an individual who had been unjustly treated prompted effort equal to that she expended on a more widespread problem. Throughout the New Deal and war years, she acted as both a spokesperson and a lobbyist for tenant farmers and African-American sharecroppers. Whether working within the administration with Will Alexander on Farm Security Administration issues or Harry Hopkins or Aubrey Williams on WPA, NYA, and Subsistence Homestead projects, Eleanor Roosevelt strove to force the administration to recognize that Jim Crow and the depression often combined to give a knockout punch to Southern African-American farmers. Outside the White House, she tried to mobilize support for sharecroppers by discussing their problems in her speeches, columns, and articles; actively supporting the Southern Tenant Farmers' Union; meeting with small groups of individual sharecroppers to discuss their plight and review their suggestions for reform; and sponsoring National Sharecroppers Week.[18]

When Randolph, Bethune, and Pauli Murray, a young African-American woman with whom Eleanor Roosevelt developed a friendship grounded in "confrontation by typewriter," informed her that sharecropper Odell Waller had been sentenced to death by a jury from which African Americans had been deliberately excluded, Eleanor Roosevelt's efforts reached new heights. She launched a one-woman campaign within the White House to commute Waller's sentence. She wrote and telephoned Virginia Governor Clement Darden to plead Waller's case, and forced FDR to follow up on her request with his own call to Darden. At the same time, she met with Waller's supporters, discussed his plight in her column, contributed to his defense fund, and advised his defense committee. When readers challenged her stance, she dismissed their objections bluntly: "Times without number Negro men have been lynched or gone to their death without due process of law. No one questions Waller's guilt, but they question the system which led to it."[19] After all other efforts on Waller's behalf failed, Eleanor Roosevelt still refused to concede defeat, and on the day of his scheduled electrocution, she repeatedly interrupted FDR's war planning meeting with Harry Hopkins until the president took her call and refused her plea for further intervention. Two hours before the sharecropper was to die in the electric chair, a dejected Eleanor Roosevelt phoned A. Philip Randolph at NAACP headquarters. As Waller's supporters listened to her over five extensions, in a trembling voice she told Randolph: "I have done everything I can possibly do. I have interrupted the President . . . I am so sorry, Mr. Randolph, I can't do any more."[20]

Although Waller was executed, the intensity of her efforts on his behalf solidified Eleanor Roosevelt's ties with civil rights leaders. Thus, despite Randolph's increasing frustration with FDR's reluctance to enforce fair employment policies, he could urge a national conference of African-American leaders to pursue a dual strategy of nonviolent direct action and working with Eleanor Roosevelt. The NAACP agreed. Walter White knew that when he phoned Mrs. Roosevelt before the 1944 Democratic National Convention to warn that African Americans might vote Republican if a strong civil rights plank were not adopted, she would not discount his analysis. In fact, she repeatedly tried to obtain an audience for White with either the president or Democratic National Committee chair Robert Hannegan. Consequently, despite FDR's thinly disguised disregard for the NAACP and the unwillingness he showed in responding to its requests, Walter White encountered no opposition when he recommended that Eleanor Roosevelt join the NAACP board of directors.[21]

Racial antagonism toward Japanese Americans proved a much more difficult and painful obstacle to confront. Eleanor Roosevelt was not as true to her convictions when the civil liberties of Japanese Americans were at stake. Indeed, her actions on this issue reflect how conflicted she felt when FDR authorized policies that treated all members of the same ethnic group as potential enemy aliens. At first, she responded in her usual fashion—press conferences, speeches, and photo opportunities. Yet, after such an immediate endorsement of the loyalty of the Japanese-American population, a strange silence overtook her. In glaring contrast to the numerous other controversial issues that she attacked during the war, such as her intercession on behalf of Jewish refugees, there is no paper trail to follow to reconstruct Eleanor Roosevelt's changing actions on internment. In fact, the dearth of evidence indicates the extent to which she felt constrained. Perhaps she and FDR never found common ground and, frustrated by his decision to defer reform, she resented the restrictions his war policies placed on her actions.[22]

What is clear is that at the beginning of the war, Eleanor and Franklin Roosevelt held opposite views on the rights of Japanese Americans. Less than a week after Pearl Harbor was bombed, Eleanor Roosevelt toured the West Coast; praised a plea for racial tolerance by Mayor Harry Cain of Tacoma, Washington; posed with Japanese Americans for photographs that would be distributed over the Associated Press wire service; and spoke out against retribution. Respecting the rights of Japanese Americans, she told readers of the column "My Day," "is perhaps the greatest test this country has ever met." "If we cannot meet the challenge of fairness to our citizens of every nationality," Americans will have "removed from the world the real hope for the future." FDR, on the other hand, determined to capitalize on the procedures he utilized to monitor his critics throughout the 1930s, immediately summoned aides to discuss the wholesale detention of Japanese Americans and German Americans.[23]

Eleanor Roosevelt never considered internment anything but an "absurd" and "vicious" policy. She thought the treatment Japanese Americans received in 1941 "pathetic," and the attack on Pearl Harbor did not change her mind. These people "are good Americans," she told FDR, "and have the right to live as anyone else."

Moreover, the policy would be countereffective. "Being bitter against an American, because of the actions of the country of his predecessors, does not make for unity and the winning of the war." Thus, when Yaemitsu Sugimachi offered a less dramatic proposal "for dealing with alien Japanese in wartime," she forwarded his plan to Attorney General Francis Biddle, and when Sam Hohri, press agent for the Japanese American Citizens League, told her that the San Francisco chapter of the Red Cross refused offers of aid from Japanese Americans "on the grounds that we might poison the medicines or bandages, treat knitted goods to injure the wearer, and deliberately sabotage its work," she appealed to the organization's national president to overturn the chapter's policy.

Eleanor Roosevelt wanted to prevent the evacuation. She worked closely with Attorney General Francis Biddle to ensure, first, that she understood how the Constitution applied to internment and, second, that the Justice

Department presented a strong case against the policy to FDR. Furthermore, since she was a faithful supporter of the American Civil Liberties Union (ACLU) as well as a close friend of its director, Roger Baldwin, she probably participated in at least a few off-the-record conversations with him on the issue the ACLU called "the worst single wholesale violation of civil rights of American citizens in our history."[24]

However, once FDR signed Executive Order 9066 and internment began, Eleanor Roosevelt fell silent. Although neither she nor the president left any record of their conversations on internment, it is safe to assume that FDR presented the same case supporting internment to his wife that he presented to her ally, the attorney general. Convinced that internment was a military necessity, which superseded constitutional protections, FDR made it painstakingly clear to Biddle and other Justice Department officials that he would tolerate no opposition to this policy. Uncomfortable with the policy, Eleanor Roosevelt nevertheless refused to continue to challenge it. She replaced the righteous indignation that characterized earlier "My Day" discussions of internment with oblique references to Japanese-American patience and patriotism. By late March of 1942, she ruefully conceded that "unfortunately in a time of war many innocent people must suffer hardships to safeguard the nation." The president won the first round.[25]

Once the relocation of Japanese Americans began, Eleanor Roosevelt tried to ease her conscience in many quiet ways. She told the *Washington Star*, "The biggest obligation we have today is to prove that in a time of stress we can still live up to our beliefs and maintain the civil liberties we have established as the rights of human beings everywhere." She increasingly linked the civil rights of African Americans to those of Asian Americans in her speeches and columns. Unable to remain aloof, she decided to act behind the scenes by monitoring evacuation procedures, intervening to keep families together, and interceding with War Relocation Authority (WRA) personnel on behalf of those few noninterned Japanese Americans who protested the treatment their relatives received in the camps. When she learned that the former assistant director of the Oriental Section of the Library of Congress, Dr. Shio Sakanishi, had been detained without having charges brought against her, Eleanor Roosevelt asked Biddle "to tell her whether the Naval Intelligence had anything" on the librarian. When internees of the Harmony Camp wrote to her, decrying their accommodations, she pushed the WRA to investigate its housing. And when a young Californian suggested that consumer cooperatives be established within the resettlement area, an intrigued Eleanor Roosevelt encouraged WRA official Milton Eisenhower to give the proposal serious consideration.[26]

The WRA was not the only organization to feel Eleanor Roosevelt's pressure. She prodded the Justice Department to investigate claims of employment discrimination and retributive violence against Japanese-American fishermen. When interned women who had cleared the FBI background checks asked her assistance in enlisting in the Women's Army Auxiliary Corps, she quickly wrote to Colonel Oveta Culp Hobby, interceding on their behalf. Moreover, when Hungwai Ching told her during a White House meeting of the attack against Japanese-American soldiers stationed in Shelby, Mississippi, Eleanor Roosevelt not only pushed FDR to act but also encouraged General George Marshall to investigate the assault, transfer the soldiers to a safer base, and send her "a report on this situation."[27]

Eleanor Roosevelt waited until late 1943 to address internment publicly. By then the vast majority of the Japanese-American population had been removed from the West Coast, and those interned in the Poston, Arizona, and Manzanar, California, camps had either struck or rioted to protest their incarceration. A concerned Harold Ickes wrote to FDR that the situation demanded attention and argued that the president must no longer "disregard the unnecessary creation of a hostile group right in our own territory." Although Eleanor Roosevelt had wanted to visit the camps in the fall of 1942, it was not until FDR, on receipt of Ickes telegram—worried that his interior secretary might be right—asked her to visit the Gila River camp on her way home from her Phoenix vacation. She agreed and, after the disturbances were squelched and tempers were calmed, announced that she would inspect the camps and report her findings to the nation.[28]

Yet instead of discussing the psychological and political climate of the camps, she wrote glowing accounts of the internees' attempts to beautify their small plots of land. She also avoided discussing the concerns about racism and resettlement the internees raised during her meeting with them. She tempered her discussion of the efforts the internees made to "take part in the war effort" with the reassurance that their "loyalty" must be authenticated by both the FBI and the WRA before they could begin work. Given her previous statements, this deliberate evasion of civil liberties stands out as a glaring omission.[29]

Despite this momentary lapse into public acquiescence, a decidedly anguished tone resonates through Eleanor Roosevelt's other depictions of internment life. The night she left the Gila River camp, she confided to a friend that she had "just asked FDR if I could take on an American-Japanese family," only to have him evade her request by rationalizing that "the Secret Service wouldn't allow it." This evasiveness hurt and haunted her. No matter how loyal she tried to be in her defense of the administration's internment policy, no matter how many times she stated that "the whole job of handling our Japanese has, on the whole, been done well," she could not temper her belief that security was not the sole motivation. Suspicion of Japanese in America increased because one region "feared [them] as competitors" while the rest of the nation "knew so little and cared so little about them that they did not even think about the principle that we in the country believe in: that of equal rights for all human beings."[30]

Moreover, when Eleanor Roosevelt tried to present the administration's case that loyal Japanese Americans were interned for their own protection, as hard as she tried, she could not completely suppress her own doubts about this argument. For example, when she tried to justify the administration's demands for immediate relocation and the "unexpected [economic] problems" this caused Japanese-American property owners by arguing that "an effort was made to deal with [their financial holdings] fairly," she introduced as many arguments questioning this statement as she did endorsing it. Finally, she lambasted those West Coast xenophobes who believed that "a Japanese is always a Japanese" by declaring that such "unreasonable" bigotry "leads nowhere and solves nothing." Consequently, despite her endorsement of the policy, Eleanor Roosevelt could never completely convince herself that internment was either morally or strategically justifiable. As she confessed to a wounded Japanese-American soldier who asked her to help expedite his parents' request for citizenship, "War makes far too much bitterness for people to be reasonable."[31]

Why Eleanor Roosevelt acquiesced in her husband's probable demand that she be silent on such issues as internment of the Japanese Americans will never be known. Perhaps she kept quiet in public so that she could be more effective in modifying the policy within the administration. Or maybe she knew that this was one time when FDR would not tolerate any deviation from his position. Or possibly she temporarily convinced herself that the suspension of Japanese-Americans' civil liberties actually protected them from xenophobic violence. Or maybe she combined the best aspects of each of the above reasons to rationalize her behavior. Or perhaps she chose to give other critical domestic issues—racial violence, labor unrest, and postwar economic planning—higher priority.

Unquestionably, Eleanor Roosevelt equivocated on the civil rights and civil liberties of Japanese Americans during the war. But it is also very apparent that she could not completely abandon her conscience and deny her convictions. Stark images reflecting her guilt surfaced in her public and private writings. She confessed to the nation that she could "not bear to think of children behind barbed wire looking out at the free world," and she confided to her friend Flora Rose that "this is just one more reason for hating war—innocent people suffer for the few guilty ones." Tormented by the policy, she conceded that "we must build up their loyalty, not tear it down." Thus, she promoted dissent and criticism as diligently as she dared. For example, when Secretary of War Henry Stimson refused quick response to a November 1943 request by Dillon Meyer, director of the WRA, to relax enlistment standards against interned Issei, Eleanor Roosevelt joined ranks with Meyer and Ickes to advocate closing the camps and proposed "a massive public education campaign to reiterate American commitment to democracy." Refusing to change course, FDR rejected her plan summarily, saying simply, "It would be a mistake to do anything so drastic." Yet by this time, Eleanor Roosevelt no longer deferred to his priorities. She corresponded with her "dear" friend Judge William Dennan of the U.S. Circuit Court of Appeals regarding his dissents in the *Hirabayashi* and *Korematsu* cases and carefully read the briefs he sent her, noting in the margins, "Thanks. I get it."[32]

What is striking about Eleanor Roosevelt's decision to support those whom the administration considered suspect patriots is, first, that in assuming such a position, she deliberately opposed her husband during the most crisis-ridden period of his administration and, second, that she refused to discount the hypocrisy inherent in her complicity with FDR's racist restrictions. She chastised herself when she chided Americans who divorced the rights of the Japanese Americans from their own rights and liberties. Reminding readers that a principle was only as effective as its practice, she subtly asked her fellow Americans to recognize that their rights would be protected only when they defended the rights of others. "We retain the right to lead our individual lives as we please, but we can only do so if we wish to grant to others the freedoms that we wish for ourselves." Many interned Japanese Americans intuited the anxiety Eleanor Roosevelt felt and continued, like their African-American compatriots, to keep faith with the first lady, even though she had not completely kept faith with them. At no time was this respect more clearly demonstrated than when Togo Tanaka, the organizer of the protest that rocked the Manzanar camp, named his first child after her.[33]

Clearly, Eleanor Roosevelt did not speak out as forcefully and as continuously on behalf of wartime civil rights and civil liberties for all races and ethnic groups as she would in the postwar era. But it is also clear that her decision to challenge FDR during the war set the precedent for her more outspoken defense of civil rights and civil liberties during the Cold War. In an early draft of an article FDR eventually overruled, she blatantly conceded that "to undo our mistakes is always harder than not to create them originally—but we seldom have the foresight and therefore we have no choice but to correct our past mistakes."[34]

The horrors of war appalled Eleanor Roosevelt. But she was equally repulsed by the ease with which the majority of Americans succumbed to racial stereotyping and political complacency. And she regretted her compliance with policies promoting such behavior. Thus, when she no longer had to defer to the constraints of the White House, the first organizations she joined, such as the NAACP, were those dedicated to civil rights; the first speeches she gave addressed racial restrictions in housing, education, and employment; and the first commissions she chaired investigated white-on-black violence, lynching, and racially biased court proceedings. And she used her column, lecture tour, and political contacts to press the Truman administration to do what her husband's staff had refused to address. She told a *New York Times* reporter who questioned her activism, "For the sake of our Souls we should live up to the way of doing things that we believe is the right and civilized thing to do."[35]

There were limits to Eleanor Roosevelt's power within the White House. Her insistence that the administration address the problems that African Americans and Japanese Americans confronted alienated many of FDR's key aides. Jonathan Daniels later admitted that while she "did a lot of good," she really was a "hair shirt" to the administration and was always complicating policy by "bringing a hell of a lot of cats and dogs" into the discussion. Thus, from the early days of the war until FDR's death, Daniels and other aides worked to keep Eleanor away from the president. She recognized this ploy but refused to give ground. Thus, the changes in policy she was able to achieve—limited intercession for Odell Waller, African-American occupancy of the Sojourner Truth housing project, protection of Japanese-American soldiers—must be assessed in light of the limited influence and power she had within the administration. With that constraint, her diligence made her more than Daniels' hair shirt or Schlesinger's political warhorse. She was more like a Sherman tank.[36]

NOTES

1. Interview with Arthur Schlesinger, Jr., June 24, 1994.

2. Allida Black, *Casting Her Own Shadow: Eleanor Roosevelt and the Shaping of Postwar Liberalism* (New York: Columbia University Press, 1996), 23–49, 88–96.

3. Ralph J. Bunche, "Memo on Interview with Mrs. Franklin D. Roosevelt at the White House, May 15, 1940," Myrdal Study, Senate Interview File, Ralph J.

Bunche papers, special collections, UCLA Library. See also Bunche, "Memorandum presenting suggestive notes on 'The Negro Worker and the Struggle for Economic Justice,' " prepared for Miss Thompson, attached to Ralph J. Bunche to Malvina Thompson, September 11, 1940, personal property of Ben Keppel of UCLA.

4. Eleanor Roosevelt, *The Moral Basis of Democracy* (New York: Howell, Soskin, 1940), 43, 50.

5. "The Issue Is Freedom," *New Republic* 107 (August 3, 1942): 147–148; draft, "What Are We Fighting For?" *American Magazine* (July 1942); "Broadcast, National Democratic Forum," February 24, 1945, Speech and Article File, Anna Eleanor Roosevelt [hereafter AER] papers, Franklin D. Roosevelt Library, Hyde Park, N.Y.

6. Eleanor Roosevelt, "Freedom: Promise or Fact," *Negro Digest* (October 1943): 8–9.

7. Eleanor Roosevelt, "Tolerance," attached to George Bye to Eleanor Roosevelt, February 27, 1945, and "Building for Peace," Speech and Article File, AER papers.

8. For representative press coverage of the article, see UPI release, dateline Chicago, October 11, 1943; Doxey Wilkerson "If She Were a Negro," *Daily Worker*, October 20, 1943; "First Lady Urges Negroes to Fight for Full Equality," *Louisiana Weekly*, October 2, 1943; letter to J. Edgar Hoover, re Mrs. Roosevelt's article "If I Were a Negro," October 13, 1943, FBI file #100-0-19681, [hereafter FOIA (Freedom of Information Act)] request.

9. "Race Riots," n.d., Record Group 44-802-167, FBI Files, FOIA request by author.

10. John Morton Blum, *V Was for Victory* (New York: Harcourt Brace Jovanovich, 1975), 200–201; and Doris Kearns Goodwin, *No Ordinary Time: Franklin and Eleanor Roosevelt and the Homefront in World War II* (New York: Simon and Schuster, 1994), 326–327.

11. Blum, *V Was for Victory*, 202–203; Goodwin, *No Ordinary Time*, 444; ER to Trude Pratt (Lash), June 28, 1943, [hereafter JPL (Joseph P. Lash Papers, Franklin D. Roosevelt Library, Hyde Park, N.Y.)] papers.

12. *Jackson Daily News*, June 22, 1943; "The Reminiscences of Virginia Durr," February 6, 1990, Southern Historical Collection, University of North Carolina [hereafter SHC]; "The Reminiscences of Henry A. Wallace," August 28, 1943, ORHO (Oral Research History Office, Columbia University); and ER to Josephus Daniels, July 23, 1943, AER papers.

13. Joseph P. Lash, *Eleanor and Franklin* (New York: W. W. Norton, 1972), 654; ER to Doris Fleeson, October 4, 1943, AER papers.

14. See folder 190.1, Criticism of the Negro Question, AER papers.

15. Pearl D. Burnette to Eleanor Roosevelt, November 10, 1944, General Correspondence, AER papers; Alfred Steinberg, *Mrs. R: The Life of Eleanor Roosevelt* (New York: G. P. Putnam and Sons, 1958), 303; Carl Sferrazza An-

thony, *First Ladies* (New York: William Morrow, 1990), 506; and *Alabama Sun*, April 28, 1944.

16. Eleanor Roosevelt, "For the Joint Commission on Social Reconstruction," October 1945, and "The Minorities Problem," attached to William Scarlett to Eleanor Roosevelt, March 19, 1946, Speech and Article File, AER papers; Eleanor Roosevelt, untitled radio address, August 16, 1943, Speech and Article File, and Audio Tape File, AER papers.

17. For her interventions on behalf of Walter White, see the Walter White folders, 1935–1945, General Correspondence, AER papers; for Mary McLeod Bethune [MMB], see Mary McLeod Bethune to Eleanor Roosevelt, November 22, 1941, and ER's response of November 27, 1941, and MMB to Malvina Thompson, March 18, 1943, Correspondence with Government Officials, AER papers; for A. Philip Randolph and Odell Waller, see Allida Black, "A Reluctant but Persistent Warrior: Eleanor Roosevelt and the Early Civil Rights Movement" in Jacqueline Rouse et al., eds., *Women in the Civil Rights Movement: Trailblazers and Torchbearers* (Brooklyn, N.Y.: Carlson, 1990). For military camps, see John A. Lapp to ER, August 12, 1942, Malvina Thompson to MMB, n.d., and MMB's reply, August 29, 1942, General Correspondence, AER papers; Bunche, "Memorandum."

18. Pauli Murray, *Song in a Weary Throat* (New York: Harper and Row, 1988), chs. 13–14; Pauli Murray interview by Dr. Thomas Scopes, February 3, 1978, transcript, EROHP (Eleanor Roosevelt Oral History Project, Franklin D. Roosevelt Library, Hyde Park, N.Y.); Clark Foreman, "The Decade of Hope," in *The Negro in Depression and War*, edited by Berhard Sternsher (Chicago: Quadrangle Books, 1969), 150–166; Eleanor Roosevelt to Pauli Murray and Murray's responses, 1940, 1941, 1942 folders, General Correspondence, AER papers; Kate Hubell to "Dear Friend," February 27, 1941, FBI file N 100-14597-0, FOIA request by author; Sylvia Bethscher to "Dear Friend," November 19, 1942, FBI file 100-135-53-44, FOIA request; and Guy Hottel to J. Edgar Hoover, April 3, 1943, National Committee to Abolish the Poll Tax File, FOIA request.

19. ER to Governor Darden, June 2 and 22, 1942, and his response, June 23, 1942, AER papers; Murray interview; Murray, *Song in a Weary Throat*, chs. 13–14; Eleanor Roosevelt to A. M. Kroeger, August 20, 1942, Personal Correspondence, AER papers; Memorandum on the Waller Case, Group II B 54, Odell Waller—1941, NAACP papers Manuscript Division, Library of Congress, Washington, D.C.; "Urge Roosevelt to Fix Waller's Fate," *New York Times*, July 2, 1941; "Darden Rules Waller Must Die," *New York Times*, July 1, 1941; "The Case of Odell Waller," a memorandum prepared by the Workers Defense League, Group II B Legal File B54, Odell Waller folder, 1942, NAACP papers.

20. Murray, *Song in a Weary Throat*, 173; Black, "Reluctant but Persistent Warrior."

21. A. Philip Randolph source, FBI files, April 19, 1944, clipping from Baltimore conference. Evidence of FDR's reluctance to praise NAACP actions can be

found in the note attached to Franklin D. Roosevelt to Arthur P. Spingarn, October 1, 1943, President's Personal File [hereafter PPF], Franklin D. Roosevelt [hereafter FDR] papers, FDR Library, Hyde Park, N.Y. "Miss Tully brought this in. Says the President doesn't think too much of this organization—not to be to[o] fulsome—tone it down a bit." Lash, *Eleanor and Franklin*, 709.

22. The written record of Eleanor Roosevelt's intervention on behalf of European and American Jews is spotty. Nevertheless, it does show the beginnings of a pattern of action. Before the war she served as a conduit between those urging relaxed immigration policies. She supported her friend Caroline O'Day's 1939 telegram to FDR urging legislation to admit refugee children and served as an honorary chair of the Non-Sectarian Committee for Refugee Children. During the lend-lease negotiations of 1940, she urged FDR to force Churchill to release British Ghana from the empire so that it could be used as a haven for Jewish refugees. And it is safe to assume that she had conversations regarding anti-Semitism with Rabbi Stephen Wise and her close friend Elinor Morgenthau. See Caroline O'Day to FDR, President's Secretary's File, Eleanor Roosevelt, 1939, FDR Papers; Official Files, Refugees, FDR papers; ER to FDR, February 22, 1939, and FDR's reply, Official File 200-MMM; FDR to ER, May 4, 1940, and Sumner Welles to FDR, May 6, 1940, President's Secretary's File, Eleanor Roosevelt, 1940.

23. "Mrs. Roosevelt Greeting American Born Japanese," *New York Times*, December 15, 1941; Francis Biddle, *In Brief Authority* (Garden City, N.Y.: Doubleday, 1962), 214; Eleanor Roosevelt, "My Day," December 15, 1941, My Day Drafts, AER papers.

24. Yet the ACLU's record at this time was not much better than Mrs. Roosevelt's. Eleanor Roosevelt to Francis Biddle, November 5, 1941, and his response, December 5, 1941; ER to Biddle, January 2, 1942, and his response, January 3, 1942; ER to Biddle, February 25, 1942; Secretary to Mrs. Roosevelt to Francis Biddle, March 3, 1942; and ER to Biddle, May 8, 1942, and his response, May 5, 1942, all in Correspondence with Government Officials, AER papers; Steinberg, *Mrs. R.*, 283–284; and pamphlet, American Civil Liberties Union, "Freedom in Wartime," Washington, D.C., 1943, author copy.

25. Biddle, *Brief Authority*, 219; Peter Irons, *Justice at War: The Inside Story of the Japanese American Internment* (New York: Oxford University Press, 1983); Roger Daniels, *The Decision to Relocate the Japanese Americans* (Melbourne, Fla.: Kreiger, 1981).

26. Secretary to Mrs. Roosevelt to Mrs. Clark, January 5, 1944, AER Papers; Janet Fukushima to ER, November 13, 1943, General Correspondence, AER papers; ER to Oveta Culp Hobby, May 6, 1943, Correspondence with Government Officials, AER papers; ER to George Marshall, May 24, 1943, and FDR to ER, May 19, 1943, AER papers.

27. *Washington Star*, December 17, 1942; Eleanor Roosevelt to Francis Biddle, December 5, 1941, January 2, February 25, and March 3, 1942, and June 16,

1943, and Francis Biddle to Eleanor Roosevelt, May 2, 1942, Correspondence with Government Officials; Secretary to Mrs. Roosevelt to Clarence Pickett, October 25, 1943, and Secretary to Mrs. Roosevelt to Mrs. Clark, January 5, 1944, General Correspondence; and Janet Fukushima to Eleanor Roosevelt, November 13, 1943, all in AER papers.

28. Harold Ickes to FDR, April 13, 1943, Harold Ickes papers, Library of Congress; and Goodwin, *No Ordinary Time*, 427–429.

29. Eleanor Roosevelt's silence on Japanese-American–induced violence was limited to actions that occurred stateside. When news that the Japanese had executed some American aviators reached her, she immediately, in the words of one reporter, "went on record opposing reprisals." "For the sake of our own souls," the first lady told reporters, "we should live up to the way of doing things that we believe is the right and civilized thing to do." "Opposes Any Reprisals," *New York Times*, May 11, 1943. See also Eleanor Roosevelt, "My Day," April 26 and 27, 1943, My Day Drafts, AER papers; "Mrs. F. D. Roosevelt Visits: Urges Wise Resettlement and Admires Evacuee Fortitude," *Gila Courier*, April 24, 1943, War Relocation Authority Files, Record Group 210, 4 (b) Box 32, National Archives.

30. ER to Joe Lash, April 22, 1943, AER papers; Eleanor Roosevelt, "A Challenge to American Sportsmanship," *Collier's* (October 16, 1943): 21, 71.

31. Eleanor Roosevelt, "A Challenge," 71; [name concealed] to ER, January 1944. I am grateful to Shelly Jacobsen for sharing this letter with me.

32. Eleanor Roosevelt, "My Day," May 13, 1942, AER papers; ER to Flora Rose, June 6, 1942, General Correspondence, AER papers; ER, "My Day," June 2, 1942, AER papers; Dillon Meyer to ER, May 13, 1943, and her reply, Correspondence with Government Officials, AER papers. See also "Japanese Relocation Centers," attached to ER to Dillon Meyer; and ER to John McCoy, June 1, 1944, General Correspondence, AER papers.

33. Togo Tanaka to ER, January 26, 1942, and her reply, February 12, 1942, General Correspondence, AER papers.

34. Eleanor Roosevelt, "Japanese Relocation Camps," attached to Dillon Meyer to ER, May 13, 1943, AER papers.

35. *New York Times*, May 11, 1943.

36. Jonathan Daniels Interview, March 22, 1972, SHC; Reminiscences of Jonathan Daniels, 1972, Southern Intellectual Series, ORHO.

Index

About the Editors and Contributors

ALLIDA M. BLACK is assistant professor of history at the University of Baltimore and lecturer in history at George Washington University, Washington, D.C. She is author of *Casting Her Own Shadow: Eleanor Roosevelt and the Shaping of Postwar Liberalism* (1996).

MATTHEW J. DICKINSON is assistant professor of government at Harvard University, Cambridge, Massachusetts, and author of *Bitter Harvest: FDR and the Growth of the Presidential Branch* (1997).

WILLIAM E. ELLIS is professor of history at Eastern Kentucky University. He is author of *Robert Worth Bingham and the Southern Mystique* (1997).

ETHAN FISHMAN is professor of political science at South Alabama University and author of numerous journal articles and book chapters. He is author of *Likely Stories: Essays on Political Philosophy and Contemporary American Literature* (1989) and *Public Policy and the Public Good* (1991).

MARTIN HALPERN is associate professor of history at Henderson State University. He is author of *UAW Politics in the Cold War Era* (1988) and of articles in professional journals.

SAMUEL B. HOFF is professor of history and political science at Delaware State University. He has contributed numerous essays to leading political science journals and chapters to edited volumes. He is a former legislative assistant to the late Senator Jacob K. Javits (R-N.Y.).

MICHAEL LEWIS is assistant professor of sociology at Wesleyan College.

WILLIAM D. PEDERSON is professor of history and social science at Louisiana State University–Shreveport. He is author of numerous essays appearing in leading journals and edited compendia. He is editor of six books including *Abraham Lincoln: Contemporary* (1995), *Abraham Lincoln: Sources and Style of Leadership* (1994), and *Great Justices of the U.S. Supreme Court* (1993).

JAMES F. PONTUSO is William W. Elliot professor of political science at Hampden-Sydney College. He is author of *Solzhenitsyn's Political Thought* (1989) and coeditor (with Mark J. Rozell) of *American Conservative Opinion Leaders* (1990). He has written numerous essays for scholarly journals and edited compendia.

MARK J. ROZELL is associate professor of political science at American University, Washington, D.C. He is author of six books including *The Press and the Bush Presidency* (1996), *In Contempt of Congress*: *Postwar Press Coverage on Capitol Hill* (1996), and (with Clyde Wilcox) *Second Coming: The New Christian Right in Virginia Politics* (1996). His articles appear in such journals as *Political Science Quarterly, Social Science Quarterly, Polity*, and *Presidential Studies Quarterly*, among others.

MARGARET C. RUNG is assistant professor of history at Roosevelt University, Chicago, Illinois. She is a specialist in twentieth-century political history, with an emphasis on state development during the New Deal and World War II eras. She is currently working on a book concerning civil servants, management ideology, and the emergence of the modern administrative state during the twentieth century.

SEAN J. SAVAGE is associate professor of political science at St. Mary's College of Indiana, and author most recently of *Roosevelt: The Party Leader, 1932–1945* (1991) and *Truman and the Democratic Party* (1997).

ISBN 0-275-95873-6

EAN

HARDCOVER BAR CODE